D1155141

THE FOURTH BRANCH

STUDIES IN GOVERNMENT
AND PUBLIC POLICY

THE FOURTH BRANCH

Reconstructing the Administrative State for the Commercial Republic

Brian J. Cook

Published by the University Press of Kansas (Lawrence, Kansas 66045), which was organized by the Kansas Board of Regents and is operated and funded by Emporia State University, Fort Hays State University, Kansas State University, Pittsburg State University, the University of Kansas, and Wichita State University.

Library of Congress Cataloging-in-Publication Data

Names: Cook, Brian J., 1954– author.
Title: The fourth branch : reconstructing the administrative state for the commercial republic / Brian J. Cook.
Description: Lawrence : University Press of Kansas, 2021. | Series: Studies in government and public policy | Includes bibliographical references and index.
Identifiers: LCCN 2020042477
ISBN 9780700632077 (cloth)
ISBN 9780700632084 (epub)
Subjects: LCSH: Administrative agencies—United States—Reorganization. | Administrative procedure—United States. | Public administration—United States. | Separation of powers—United States. | Constitutional history—United States.
Classification: LCC JK421 .C636 2021 | DDC 352.3/670973—dc23
LC record available at https://lccn.loc.gov/2020042477.

British Library Cataloguing-in-Publication Data is available.

Printed in the United States of America

10 9 8 7 6 5 4 3 2 1

The paper used in this publication is acid free and meets the minimum requirements of the American National Standard for Permanence of Paper for Printed Library Materials Z39.48–1992.

For Brielle and Emmeline
So that you never have to worry about it

The theory of our constitution needs to recognize and understand the working and the potential of our great fourth branch of government, taking a rightful place beside President, Congress, and Courts.

—Norton Long

CONTENTS

PREFACE AND ACKNOWLEDGMENTS

What kind of nation, what form of self-government, do Americans desire? If Americans had the chance today to choose how they wanted to govern, what would be their choice? As the United States approaches its 245th year a debate has erupted about whether the nation is a republic or a democracy. Some say it is both, in the sense that the terms today are virtually interchangeable. Others, claiming to take an "originalist" position, insist that the United States is a republic, emphatically *not* a democracy. For some zealots, the latter term should, among other things, be excised from textbooks (Bernstein 2019). Although this particular dispute may seem silly to many, it suggests, at least among those citizens willing to give it some thought, that there is considerable confusion about how to answer the questions I have posed. Moreover, it seems incredibly difficult, not to mention potentially very tedious, to get consistent answers, or any useful answers at all, by consulting the past (Cotlar 2013). Many people are inclined, therefore, to throw their hands up in frustration and go shopping. And there is the answer to those questions.

Americans aspire to a distinctive political system—call it a commercial republic—in which they have combined a particular set of political institutions with a market economy. It is this combination that they have hoped would fulfill their aspirations to self-government while at the same time enabling them to seek material comfort through the satisfaction of their acquisitive desires. Americans have been fashioning and refashioning their commercial republic almost continuously over the last two and a half centuries. They have come to venerate more and more, nearly to the point of self-delusion for some, the designs underlying their peculiar form of self-government even as they have repeatedly confronted its shortcomings and faced frustrations large and small down to the present day. They are deeply wary of abstract thinking and firmly believe in their pragmatic capacity to fix what is wrong. Yet they reject wholly expedient repairs that they perceive as lacking anchors in their most cherished myths about basic structures and principles. Those structures and principles are both a benefit and a burden, keeping formless change from taking hold, but inducing fear of consequences from any steps outside the charmed circle of the venerated founding and what it allegedly wrought. Thus, like astronomers trying to work with Ptolemy's geocentric model of the solar system, they overlay new spheres in order to keep the mechanics of the system in equilibrium, dismissing a full confrontation with what really ails their regime as too radical to contemplate.

The stresses and strains, contradictions and flaws, of the design-in-practice of American governance—the "working constitution" (Long 1952, 10; Elkin 2006, 53)—have, nevertheless, become magnified to the point that regime failure is now something more than merely a dystopian fantasy. To understand why, and what more far-reaching reconceptions of the regime might be worth considering, requires reexamining the bases of the American commercial republican design and the ensuing struggles with the design over the course of American political and economic development. To undertake an effective examination of this sort requires a distinctive theoretical lens that casts a harsh light on design fundamentals. The result, not for the faint of heart, points to the need for a more sweeping proposal for constitutional redesign. This redesign deserves a hearing for how it might get the regime out of the problematic condition into which its founding design and developmental struggles have led it. The redesign is drastic in that it questions the sacrosanct tripartite separation of powers allegedly at the heart of the constitutional defenses against tyranny. What may prove even more alarming to many, the proposed redesign brings forward as the chief constituent of change in the separation of powers structure what American tradition has seen as one of the most potent possible sources of tyranny: bureaucracy, or, more expansively, an administrative state. Administration, organized into an administrative state, has been a crucial yet problematic element of the American commercial republic in design and practice from nearly the beginning. Taking account of the structures and functions of this administrative state, the roles it has played, the problems it has posed, and the opportunities it offers with respect to the design, development, and redesign of the American commercial republic in the face of a working constitution increasingly adrift is the central object of this book.

This is not an exercise in refining constitutional or administrative law or even theorizing about constitutional or administrative law, although it draws on prominent analyses and debates in those areas. It may be closer to constitutional theory, or political theory. Calling it theorizing may be too grandiose, however. It is simply an effort to sift through a great deal of illuminating prior scholarship in history, political theory, and the study of politics, law, government, and administration to probe the possibilities of designing, redesigning, and improving the American commercial republic. At its heart the book is an attempt to think about the theory and design of a commercial republic without the constraints of concern for politically acceptable solutions, none of which so far put forward has proved adequate for the challenge, while staying true to the fundamental American aspirations to create and perpetuate a just and effective form of self-government. "Government is meant for the good of ordinary people, and it is for ordinary people that the student should elucidate its problems," Woodrow Wilson once asserted (Link 1968, 399). As hard as it sometimes is for Americans to accept, this means taking full measure of the power of administration, not just the problems and dangers it poses but also its potential for good—good service, good social, economic, and political relations, and good and just governance.

Several times through its history the American people and their political leaders have regarded the American experiment in republican government as on the brink of calamity. This book took shape in the most recent of such times—and one that many regard as among the most precarious. The American commercial republic presently faces an onslaught of corruption, cynicism, deep political and cultural divisions, and spreading nihilism. It also faces several present and near-future global-scale dangers that are well understood and confirmed in general terms, and increasingly and tragically evident in their particular forms and effects. The book offers virtually nothing of immediate practical use for any of these serious threats, but if it happens to spark ideas about the links between what is offered here and actions to address those problems, it will have far exceeded its modest aims. Those aims concern an elucidation of the regime of self-government that Americans now have, but much more of the one they might still aspire to realize were they able to pause long enough to consider how better to constitute a commercial republic, one that enables private lives of comfort and consequence, and public lives of fair-mindedness and effective self-rule.

Most authors have stories to tell about the idiosyncratic circumstances in which they wrote their books. Mine are probably more mundane than most. I wrote one book on a desktop computer with 256K of RAM in a small faculty library study, another in the living room of a modest three-bedroom cape on a dead-end street in Worcester, Massachusetts, and edited two others at home in my office/guest bedroom in Blacksburg, Virginia. In all those instances the wider societal conditions, while hardly benign, were reasonably stable and rational. The book you are now holding or peering at on a backlit screen came to completion under conditions far less constant, including a global pandemic of such proportions as had not been seen for over a century. That pandemic has proven so deadly and disruptive—particularly in the United States because of the disastrous incompetence, indifference, and hatred of a political party in control of most of the levers of national governance—that it has left no individual, no family, no profession or social endeavor untouched. And it has disoriented the intellect and emotions of even the smartest, most level-headed, and fittest members of the human race. The effects of the virus on the body and mind are widely varying and shockingly random. The effects on already weakened institutions have been sweepingly destabilizing. All those who successfully navigate the treacherous waters of these times will be called upon to build a better world.

As a part-time graduate student in government and politics at the University of Maryland in 1979, I managed to find the courage to knock on the office doors of several faculty, seeking help in getting my bearings. A couple shooed me away, but one was willing to talk with me briefly, despite the fact that I interrupted a phone call he was on. I have no recollection of the ensuing exchange, but somehow I convinced Steve Elkin that I was worth a bit of his time. Not all of the developments in my subsequent scholarly career reflect the influence of his teaching, advising, ideas, and distinctive style, but this book certainly does, more than any other source. It is his theory and analyses on which I have drawn most extensively. Whenever I struggled to work out the logic and compositional challenges for a particular part of the argument, I returned to his work for orientation and inspiration. During several long conversations at a little bakery and coffee shop on Connecticut Avenue in Washington, DC, Steve helped me work through many of my key ideas and claims. It was only a little more casual than the oral defense of a comprehensive exam, and in the end the project received Steve's imprimatur. He understandably prefers to remain in blissful ignorance about whether I have made a hash of things in trying to build on his work. This book, whatever its remaining imperfections, would have been inconceivable without Steve's powerfully insightful, principled foundation.

I am also greatly indebted to my friend and fellow traveler in public administration and political-economic history and theory, Rick Green. His masterful examination of Alexander Hamilton's public administration was also a source of inspiration. More than that, Rick was willing to read and critique the manuscript at various stages of development. Rick saved me from errors of omission and commission, forced me to better articulate several key points in the analysis, and gave me encouragement when I was struggling. I am grateful for the time and energy that Rick invested in providing such valuable intellectual and collegial support.

David Lewis also read a full draft of the manuscript and invited me to discuss it with his summer graduate student reading group. David's feedback, and that of his students, was careful and thorough and pushed me to be clearer about the meaning of key terms, the structure of the argument, and links to a wider range of scholarship. I was not able to respond adequately to all of their criticisms, but the adjustments I did make improved the manuscript in important ways.

Others who guided the way with challenges to my thesis, substantive ideas and suggestions for improvements, or meaningful encouragement include Doug Morgan, Ken Meier, and Mike Spicer, Greg Cawley, and Hugh Miller. The two anonymous outside readers of the manuscript offered very positive assessments as well as key suggestions for improvements. I hope they find that I responded to their suggestions satisfactorily.

It is impossible to thank individually the many, many scholars in public administration, administrative law, history, political science, and other fields whose research and publications taught me much and guided me to a more well-informed and more finely fashioned final product. Thank you all. I am sure you will tell me if you do not like how I have used your scholarship. Of course, none of those named and unnamed bears any responsibility for the errors and shortcomings that remain.

I owe a very special thanks to David Congdon, who found my book idea worthy of possible publication with the University Press of Kansas. David's support for the project, and his encouragement, responsiveness, and feedback challenging me to make improvements at several stages, has made publishing with the Press a rewarding experience. The production team of friendly, accessible professionals enriched that experience even more. Aimee Anderson edited the manuscript with a keen eye and firm but gentle hand, bringing me both relief and gratitude for the many errors, omissions, and obscurities in composition that she found and corrected. Karl Janssen designed the cover, helping me sort through options that led me right back to his original design. Michael Kehoe and Derek Helms guided the marketing and publicity. Kelly Chrisman Jacques oversaw the editing and production with efficiency, thoroughness, and infectious enthusiasm. I am honored that the book is joining the Press's very impressive catalog of scholarly works.

It may not have taken an actual village to write this book, but it did require a loving family, especially my wife and partner, Ruth, who kept me going many a time simply by listening as I voiced the inevitable trials and tribulations. She expected me to finish it and publish it. She is always right.

THE FOURTH BRANCH

Introduction:
Challenges in Commercial Republican Regime Design

Local controversy flared in Washington, DC, during the summer and fall of 2019 concerning access to public athletic facilities (Nirappil 2019). The city's parks and recreation department announced that it was extending a 2009 no-bid contract with the private Maret School to 2029 for upgrades and maintenance of the Jelleff Recreation Center in the city's Georgetown neighborhood. The private school with a $34 million endowment had spent $2.4 million on new turf and lighting for sports fields and a remodeled outdoor pool under the original contract terms, and it agreed to continue to spend $950,000 annually for maintenance. In exchange, the school secured exclusive access to and use of the Jelleff facilities during prime after-school hours through the life of the contract. Public schools and after-school programs in the neighborhood, including Hardy Middle School across the street from Jelleff, are barred from using the facilities during the hours dedicated to Maret School use. They must limit their activities, use nearby public facilities in poorer condition, or wait until evening hours to access Jelleff. Some opponents of the contract pointed out that it seemed designed specifically to fall below the total dollar threshold that would have triggered city council review.

Proponents of the contract extension, including the city officials responsible for the contract, offered many good reasons for the arrangement, including that the Jelleff facilities might not even exist without the deal. Beyond the conflict over the access restrictions, however, opponents railed against the implications of the contract, pointing out that the business involved—and the private school is a business even if it is a not-for-profit entity—was able to wield resources to reach a deal with city bureaucrats that essentially kept the transaction uncompetitive and free of scrutiny. The private school's resources were far in excess of what the city's own schools, and the parents and students associated with them, could ever muster. At a DC city council hearing on the matter in October 2019, proponents and opponents of the renewal of the city's agreement with the Maret School sensed the linkage with national concerns and controversies. A Maret School parent observed that the fight over facility access "bears a resemblance to our nation's divisive political landscape," while a neighborhood association representative denounced the private school's attitude of "a kind of noblesse oblige that I guess is kind of typical for this new gilded age" (Vyse 2019).

Perhaps the Jelleff facility controversy in Washington, DC, might not have grown so heated were it not that, entering the third decade of the twenty-first century, the United States finds itself in a precarious condition, one of extreme social, political, and economic tumult. At the heart of the turmoil is a sense of economic insecurity and political impotence among many citizens even as the nation as a whole remains the richest in the world. The distribution of the nation's wealth and income have become extremely skewed, and the holders of the lion's share of wealth seem able to deploy it with impunity for their own selfish interests and at the expense of almost everybody else (Baker 2016; Pistor 2019; Standing 2016). The appearance in early 2020 of a novel coronavirus that quickly swept through a immunologically naive population worldwide magnified the inequality of economic and social conditions everywhere—but most dramatically in the United States. Now more than ever it is clear how the holders of exceptional wealth use it to elect legislators and chief executives who shape public policy to further serve the interests of the already wealthy and expand their wealth and power even more (Formisano 2017). Perhaps most disturbing is that the wealthy and powerful few seem to have neutralized or even gained substantial control over the levers of government, including those regulatory agencies and other administrative entities supposedly responsible for ensuring the public interest is served—including through basic public health and safety protection—by restraining the behavior of the most powerful economic organizations. These corporations of remarkable variety, size, and complexity have served as the vehicles by which the wealthiest have extracted their riches. In short, the so-called administrative state has been "captured" (Lindsey and Teles 2017; Rahman 2017). Or, if not exactly captured (Carpenter and Moss 2014), regulatory agencies have become at least so intertwined with business and industry that this administrative state provides the primary and most opaque pathway by which "large-scale controllers of capital" with "narrow interests" readily "gain the benefactions they seek" (Elkin 2006, 58, 59). If this is indeed the case and not just the feverish nightmares of losers in the great and perpetual struggles of the free market, then further inquiry into the matter is imperative.

WHAT IS AN ADMINISTRATIVE STATE?

The controversy over the Jelleff Recreation Center in Washington, DC, suggests close ties between some city bureaucrats and a privileged private business that many of the affected citizens have found extremely discomfiting. The arrangement reflects at the local level the worrisome interconnection between business and the administrative state evident across all levels of government in the United States. It is relatively unusual to associate local government with the administrative state or to suggest that local government exhibits the characteristics of an administrative state. However, municipalities, at least mid-size and larger cities, have substantial administrative structures that interact extensively with economic actors of all kinds. They have especially strong connections to the largest and most powerful drivers of their local and regional economies (Elkin 1987). City bureaucracies may thus exhibit an administrative-state "ethos" (Kathi and Cooper 2005, 560–561). Still, the "administrative state" label is usually reserved for characterizing the structure and power-wielding features of a national government. In its most prominent usage, at least in public administration, political science, and constitutional- and administrative-law scholarship, it refers to the emergence in the United States during the early to mid-twentieth century of a national government dominated by large, bureaucratically organized administrative agencies delegated a combination of powers to regulate a wide array of social and economic functions and to deliver a broad set of public services (see, e.g., Waldo [1948] 2007; Rosenbloom 1983; O'Toole 1987; Roberts 2020). The idea, structure, and substance of an administrative state need not be so contextually confined, however, especially for theorizing about constitutional design and constitutional governance.

In one nontrivial respect the phrase is redundant (Waldo 1984). All modern states are essentially administrative in two important aspects. First, the largest component of government is administration, often bureaucratic in form and character. Even the institutions of government not normally considered administrative—legislatures and courts—are organized bureaucratically—or at least have bureaucratically organized support, such as the administrative support that enables courts to function. In liberal democracies elections are also largely an administrative function and process, usually bureaucratized, including the collection and counting of votes. It is only at the precise point where the individual voter makes candidate selections that elections are not bureaucratized. How those candidates come to be on those ballots is almost entirely an administrative process as well, and candidate and party campaigns are in many cases at least quasi-bureaucratic.

Second, the primary responsibility of most modern liberal-democratic states is to organize and manage major social and economic institutions and functions and the relations with individuals and groups pursuing their private aims and purposes, making them fully articulated in structure and purpose (Rubin 2005a, 25–29). Much of this state organization and management is bureaucratic in form. The extent of the state's organization and management of society and economy is mildly disturbing to many, deeply unsettling to some, and this discomfort is aggravated by the highly bureaucratic nature of the enterprise. Whatever its functional advantages, bureaucracy seems to be deleterious to individual psychological well-being and to a healthy culture and social relations as well (Hummel 2008). A big state with a long reach and extensive knowledge and capabilities, even (or especially) when those characteristics are directed toward the welfare of individuals and the improvement of society, is for some a fearsome thing that has prompted dire warnings about the potential for oppressive government (e.g., Tocqueville 2000, vol. 2; Hayek 1945).

If this is the portrait, with some variation, of all modern states, what specifically is an administrative state? One way to think about it, and the primary usage in what follows, is that an administrative state is not the whole state, but the most prominent feature of a modern state, and the primary setting within which governance takes place on a day-to-day basis. The primary reason for isolating and naming this characteristic is that it poses a problem for governing theory and practice, especially for liberal democracies. Hence, a modest effort to define terms is necessary to explain the problem while avoiding a plunge into the deep and murky waters of social-science scholarship on the nature of the state.

A state is a central government, or a combination of central and regional governments as in a federation, that holds recognized sovereignty over a defined territory. Coordination with some nongovernmental organizations may also be present. Sovereignty is recognized internally by the people residing within the borders of that territory when they accept the state as having the capacity and legitimacy to exercise that sovereignty, that is, to govern (Barkin 2016). This is so even if a particular state's theory of governance is that the people are "that pure, original fountain of all legitimate authority" (*The Federalist Papers*, no. 22). The extent to which the people select the leaders of that government or combination of governments, or otherwise participate in governing, will vary across states. There are multiple ways by which a state's sovereignty is popularly legitimated and tacit compliance with law habituated. A state's sovereignty is also recognized externally by other sovereign states that honor that state's claims about the borders that define its territory, and its claims about its legitimacy and capacity to govern within those borders. Those claims encompass extensions of governance beyond a state's borders, such as embassies and military bases. Other states employ, recognize, and accept such sovereignty claims for those extensions as well.

This sovereignty that states embody, this governing that states undertake, comes in many concrete forms in complex combinations. The foundations of these developments owe much to the work of Emer Vattel in the eighteenth century (Vattel 1835; Beaulac 2003). Over a century later Woodrow Wilson offered a simple yet powerful way to categorize the concrete forms of state sovereignty and governance in Western civilization. He distinguished between constituent and ministrant functions. Wilson defined constituent functions as those that constitute the state, that make it what it is. These are functions that preserve economic and social integrity, such as the protection of life, liberty, and property. These functions are "necessary to the civic organization of society"; they are "not optional"; they preserve "the very bonds of society"; and thus embody the state's existence (Link 1968, 670–671).

Wilson defined ministrant functions as those that were not formative of the state and society but enhancements of the basic order of society. These are optional, "advancing the general interests of society," but "necessary only according to standards of convenience or expediency, and not according to standards of existence" (Link 1968, 671). Ministrant functions might include the regulation of industries and labor as well as social welfare and natural resource conservation. Wilson admitted, however, that "the line of demarcation is not always clear" between the two (672), for "even among these ministrant functions there are some which everybody recognizes as habitual with most governments" (677).

Wilson contrasted constituent and ministrant functions in order to draw attention to a shift in the orientation of states that raised the prominence and importance of ministrant functions and of administration. States throughout history had to minister to their societies with respect to convenience and expediency and thus toward societal betterment. In that sense, then, ministrant functions have not been optional. Yet they have not been among the elements that gave a state the minimum requirements for existence. Modernity, at least in the West, brought about a change in "morals and the conscience of government." States ministered to their populations in the context of "new ideas as to what constitutes social convenience and advancement." The individual rather than the state was now at the center, and the state had to navigate the complexities of modern conditions in ways that would foster individual development (see also Maritain 1951). Modern governments could no longer "administer" the lives of individuals directly by treating them as indistinguishable parts of a whole (Link 1968, 689). Individuals qua individuals needed autonomy and social space to develop outside the state. States still had to provide support in many forms, however, that would both overcome substantial barriers to, and create new opportunities for, individual development. New state structures and capabilities were required as a result, forcing states to reengineer and expand their administrative structures and capacities, setting in motion the rise to prominence of distinct administrative structures and functions within states. If such structures and functions exhibit three key characteristics, they constitute an *administrative* state within the state.

The first characteristic is that administration is the most prominent governing component of the state, in terms of human and fiscal resources and the reach and regularity of its activity. It also exercises many of the state's constituent functions and most of its ministrant functions. Second, to some identifiable extent validated in law, the units of the administrative component of the state are authorized to exercise in varying combinations all the basic powers of government—policy making, policy execution, and adjudication. Third, administrative units exercise these powers with at least some independence and self-direction. That is, they can fulfill their functions and responsibilities without constant command from any other governing component of the state. This may be called administrative discretion, but there is no need to engage in an effort to define that term precisely, and it suffers from descriptive and analytical weaknesses (Rubin 2005a, 85–91; also see chap. 6). Administrative units may or may not have acquired political autonomy in some form (Carpenter 2001, 14–18; Adler 2012), but evidence of sustained striving for such autonomy in many administrative units is a good indicator of the existence of an administrative state.

Whether bureaucratic organization of administrative units is a necessary condition for there to be an administrative state is debatable, but it seems highly unlikely that any modern state would organize administration in any other way. What constitutes bureaucratic organization is also subject to plenty of debate, but again, no definitive definition is necessary for recognizing the existence of an administrative state. It is helpful to point out, however, that administrators may be elected, or appointed either by political criteria or merit criteria, and the structures of administration in any given administrative state may have all three in varying combinations.

Finally, states can vary somewhat in how extensive their ministrant functions are and how much those functions have been delegated to the administrative component of the state. In other words, states may vary in the extent to which they are so-called welfare states. What matters most, however, in recognizing the existence of an administrative state in a modern liberal democracy is that the administrative component of government is prominent enough that it has *constitutive* effects on the state and the larger political regime. It is both an instrument of the state and regime and in its form and actions helps *constitute* state and regime. It actively shapes and reshapes political relations and public purposes. It thus exhibits "co-causal interaction of structure and intention" (Rubin 2005a, 29). In perhaps the simplest but most powerful effect, citizens—as individuals but more importantly when organized into social and economic organizations—come to think of the state, and their relations with it, primarily on the basis of their interactions with administration. This then has downstream effects on how administration is structured and operates interactively with other components of the state, society, and economy.

Administration as the primary frontier of contact between the state and various elements of society is the core theoretical and practical problem that administrative states pose for liberal democracies. This is so first because citizens in liberal democracies expect to enjoy considerable freedom to organize their lives and social relations as they see fit. They may construct their own organizations for such purposes without the involvement of the state. Such endeavors fall under the common rubric of civil society. The looming presence of state administration, whether modest or substantial, is in serious tension with such citizen expectations and activities, however. Second, liberal democracies rely on, indeed may be defined in significant part by, the "division of labor between market and state" (Elkin 1985, 179). A major part of the relatively unfettered pursuit of life goals by citizens in liberal democracies is the satisfaction of acquisitive desires in a market economy. Markets also perform society-wide functions, however, by generating material wealth and general economic well-being for the populace. Markets are thus of central concern to the state, creating additional tensions as the administrative apparatus of the state monitors—and when deemed necessary intervenes in—the market to ensure that it performs at least minimal levels of its society-wide functions. Governance in liberal democracies is thus prominently defined by the evolving patterns of interaction between state and market. Some civil society organizations serve as moderators of this extensive and complex space where market-state interactions occur.

MARKET-STATE RELATIONS AND THE PUBLIC INTEREST

The essential challenge of liberal democratic regime design and practice is to define, and redefine as necessary, how the primary organs of the state and the primary organizing structures of the market are to relate to one another. The central concern this challenge raises, in other words, is the structure and substance of market-state relations because "there is a deep connection between how we organize ourselves to pursue economic, social, educational, and other private and public goals, and how our democratic system of politics functions" (Hennessey and Wallis 2017, 78).

What especially drives the challenge posed by the market-state division of labor is the commitment of the state to satisfy public desires and demands for an adequate form and level of economic well-being. This is, in a very real sense, the primary ministrant function of the state in liberal democracies. As noted, however, in most liberal democracies the state has ceded considerable control over the creation and use of productive assets to the market and the businesses that operate in the various market sectors. The United States of the twentieth and twenty-first centuries is a relatively extreme case of placing control of productive assets in the hands of private actors, and thus constructing a political economy with distinctive public and private institutional and organizational structures and relationships. In every liberal-democratic case, however, the state's commitment to provide a satisfactory level of economic well-being for most of a nation's residents requires close and continuous contact between market and state. These contacts primarily take the form of strategic interactions and negotiations concerning economic performance between elected and unelected public officials, a multitude of business owners, investors, and managers with discrete and narrow interests and the associations that claim to represent such interests. A variety of nongovernmental or nonprofit organizations are also engaged in these interactions as extensions of the service functions of the state. Some operate, for example, within the market to reduce information asymmetries between producers and consumers, or as vehicles by which businesses try to evade some of the taxing and regulating initiatives of the state.

Business control of productive assets means that business has discretion in how to deploy those productive assets. How business uses that discretion in turn has considerable effect on general economic well-being. Businesses will engage in some investment, hiring, production, and output on their own. Entrepreneurs are, after all, driven by the desire for material gain, and a few even have a social conscience. Overall, however, the unprompted effort by business is unlikely to fully meet public expectations for a satisfactory level of economic well-being, at least because the risks of miscalculation and business failure are high in competitive markets where exogenous factors are numerous and hard to control. A truly free market, one in which the state exerts little effort to restrain those exogenous factors, or endogenous factors for that matter, will fail to adequately meet a society's collective material needs and is thus inconceivable as anything other than the graveyard of advanced capitalism.

Furthermore, public officials cannot simply command business performance when the state has ceded to business primary control of the use of productive assets. Property rights are a central constraint on what public officials can do to direct businesses in the use of their productive assets. Business discretion in the use of productive assets is also constrained by market competition. To meet the state's commitment, therefore, public officials must and will worry considerably about how to encourage sufficient business performance to meet citizen expectations for an acceptable level of economic well-being, the relative equity of its distribution across the populace, and its relative stability over time. The failure of public officials to meet citizen expectations for economic performance, or to at least appear as if they are meeting those expectations, means at least some elected and unelected officials will be searching for other lines of work.

Under these conditions the incentives for businesses to seek *inducements* (Lindbloom 1977) and for public officials to grant them are considerable. This does not mean that public officials are in the pockets of robber barons, at least not continuously. Instead, the relationships between businesses and public officials are complicated, dynamic, and often conflictual. It is a "process of mutual dependence and control" (Elkin 1994, 119) that is stable in its essence but can shift in its particulars in the relatively short run as internal and external conditions change. Moreover, neither the market and business, nor the state and public officials, are monolithic. Businesses are often in conflict among themselves over what public inducements are wanted or needed. Also, some citizens will be critical of business in various ways, while others will be unwavering supporters. Because in a liberal *democracy* public officials are attentive to citizen concerns and demands at least some of the time, and because they will have considerable self-regard given their election or selection to powerful public posts, they will have their own ideas about what will encourage an acceptable level of prosperity and the forms and levels of business performance that will achieve and sustain it. Public officials must, nevertheless, obtain at least tacit business consent to particular actions. Business views will thus carry considerable weight in the deliberations of public officials on public policy, even in policy domains that do not bear directly on economy and finance. Policy debates in these other areas of public concern often include extensive consideration of the effects that various policy options will have on "business performance" (Elkin 1994, 118) or the broader notion of economic growth.

Business demands for performance inducements take the form of policies "directed at facilitating large-scale [business] investment, with the control of risk, the ample size of rewards for succeeding, and compensation for failure being central." Public officials respond with such policies "to avoid reducing the confidence" of business and to stimulate performance beyond what business would otherwise do (Elkin 1987, 131). Confidence comes from stability and certainty in public policy, and performance comes from properly calibrated rewards for success and compensation for failure. Furthermore, as markets and states in most liberal democracies have progressed, control and modulation of the structure and substance of business inducements have flowed into the hands of unelected officials. Elected officials have driven this development in an effort to push decision responsibility and the inherent risks of miscalculation onto officials with greater specialized expertise who are more insulated from direct democratic control. The result has been the emergence of "an extensive pattern of informal contacts" between market actors and less publicly prominent administrative officials, enabling discussions that "can be carried out largely shielded from public view" (Elkin 2006, 57). It helps that what remains of traditional journalism rarely finds newsworthy the day-to-day machinations inside administrative agencies. As globalization has progressed, moreover, national and international technocrats have gotten themselves and their regimes in trouble by attempting to "discipline" democratic control (Roberts 2010) to further shield the structures of inducement from public disaffection.

Some may object that all this concedes too much to business, giving it far too much influence at the expense of citizens and the idea of popular sovereignty.

Alongside such normative objections are practical questions concerning what relationships exist in particular instances and what the results have been. In general, however, "from the viewpoint of citizens it is rational for officials to listen carefully to what businessmen have to say, in short to give them a privileged voice. This simply follows from it being rational to give whoever controls productive assets—whether public or private—a special place in government councils. Public officials then are simply doing in effect what rational citizens would command them to do" (Elkin 1994, 122), at least up to a point. Furthermore, public officials, like all humans, have cognitive biases, and there are other limits to their rationality. "They are often divided and confused. What they do know is that they need economic performance from [business] and that it would be best if they could get [its] cooperation" (118) in achieving such performance. Even the most expert among public officials or those who advise them can also miscalculate, especially because capitalists themselves do not always know what will ensure satisfactory economic performance.

Finally, business "will not win all battles" despite having privileged access to public officials and "control of capital" and other resources (Elkin 2006, 57). Public officials have the "resources of law and public will" (57) to counter business demands for inducements. Public officials may deploy them if they find business demands excessive or unreasonable, or simply to signal their independence and power. Hence, the substance or duration of the inducements to business are not predetermined. They will be the product of the unique "depth and breadth" of the mutual dependence between public officials and business as shaped by the prevailing theories and practices in a given liberal-democratic regime.

The mutual interdependence of market and state in liberal democracies is a fundamental regime design problem, akin to the problem of self-interest and faction with which the American framers struggled so mightily. Indeed these two design problems are closely related. Like the problem of faction, market-state mutual interdependence cannot be willed away, or one side of the dyad sacrificed to the other, if the kind of regime to which people of liberal-democratic leanings aspire is to be realized and maintained. The mutual interdependence thus must be regulated, like faction, and how to do this is part of the larger set of questions concerning how to design a regime and put that design into practice.

THE COMMERCIAL REPUBLIC AND THE PROBLEM OF ADMINISTRATION

If market-state interdependence was all there was to the nature and extent of liberal democracy, it might satisfy some, but it is a good bet that most would regard it as a pretty sorry form of governance, neither sufficient nor inspiring. Worse, it would leave completely unfulfilled several centuries of rising democratic expectations. Liberal democracy thus aims for much more, most especially some form of genuine self-rule. This includes creating necessary space for social interactions outside the market and beyond the general reach of the state. In the case of the United States, the aspiration from the beginning has been toward a particular form of liberal democracy—a commercial republic (Elkin 2006, 5–11). Across their history from the founding to the present, the American people and their leaders have aspired to a form of self-government in which individual rights are protected, a wide sphere of autonomous choice of life purposes is honored, and the general welfare is secured. All along, the central puzzle has been how to connect the deep-rooted American desire for self-government to the equally deep-rooted acquisitiveness of the American people and how to sustain a positively reinforcing version of that connection across time. To state it differently and in a more familiar form, the challenge is to find ways to harness the desire for economic gain, and self-interest more generally, so as to secure, sustain, and perhaps even enhance republican government—democracy with limits. This aspiration is ultimately for a form of self-government with a politics of self-limitation at its core (Elkin 2006, 290). Otherwise stated, the aspiration is to realize the commercial public interest, or more generally, the *public interest,* which at its heart concerns creating and sustaining the institutions that constitute a politics of self-limiting popular sovereignty (144–145). Such a self-limiting regime politics ultimately aims to realize "a defensible conception of justice" and thus a particular form of a good political regime (94).

The attentiveness of public officials to public concerns about the level and distribution of economic prosperity, and thus their concern for business performance and the need for inducements to stimulate sufficient business performance to meet public concerns, is a central part of the effort to promote and sustain a commercial society. The critical question is whether public officials, and citizens more generally, are in any way cognizant that "attending to the commercial public interest requires that inducing business performance be seen in the larger context of securing republican government" (Elkin 1987, 144). A commercial republic is not principally about serving business interests or even inducing satisfactory business performance. Public officials must somehow recognize the need "to maintain the distinction between the essentially political reasons for a commercial society and how to contrive a happy environment" for business (144). A critical component of commercial republican regime design is thus to create the institutional arrangements that generate and sustain the necessary incentives for public officials to recognize and hold on to the "larger, more political view" and purpose (145) of their attention to promoting a commercial society. Because administration is so central to the workaday operation of a modern liberal democracy, the question of how some form of an administrative state is to fit into such institutional arrangements is a particularly important regime design problem.

In the case of the American republic, repeated confrontations with these realities and challenges of liberal democratic regime design have sent reverberations across its unfolding history. The framing of the US Constitution, the early conflicts between Federalists and Jeffersonians, the triumph of white, male majoritarian democracy, westward expansion, the existential conflict over slavery, the collapse of Reconstruction, the emergence of a fully industrialized economy, international conflicts, and adjustments in response to globalization are all heavily marked if not centrally defined by the struggles of political leaders, other public officials, business leaders, and ordinary people to respond to the challenges of creating a commercial society that serves and strengthens republican self-government rather than subverting it (Elkin 2006, 7). Because the ongoing interdependence of market and state, and interactions between public officials and business, have increasingly become the responsibility of administrative officials in the form of an administrative state, questions concerning how administration has been conceptualized and structured, what its effects have been, and what its potential role could be are central to any inquiry about the ongoing challenge of creating a commercial society and successfully holding onto its larger, political meaning and purpose. In the case of the United States specifically, it is an inquiry into the place of administration in the design of the American commercial republic in theory, and in practice through its working constitution.

The first part of this book offers an analytical and historical synthesis that broadly traces the American republic's evolving struggles with the continuing challenge of market-state relations and public administration's rising place in those struggles. The second part, and the more general aim of the book, is to advance the inquiry into "a theory of the political constitution of an American commercial republic" (Elkin 2006, xi) by considering specifically administration's role in and contributions to the political constitution of such a regime. An initial presentation of the underlying theory and its component concepts is therefore necessary to properly frame the structure and content of the book.

OVERVIEW OF THEORY AND CONCEPTS

A theory of political constitution of an American commercial republic is not simply about the US Constitution, and certainly not primarily about the Constitution as a legal document or plan for a government. It is instead about "thinking constitutionally" and therefore theorizing about what is necessary to design, or constitute, a whole regime (Elkin 2006, chap. 1). It is also about considering the possibilities for improving the political order that are reasonably consistent with the broad history and traditions of the regime. The particular regime in question, again, is a *commercial republic*. It conjoins popular, limited, and active government, a lively sphere of public associational life beyond government, and a market system anchored in a broad domain of private property rights and centered on business enterprise. The businesses occupying the market domain control most of society's productive assets, thereby driving economic activity through investment and response to consumer demand. Chapter 1 provides the historical and theoretical explanation and defense of the American regime as a commercial republic.

Because it is a form of liberal democracy, the American commercial republic seeks a public life of well-adjusted relationships across society, state, and market, especially the creation of "mass well-being" and the attainment of "liberal justice." This is a form of justice, or just politics, in which "people stand in relation to one another as free and equal" (Elkin 2006, 11). This means that people are equally free to choose their own life courses, and they are equal in their standing "before the state and its law" (12). For the widest cross-section of people to share this experience, government must actively inhibit extreme discrepancies in wealth, social standing, and quality of life, and ameliorate such conditions when they arise. However, there are limits on what government can do in this regard, and a self-governing people committed to liberal justice through a commercial republic accepts that the tools and powers of government must not be used to force absolute political or economic equality. Such a result would be neither a liberal democracy nor a commercial republic.

The theory of political constitution of a commercial republic is concerned with the design and practice of a regime with the qualities necessary to facilitate liberal justice. These concerns encompass the nature of the public interest, the modes of association among citizens, between citizens and lawmakers (broadly defined), and among lawmakers, the nature and form of political, civic, and economic institutions, and the nature and form of political leadership. Thinking constitutionally is thus about how these various components might best fit together to constitute, again not just a government, but a whole regime with the desired qualities.

The theory is not just concerned with the abstract arrangement of components, however. It must also consider the "actual practices" (Elkin 2006, 52) that unfold under color of the design, give it life and substance, and adjust the design to changing circumstances. This is the *working constitution*, which is the ongoing, shifting assembly of structural and procedural additions, enhancements, alterations, and extensions achieved through statutes, administrative rules, and legislative, executive, and judicial interpretations. The working constitution also encompasses the "working attitudes towards the rule of law, civil liberties, and due process," among other design principles and features (Long 1952, 816), and the "working interaction" among the primary governing institutions that "makes the constitutional system a going concern" (813). The idea of "small 'c' constitutionalism" as "a modality of public life and discourse, facilitating the building and editing of structures within which . . . citizens can live flourishing lives" (Eskridge and Ferejohn, 2010, 1–2) is similar in concept to the working constitution.

Recognizing institutional interaction as central to shaping a working constitution points to political institutions as vital to determining the character of a regime. From a design perspective, political institutions are the principal components of a regime. The type of rule a regime embodies is expressed through its political institutions. A regime and its type of rule are not relegated to one fixed arrangement of political institutions, however. For example, liberal democracy is a type of rule and thus a generic form of regime. All liberal democracies must contend with the problem of faction. Not all liberal democracies design and fit together their political institutions in the same manner as the United States to cope with the problem of faction, however. In fact, most do not. It is therefore not only appropriate but essential to delve into the reasons and actions that led to a specific regime's institutional forms and arrangements, what the consequences have been, and what alternative institutional forms or arrangements might be possible to address worrisome consequences while preserving the essential character of the regime.

In addition to treating regimes as "packages" of political institutions (Elkin 2006, 88), the theory of political constitution under consideration also regards the essential nature of political institutions as constitutive. They are "not just bundles of formal rules" but also "patterns of political behavior" (92). They have an instrumental function, but they are not interchangeable means for attaining designated ends. Each political institution "has a specific job to do" and in doing that job it creates and sustains a "mode of association" (111). These multiple institutional modes of association, or political relationships, when fitted together constitute a "political way of life" or a particular kind of regime politics. The political institutions of a regime and the nature of a people individually and collectively immersed in it have formative effects on one another. Thus, political institutions are both instrumental to and constitutive of a political regime. They work to realize public aims and purposes, but they also shape and reshape those purposes. The US presidency, for example, is designed to enable prompt national government action, especially in response to external threats to the nation's security. Yet its structure and evolution, driven in part by those who have held the office, toward a "plebiscitary" form (Lowi 1985) has reshaped public understandings of national political representation and leadership.

Public administration is a political institution in its own right and thus both instrumental and constitutive in its role and effects. Through its many component organizational units, public administration is most often the primary means by which a given regime governs at ground level in the sense of translating law and policy goals and objectives, stipulations and restrictions, into action, and action into outcomes. All organizational units in public administration operate primarily through instrumental rationality. That is, they recognize and embrace a primarily instrumental role of matching means to ends. In most instances they also operate through the organizational form that is the most powerful expression of instrumental rationality yet devised—bureaucracy. Although instrumental in its view of the world, bureaucracy is nevertheless a mode of association and therefore constitutive of administration and of the larger politics of which administration is a part. This sets up considerable tension within any administrative organization, specifically that between its prominent instrumental orientation, its purpose or mission, and its constituting effects. Such effects may be intended through policy or organizational design, although often only vaguely so. Or they may be unintended, with positive or negative consequences, and sometimes both. In any case, public administrators must grapple with this tension on an ongoing basis even if they don't consciously recognize it as such. But they surely do recognize that, in a human service agency for example, the rules they write to implement a statute and how they interpret and apply those rules affect the behavior of their clients, to which administrators in the agency must then adapt and respond. Such a mode of association is an often complex and fraught pattern of behavior, and highly political, as the impacts of policy design and implementation, including the "street-level" interpretation and application of rules, reveals. These "feedback" effects (Béland and Schlager 2019) are inescapably political because they reverberate out into society, affecting how the agency's clients relate to others, how they think about their place in society, their sense of citizenship, and how as citizens or noncitizens they relate to government.

Beyond the internal constitutive effects that an administrative organization has on its members and on its association with other actors in its environment, especially other political institutions, administration as a collective entity, no matter how fuzzy its boundaries, is constitutive of the regime in which it operates. It has a specific job to do, and no other political institution can do that job, especially in the ways a modern, bureaucratized public administration can. At least for liberal democracies, this may be the most essential message of Max Weber's writings on bureaucracy (Weber 1968). Public administration is indispensable to the operation of liberal democracies, including grappling with the challenge of market-state relations. Administration, in the form of an administrative state, thus contributes unavoidably to constituting those critical relations, for good or ill. Liberal democracies can vary in the structure and treatment of administration and its fit into a particular arrangement of political institutions. Whatever the administrative structure and institutional arrangement, however, administration is constitutive of the regime of which it is a part. This further reinforces the point that in a commercial republic, the design of administration and its fit into the regime design, and how it operates in practice, is a crucial consideration for ensuring that the larger, political view of the value of a commercial society is given due consideration.

The theory of political constitution of the American commercial republic framing the historical and theoretical analysis that unfolds in the chapters that follow draws on the "neo-Madisonian" theory developed in Elkin (2006), but modified and extended with neo-Hamiltonian elements drawn from many sources. The modifications and extensions reflect the layered regime design for a commercial republic that emerged from the sometimes cooperative, sometimes sharply conflicting ideas and actions of those prominent framers. The theory provides the lens through which the book considers the role and contribution of administration and an administrative state in the American commercial republic historically, and theoretically as one possible corrective to a working constitution that has veered "down the road to factional rule" (68). In applying this theory of political constitution of the American commercial republic to explain the emergence of serious distortions in the structure and operations of the market, the state, and the relationship between the two and how those distortions might be rectified through politics and political design, this book bears some affinity with the appearance of what might be called a new republican synthesis reflected in the work of Ackerman (2010), Petit (2012), and Ginsburg and Huq (2018), among others. With its special attention to the design and role of administrative agencies as a potential corrective to the particular distorting effects of business interests and economic power, this book is especially in accord with such work as that of Michaels (2017) and Rahman (2017). Nevertheless, the present book stands apart in its focus on whole regime design, the commercial republic as the distinguishing feature of the American liberal-democratic form, and administration as a distinct political institution situated at the center of struggles to keep the political value of a commercial society in view.

PLAN OF THE BOOK

The book is structured in two parts. The focus of Part I is on the original ideas and debates that shaped the design of the commercial republic, the tensions in the design that emerged, and the methods by which successive generations of public officials and the engaged public have grappled with that design as they confronted the challenge of structuring and managing business-state relations while keeping an eye on the public interest. Part I begins, in chapter 1, with attention to the design of the American commercial republic in theory and in its early practice, including its historical roots, design features and flaws and attempts to ameliorate them, and the conflicts that ensued. Overall, the chapters of Part I explore the design of the American commercial republic and how political, social, and economic developments and critical decisions in response to such developments have by the present moment weakened the incentives for public officials to hold onto the larger, more political view of a commercial society and to hew to the essence of the public interest. In a grand version of goal displacement, serving business interests and sustaining business political privileges have become the central aim of national governance, exactly what the admittedly "delicate operation" (Elkin 2006, 75) of the regime's original design was meant to avoid.

What distinguishes Part I from many other treatments of American political and economic development is not only the focus on the fundamental challenge of republican regime design and practice but a particular attention to the political treatment of and actions by administrative institutions and administrative officials as part of the working constitution of the commercial republic. Chapters 2 and 3 offer portraits of two distinct but not entirely disconnected working constitutions and their administrative states, the first associated with the nation building era and the second resulting from the consequences of the first. They both reflect the complex struggles of legislators, elected executives, judges, public administrators, and business to keep a fix on the political institutional heart of the public interest of the commercial republic. As chapter 3 shows, it is primarily through additional developments in the transformed political economy and second administrative state that in the present moment the constitutive institutions of the regime too often fail to serve the public interest. They now magnify far more than they counterbalance the tendency to make serving business interests and inducing satisfactory business performance an end in itself.

Given the reality and current character of the commercial republic and the second administrative state, the chapters of Part II constitute an argument for redesigning the regime to incorporate an administrative state into fundamental law and thus better enable it to serve the public interest. The primary attention of Part II is on the theoretical accommodation and enabling of a fourth administrative branch as part of the theory of American political constitution. What such accommodation means in practice is also considered, however. Chapter 4 presents the normative case for the creation of a fourth, administrative branch as part of the root institutional structure of the regime. The case for a fourth branch is substantial, including improvements in the functioning of the separation of powers and increasing the chances that the public interest will be realized by broadening the currently very narrow interests of corporate capital, the primary controllers of productive assets in the regime. Drawing an engaged public into governance more broadly is also a strong possible effect of creating a fourth branch. There are, however, many alternative and competing solutions on offer to address the difficulties the commercial republic and the administrative state in their current guises pose for good governance. Chapter 5 examines several of the most elaborate and thought-provoking alternative solutions. None of these alternatives fully grasps the fundamental political meaning of the commercial republic, however, nor do they acknowledge the essential reality of administration as a constitutive institution of the regime and what that requires to incorporate the administrative state into the regime in such a way as to ensure a continuing concern for the public interest. Hence, questions about the specific structural features of a fourth branch, or at least the principles on which those features might develop, deserve consideration. This is the task of chapter 6. The conclusion briefly considers the fundamental meaning of and prospects for a redesign of the regime that would place public administration alongside the other constitutive institutions to advance the promise of the American commercial republic.

PART I

Searching for the Commercial Public Interest

1. The Political Constitution of the American Commercial Republic

In the most common version of the myth of Pandora, Hephaestus creates the first mortal woman on Zeus's command. To counterbalance Prometheus's gift to mortals of fire, Zeus arranges for Pandora to receive a *pithos* filled with scourges. At first fearful of what might be inside, Pandora's curiosity eventually overcomes her fear. She opens the vessel and out fly many banes and curses, psychological and physical, including many phobias. By the time Pandora clamps down the lid she captures only hope inside. Thus, in transcending her own fear, Pandora let loose other fears upon the mortal world.

Considered from a particular perspective, the founders of the American republic acted much like the mythical first woman. They overcame their fear of popular rule, a fear of unrestrained passions and anarchy, evidence of which seemed far too prominent to ignore in the history of failed popular regimes. As Publius astonishingly declared in *The Federalist Papers*, "In all very numerous assemblies, of whatever character composed, passion never fails to wrest the sceptre from reason. Had every Athenian citizen been a Socrates, every Athenian assembly would still have been a mob" (no. 55). Yet many in the founding generation had hope that the banes and curses of popular government could be arrested. Among the many competing views of the possibilities, that of the learned and perpetually well-prepared James Madison was so bold as to contend that a larger, more "extended" republic would be far more effective in navigating the pitfalls of popular government.

Many of the supporters of this new kind of republic carried with them the Whig, or Commonwealth, sensibilities of Englishmen who most feared a "court party" faction. Their fear was that such a faction would use governmental authority to derange the English constitution so as to keep themselves in power and abuse the liberties of fellow citizens. In this account of the "ideological origins" (Bailyn 1967) of the American revolution, further bolstered in a "Republican synthesis" (Lowery 1993, 183; see Wood 1969; Pocock 1975; Banning 1978), the fears of the Whig perspective not only animated the break with England but also informed the critiques of the Articles of Confederation and guided central design elements of the new version of the American republic. Like Pandora's fateful move, however, particular Whiggish fears were loosed upon American society, affecting the design of the republic in ways that would plague its practical unfolding in a working constitution.

Two of these fears were of organized interests formed into durable parties—factions—and of corporations as particularly insidious vehicles for factional control and corruption. Because such forms of political and economic organization nevertheless came to dominate the American political economy, the underlying fear of them and thus the "founding errors" (Wallis 2008) of resistance to planning for their subsequent rise colored the efforts of several successive generations of political leaders to flesh out the practical workings of the republican design of 1787, including the relations between an emerging capitalism and a constitutionally restrained state.

A third fear was of bureaucracy, or administration. For Americans of Whiggish predilections, administrative agents were, like corporations, particularly dangerous because they could serve as a vehicle for upsetting the balance of powers in a republican constitution, depriving citizens of their liberties (Lowery 1993, 187–188). Administration, or the "ministry," was dangerous because it could threaten individual liberty "through interference with the personal affairs of citizens via the agency of administrative action" (188). Administration could also threaten the basic balance and structural protections of republican governance on its own through its special expertise and control of information, or as an instrument of oppression in the hands of the executive or the legislature (188–197). Much of the danger posed by these latter systemic threats stemmed from the potential use and abuse of patronage—the control of government jobs, privileges, and contracts—to cater to narrower interests as against the public interest, perpetuating rule by such interests and enabling them to inflict ever greater and harsher deprivations on their opponents. These narrower interests were primarily "monied interests" that a "designing ministry" could corruptly manipulate to serve its own purposes, including corrupting the legislature (McCormick 1981, 254).

All these fears and the responses to them can be seen in the articulation of designs for the American commercial republic formalized in the Constitution and in the struggles and conflicts to elaborate on those designs in an initial working constitution in the early years of the republic. The best starting point to delve into the struggles and conflicts is James Madison's vision for an American commercial republic and the theory of political constitution of the regime he articulated.

THE MADISONIAN COMMERCIAL REPUBLIC

James Madison remains "the leading architect of American political institutions and their most persuasive defender" (Elkin 2006, 20; also see Reimer 1958). It makes good sense, then, to attend first, and carefully, to his thinking in any exploration of the evolving American commercial republic, its character, and its difficulties. The standard approach in political science and constitutional law is to treat Madison's thought as centered on, if not exclusively about, institutional arrangements, especially the separation of powers. Yet Madison was concerned with the design of a whole regime, not just the structural mechanics of republican government. He was concerned with "how to constitute a politics whose defining feature is a self-limiting popular sovereign" (Elkin 2006, 20) and how to do that given the commercial character of American society and his own vision for a distinctly commercial republic.

The question of the commercial nature of the regime may very well have been the most serious point of contention during the constitutional convention and the battle between federalists and antifederalists during the ratification debates. Because it related so closely to those old Whig fears of parties, corporations, and administration, the character of an American commercial republic also became the central source of friction between James Madison and Alexander Hamilton and the ultimate cause of their permanent fracture in the political war between the Federalists and the Jeffersonians. Finally, if the heart of the American experiment is to test the long-run viability of a commercial republic, then any further theorizing about bettering this particular form of republican political constitution must take up the challenge of preserving the rewards of a commercial society and the particular form of a liberal justice to which it aspires in the context of administratively centered modern governance. To respond to that challenge requires a consideration of and appreciation for original thinking about the rewards and aspirations associated with republican rule, the designs and design flaws emanating from that thinking, and the consequences that have followed.

Primary Dimensions of Commercial Republican Regime Design

Madison's theorizing about a commercial republican regime was multidimensional (Elkin 2006, chap. 2). The first five dimensions are most familiar to students of the Constitution and its sweeping defense laid out in the *Federalist* essays. The sixth dimension of Madison's theorizing, the social basis of the regime, is the most complicated facet of Madison's thinking, but it is also what makes Madison's thinking a more holistic endeavor to fashion and defend a commercial republic.

The first, most familiar, and to many the most prominent feature of Madison's thinking is the set of institutional arrangements that takes aim at the dangers of factional government. To know that at the root of this dimension in Madison's design is the Whiggish fear of a dominating court faction that can subvert the public interest and perpetuate its rule is to highlight that this aspect of Madison's design is about more than the tripartite separation of powers and its complement of checks and balances. As Madison made clear, the underlying problem was multidimensional, requiring a broader and more complex set of institutional arrangements. The separation of powers was an important component, but it was to be an "auxiliary" precaution, for the threat of factious government was not just that it puts rights in jeopardy. It undermines more insidiously any effort to reason about the public interest and deliberate about its concrete meaning. Factional government has this effect by substituting the interests of some for the "permanent and aggregate interests of the community" (*The Federalist Papers*, no. 10). Separation of powers alone would not counteract the threat.

Madison acknowledged that a group of citizens of factious spirit could "[amount] to a majority or a minority of the whole" (*The Federalist Papers*, no. 10). He regarded the threat of the latter as largely neutralized by the "republican principle," that is, majority rule by a properly informed and civic-minded citizenry. By the time of his rift with Hamilton, Madison had come to see the threat of minority faction as a far more serious problem. He thus insisted that special effort was imperative to ensure the strength and resilience of majority rule. Before that realization, however, Madison's thinking about institutional designs for coping with the threat of faction reflected the general fear of the founders regarding popular government. Hence his design components intended to confront the problem of faction were generally aimed at diminishing the chances and, failing that, controlling the effects of majority factions seizing control of the whole government. The components he promoted, incorporated into the Constitution's structure, were a system of representation, the extended republic, and the tripartite scheme of separated institutions sharing governing powers.

Madison proposed a particular structure of national representation, and he presented the idea of the extended republic with the specific rationale of decreasing the chances that a majority faction would ever arise. For a national legislature to function, the number of representatives would have to be small enough, and represent districts large enough, that single factions having the political power to choose the representative from any given district would be less likely. Extending the republic over a large territory, and dividing sovereignty between the states and the national government, would multiply and diversify interests. Should a particular faction overcome these barriers and gain the support of a majority of citizens, the separation of powers, with its multiple forms, timing, and manner of election and selection of the occupants of the distinct institutions, would then serve as a second line of defense to divide and frustrate a factional majority by making it hard to gain and keep control of the whole government, deploy the government to serve its own interests, and oppress opponents.

It is thus a serious misunderstanding of Madison's design ideas to treat the separation of powers as the essence of his theoretical and practical thinking about the design of a commercial republic. Madison specifically derided mere "parchment barriers" between the primary governing institutions as insufficient defense against factional rule (*The Federalist Papers*, no. 48). It is critical not just to allocate different powers to different institutions. These powers must overlap to some extent because the aim was not only to stop bad things from happening but also to increase the chances that good things would get done. As Madison stressed, a principal problem with the Articles of Confederation was that it structured the primary components of government and allocated powers among them ineffectively for both restraining faction and facilitating necessary action. Out of the research he undertook in preparation for the constitutional convention, Madison came to be equally concerned with enabling good majorities to arise and to govern. A particular form of separate institutions sharing power was meant to further that aim (Elkin 2006, 27). One of the principal advantages of the scheme was that it would encourage representatives of various sorts to interact and collaborate in ways that would enable them to reason about the public interest and how to give it concrete meaning on a given question. They would be more likely to deliberate, not just rule. Certainly the institutional occupants would bring their self-interested motivations into office. Their ambitions to govern would nevertheless push them into cooperation in order to avoid total frustration of their governing aims by complex structures and processes.

Madison acknowledged that the science of factional control was imprecise, and thus the Constitution's institutional designs "must be relatively crude, with the result that some good majorities will be impeded along with reprehensible ones" (Elkin 2006, 28). Experience with their operation would show what adjustments might be necessary to refine them and shore up their weaknesses. He eventually pivoted to extraconstitutional arrangements—particularly the political party—in this regard. It is also worth noting that Madison firmly believed that the Constitution's amendment process, which was to be used only sparingly and carefully, was nevertheless practicable. Design adjustments that showed promise in enabling good majorities to arise could be cemented in place through the amendment process (McCoy 1989, 71–73). More important, the unavoidably crude institutional arrangements, including lines of division and allocation of powers within government, were not to be left on their own as the bulwark against threats to liberty. They had to be fitted together so as not to completely frustrate good majorities and paralyze government action. As a result they would be only weak barriers to factional rule absent other design features that would complement and indeed would be more crucial to ensuring a stable, peaceful, and sustainable regime of self-government.

The second key dimension of Madison's theory is the rule of law. For Madison, this meant that any law enacted must apply to the lawmakers as it would to all other citizens. It also meant that law was to be the product of a public, deliberative process, requiring lawmakers to give reasons for their support of a proposed law. Madison conceived of the rule of law as a particular complement to the devices for regulating faction (Elkin 2006, 29). Rule of law made the enactment of laws granting special privileges or exclusions, or otherwise giving one group better or harsher treatment, less likely. Likewise, inhibiting factional influence reduced the possibility that lawmakers would exempt themselves from the laws. Still, like the institutional designs meant to regulate the threats of factional government, rule of law is only a rough barrier. The US Congress has exempted itself from many laws over the course of American political development. A concerted effort via the Congressional Accountability Act of 1995 (2 U.S.C. 1301) and its small policing agency, the Office of Compliance, has only relatively recently aimed to reduce these violations of the rule of law principle. On the executive side, the president's pardon power (Article II, Section 2) has been used to circumvent the rule of law for seemingly noble ends as intended (*The Federalist Papers*, no. 74), as well as more nefarious aims (Crouch 2008). These instances of actual practice are an indication that unless other elements of a regime design create institutions that are effective in facilitating the development of supplemental norms and the incentives to adhere to them, those norms will be only weak complements to and lubrication for the effective function of the more structural features of a regime design.

The third element of Madison's regime thinking, the public interest, is rarely singled out in treatments of Madisonian theory. Yet Madison was clear that his designs for the American republic were not merely intended to inhibit factional strife and prevent disastrous violations of rights. The intent of the regulation of faction was also to give lawmakers some breathing room so that they might at least occasionally consider what serving the permanent interests of the community would mean in various circumstances. In other words, for republican government to succeed, institutional design must facilitate, at least some of the time, the emergence of a common understanding of the public interest (Elkin 2006, 30–31). This would vary by circumstance and would still be an iffy proposition under even favorable conditions, many lawmakers being of factious spirit despite the best efforts of system designers and thoughtful citizens. Therefore, some understanding of the substantive content of the public interest must obtain. Madison "said surprisingly little about the content of the permanent interests of the community" (Elkin 2006, 30), however. There are indications, nevertheless, that Madison regarded securing rights, maintaining stable government, and promoting a commercial society of a particular kind as among the common interests of the American community.

Further inquiry into this last aspect of Madison's thinking about the public interest follows shortly.

Increasing the chances that lawmakers would thoughtfully deliberate about elements of the public interest is the fourth element of Madison's thinking (Elkin 2006, 33–36). Like the public interest element, promoting deliberation reflected Madison's contention that regulating the clash of factions was not sufficient to ensure good government in a popular regime. Aggregating interests into a majority coalition was not enough either. On matters of national import, lawmakers must find their way to a view of things that transcends their narrow interests.

It was important to Madison that lawmakers not be abject scoundrels, but he also thought that they need not have much in the way of broad visions of the public interest. Indeed, it might be better that they not be visionaries, as long as they were ambitious enough to pursue their interests into the public councils. There they would confront others of similar character in the context of the separation of powers and other institutional devices. Those design features would force them into public exchanges in which they would have to explain how the aims they sought served the public good. The process might nevertheless be dominated by bargaining and vote trading serving particularistic interests rather than producing clear public interest outcomes. Many Americans today seem convinced that the nation's political history is littered with corrupt bargains large and small. Yet Madison suggested, at least in *The Federalist Papers*, that the Constitution's design and its underlying supports would increase the chances that bargaining and interest exchange would not be the only outcomes of the lawmaking process. Further inquiry into this aspect of Madison's thinking also follows later in the chapter. It is useful here to note, however, that after his own service as a representative in the First Congress, and upon further reflection after he had retired to his Virginia homestead, Montpelier, Madison was far more guarded in his views about the possibility, and necessity, of deliberation in lawmaking (Bailey 2015). Whatever sample of Madison's thinking one takes in this regard, however, it is reasonably clear that he saw the general character of representatives, and the chance that they might deliberate about the public interest on occasion, as critically linked to the general aptitudes of the citizenry.

Thus, a "capable citizenry" is the fifth element of the Madisonian design (Elkin 2006, 36–38). This concern about the capabilities of ordinary citizens as a matter of regime design centers on the expectation that there would be sufficient "virtue" among citizens such that they would be capable of distinguishing potentially effective representatives from the knaves and demagogues of factious spirit always attracted by opportunities for controlling public power. Such virtue not only encompasses a minimum level of political astuteness but also a public spiritedness such that, with the help of other design elements such as large electoral districts, good or "civic" as opposed to factional majorities would be more likely to form. Madison regarded republicanism and public spirit as mutually reinforcing. Public-spirited republican citizens would understand that they had duties concomitant to their rights, "that self-governance demands a vigilant, continuous participation in the public affairs," and that they are part of a "collective consciousness" that all citizens are "embarked together, as individuals and equals, on a common quest for happiness and justice" (Banning 1995, 90). An ennobling vision for sure, but how would this "necessary character of the citizenry . . . be fostered without an intrusion into the lives of the citizens" (Elkin 2006, 37) that a liberal-democratic regime would want to avoid? Madison tried to address both the character of the citizenry and the last facet of his regime theorizing—the social basis of the regime—by connecting them to the specific kind of commercial republic he sought to create and sustain.

THE SOCIAL BASIS OF THE REGIME AND A POLITICS OF CLASS INTERESTS

Given Madison's considerable expectation for and reliance on the self-interested behavior of citizens and those whom they would elect to various national offices, under what conditions would civic majorities—those with an eye toward concerns that transcend faction—form? Madison's answer came in several parts beginning with provision for a particular "social basis" for the regime (Elkin 2006, 38). Madison's "political sociology" connected the regime's success to a dependence on harnessing not just self-interest generally, but the self-interest of a particular class. The general theoretical proposition for a theory of political constitution of a commercial republic that builds on this feature of Madison's thinking is that a "politics of the public interest includes, then, not only a politics of deliberation but also a politics of class interests" (114).

Madison had in mind as the social basis of the commercial republic the class of large property holders. Securing commitment to the regime from a class of major property holders was most likely to secure the regime's long-run viability (Elkin 2006, 38–42; also see Nadelsky 1990). Thus, Madison's designs intended to harness self-interest were oriented toward—would work best with—the self-interests of a property-holding class. This required that holders of property be given disproportionate political advantages. They were a critical minority in that they controlled land, society's most important productive asset. They had to be coaxed into committing to a regime in which they would be politically outnumbered. Giving them political advantages in the regime's design would thus reinforce the regime's commitment to protecting property rights against factious majorities, which were likely to be combinations of the "little propertied and the unpropertied" (Diamond 1959, 64). Protecting property was in turn a critical element in the larger protection of rights associated with the substance of the public interest.

But wait, wouldn't this rich, propertied minority simply hijack the government to serve its own narrow ends, leaving the majority increasingly impoverished and open to manipulation that would coax it into voting against its own interests? Gouverneur Morris thought so, but his primary response to the problem was to restrict the broad public's access to power (Nadelsky 1990, chap. 3). Madison also recognized the risk but concluded that large landowners whose fortunes were tied to stable land values, and thus a stable regime, were most susceptible to enough broadening of their interest orientation through the institutional designs of the constitutional scheme that the risk of an overbearing minority of the propertied was considerably lessened. These design features, particularly elections from large districts and the separation of powers, working on the interests of the propertied, would encourage civic rather than factional coalition building. The propertied, likely to be well represented in the public councils, would sometimes be forced by the Constitution's design to engage in public deliberation about the public interest, or at least to put on a show in that regard—which might amount to the same thing. Furthermore, to enjoy both the material and the political advantages the regime offered over the long term, maintaining republican government would be in their interest as well. Whether the potential for a broadening of the interests of a particular class in favor of the public interest, or just the superficial trappings of republicanism, would be realized was an open question. The former would certainly require the development of citizen capacities to choose representatives who would be susceptible to interest broadening. Although worried about the future, Madison was nevertheless guardedly sanguine about a property-based system of political advantages when it was combined with a sufficient reservoir of citizens whose virtue would be developed because of their ties to the land, such that the regime would be truly republican in the way he and others envisioned it.

It is important to highlight here a particular concern of Madison's regarding the deprivations stemming from the instability of arbitrary rule. A society cannot prosper and enjoy the many fruits of civilization if the law is erratic and easily manipulated, whether because of the rule of a few or of the many. Madison's design aimed to create a regime that was popular but limited as a solution to arbitrary rule (Elkin 2006, 46). It could only be so if it was energetic enough within its sphere not only to prevent factional rule but also to provide the stability, order, and prosperity that would allow the great bulk of the people to enjoy the peace and tranquility necessary to seek and achieve their own purposes. The limits, while not excessively constraining, must still be real. If citizens regard government as merely an instrument for satisfying private desires by having someone else pay for them—the very essence of faction—they will conclude that the race for benefits will always go to those best organized and most motivated by the size of the gains. They will then see self-government as a folly to be avoided (Elkin 2006, 48). Hence, the central constitutional problem is to sustain "the creative tension between popular government and rights and permanent interests," to realize a government that is "active in pursuit of its limited purposes" (49). The creative tension is especially acute in a commercial republic, which privileges a particular class in order to gain its commitment to the regime and bring its energy and interest-broadening potential into government, sometimes pitting it against the general citizenry in the process.

Madison's response to this problem, remarkably creative, was also unavoidably rough and imperfect, however. As Madison recognized, political leaders would have to be mindful of what was working and not working as parchment turned into a working constitution. Not surprisingly, Madison was in part thinking of himself, and he contributed to this effort through the various public offices he held, in ways perhaps as far-reaching as his theorizing. Others of his generation made major contributions too, not all of which Madison agreed with. Regarding the central challenge of liberal-democratic regime design, market-state relations and inducing business performance, and thus in the American case the nature of the commercial republic, there is reason to look more closely at Madison's thinking and its limitations, in part by comparing it to the most distinctive alternative vision, that of Alexander Hamilton. Madison's design was for a particular kind of commercial republic that he readily acknowledged could not last forever—and might not even last more than a few generations. Hamilton sought to lay the foundations for a design that would last much farther into the future. The contours and substance of their contrasting designs and the debates surrounding them during the founding and the early years of the republic about the proper social basis of the regime, and the political economy best suited to an American republic, centered on who would have favored status in the regime and what role the general citizenry would play. The uneasy fit of the competing visions did much to orient the character and long-run development of the American experiment with the republican form.

MADISON: LANDED PROPERTY, VIRTUE, AND THE AGRARIAN COMMERCIAL REPUBLIC

The commitment at the founding to form a commercial republic was widespread. It is not too much of an exaggeration to suggest that it was inconceivable to those of the founding generation that an American republic would be anything else. Despite the noncommercial origins of a few of the early colonial ventures in

North America, the American colonies were consolidated on the foundation of commercial enterprise. Trade was the primary relationship between Europe and the American colonies, England paramount. Commerce and trade were already deeply ingrained in the American way of life when serious talk about how the new nation might reconstitute itself arose in the 1780s. The great question was what kind of political economy would enable the United States to avoid, or forestall as long as possible, the decadence and decay of the political economies of the old-world powers, with their corrupt court politics in their capital cities, their permanent underclass of landless poor, the manipulations of trade to keep court parties in power, and the nearly constant international conflict tied to a wasteful mercantilist trade system.

Nearly all who were engaged in the debates agreed that an American republic could avoid the worst of the old world's flaws and excesses. Madison's design for an extended republic as the foundation of the new constitution, and the subsequent success of the new governmental design in the ratification debates, masked to some extent the divergent views about the social basis of the regime held by the new design's foremost theorists and advocates. These divergent views became dramatically clear after Alexander Hamilton took the reins of the newly created treasury department. Before that, however, the imperative of constructing a new design for the American commercial republic and getting it ratified kept more serious conflict over the critical question of the social basis for the regime contained.

The social basis of a commercial republican regime as Madison envisioned it was grounded in his conception of future development "across space rather than through time," anchored in "the principles of commercial liberalism" and "the promise of a new, more open international commercial order" (McCoy 1980, 121). Like the views of others—including Benjamin Franklin, who followed the views of François Quesnay and the French physiocrats—Madison's aim was to keep "America . . . young and virtuous, while offering both a haven for the landless poor of Europe and a bountiful market for the advanced manufactures that a fully peopled Europe was forced to produce" (121). Westward expansion would sustain America's agrarian character. A nation of industrious farmers would produce abundant agricultural surplus to sell to the teeming nations of Europe and obtain refined, manufactured goods in return. This would forestall the need for America to develop its own substantial manufacturing base beyond the necessities that Jefferson described as "coarse and middling goods" (227). Landed property was central to Madison's design for a stronger central government because that particular social basis of the regime would not only protect the property rights of the virtuous agrarian freeholders, it would also provide the energy in government to enable the United States to succeed in dismantling the old, corrupt mercantilist system in favor of a more open and balanced international trading order. Madison thus argued for property as a qualification for suffrage, because those industrious farmers who were concerned with and committed to the land as the basis of wealth would be best able to discern who was qualified to represent them locally, in state capitals, and in the new national government, the new federal Congress in particular.

Because "landed farmers were beholden to neither an employer nor the government," they were the natural promoters of "public liberty" and the natural defenders of "public safety." Because they "enjoyed the benefits of health, virtue, intelligence, and happiness that were less evident in other occupations," they were most likely to preserve and perpetuate the virtues of a republican way of life (Gibson 1993, 526). They would also be able to discern who among the elite property holders and men of high regard in the community should be their representatives because these men would be most likely to fulfill Madison's conception of representation as impartiality, or the pursuit of the public good rather than service to their own or their local community's interests. They would thus be more likely "to deliberate about the ends and goals of public policy" (525).

Madison's concern for giving special political advantages in his regime design to holders of landed property was thus about ensuring that these men who would be more receptive to a broadening of their interests toward the common good and permanent interests of society, and more likely to deliberate on what the public interest might be on concrete questions of public policy, would be well represented in the councils of the national government. This was especially necessary because it was inescapable once new land was no longer available for sustaining a growing population and a largely agrarian political economy. This would lead to "the formation of a propertyless poor who would seek refuge in the cities and eventually become a threat to the property rights of landed interests" (Gibson 1993, 514). A threat to landed interests would also be a threat to the base of citizen virtue necessary for a true republic to endure. Providing political advantages to those landed interests would ease their way into government. Even if they arrived with strictly self-interested aims, the source of those interests combined with the separation of powers and other features would give them the incentive to deliberate on and craft public policy to serve the permanent interests of the nation. The primary public interest was to extend the life of the American republic's special character, holding back the inevitable forces of urban population concentration and social decay for as long as possible and cushioning the impact of their eventual arrival.

To state the concept of the social basis of a regime in more general regime design terms, "a regime is a set of institutions harnessed to a conception of justice consistent with the one held by the powerful social strata of the regime" (Elkin 2006, 38). Madison looked to a particular social stratum he thought most likely to exercise the kind of impartial judgment in lawmaking and governance that he regarded as essential for the protection of rights and the commitment to vital common interests. Madison's design relied primarily on the extended republic to draw from this stratum the representatives and lawmakers who, when gathered together in Congress, would deliberate impartially rather than wholly on the basis of local interests (Gibson 2012; but also see Bailey 2015, chap. 3). They would thus give form in word and action to their conception of justice.

Initially, the extended republic was Madison's invention primarily to ensure the security of a universal veto over state laws, which he sought to incorporate into the Constitution. He promoted "expanded electoral districts" as a way to "block the spread of factious majorities and promote the formation of impartial majorities within Congress." Larger electoral districts would "create competition among a stable number of enlightened and virtuous statesmen" for a more limited number of legislative offices, increasing "the likelihood of a 'fit' choice" (Gibson 2012, 199). This would validate the normative and practical worth of the universal veto. The universal veto failed to win approval at the convention, however, forcing Madison to revise his thinking about the role that the extended republic would play in his regime design. Through that rethinking the extended republic became central to his design for getting into Congress those who would be most open to articulating a broad conception of the public interest, including, of course, preservation of the nation's republican character. The extended republic would create in Congress the conditions by which lawmaking would be collectively impartial "even though individual legislators" would be "judges in their own causes and interested parties on some issues, some of the time" (191n6).

What is most important to understand about Madison's reliance on this design feature is that, because he expected it would greatly reduce the chances that a majority faction would ever show up in the national legislature, the extended republic would establish the conditions for deliberation. That in turn would lead to identification of the true common interest on any question of national import. The dynamic would involve a kind of majority cycling in which majorities would nearly always be composed of those lawmakers with little to no personal or local constituent interest in the question before them. This would be both the outcome of and input into deliberation, which "would create a broadening of the coalition necessary to form a majority. Aware that they could not successfully advance purely partisan or partial schemes, representatives would develop an enlarged understanding of what policies were in the interests of the whole nation on the basis of a more accurate view of and sympathy for those interests" (Gibson 2012, 201). Deliberation that moved toward revealing the common interest was the result of representatives making "mutual and equitable sacrifices" (201) because they would be "in an equal position within a legislative body in which there is [already] a commitment to the collective interest" (202).

This was the logic in context behind Madison's choice to make men of considerable landed property holdings the social basis of his regime design. These men most likely embodied the character of the virtuous agrarian republic, which in turn would make them the individuals chosen by other enfranchised citizens—conscientious landowning farmers all—to be their representatives. They would also embody and vigorously defend the kind of property that Madison regarded as "most sacred" because it reinforced those "faculties of mind, which included the rights of conscience and the communication of opinions" (Gibson 2012, 195) that define a free people. This in turn would reinforce the link with Madison's commitment to a form of self-government anchored by a well-cultivated and discerning public opinion.

Madison's extended republic, combined with the creation of larger electoral districts, would privilege the selection of men from the landed elite as national legislators—not to mention as judges, chief magistrates, and public ministers. These men would already be oriented to serving the public interest because it was commensurate with their interests in prolonging the existence of an agrarian commercial republic, because they would less likely be part of a factious majority and because, with the threat of majority faction much reduced, they would be able to deliberate as equals to find the common interest with respect to protecting rights and sustaining the special prosperity that an agrarian commercial republic would bring. The other branches would also constitute a more effective check against any remaining threat of majority faction, or the effect of short-term public passions that might arise in Congress as the national institution most energized by popular opinion. The compound republic would provide a further constraint, especially as it would "[preserve] a limited scope for federal responsibilities" as well as "increasing the distance between the people and their representatives" on questions of national import that fell within that limited scope (Gibson 2012, 204). This is how Madison envisioned structural and social elements fitting together to form a regime of popular rule and vigorous but limited government. He envisioned government as "part of the solution of the problem of arbitrary rule" (Elkin 2006, 47), whether that arbitrariness came from government officials themselves or popular majorities with a penchant for oppressing minorities, especially a minority holding a disproportionate share of the means of production.

Madison's regime design was therefore based on a particular conception of the social and economic nature of American society and the necessary devices for preserving it as long as possible, despite his acceptance of the inevitable forces of economic development that would eventually overcome America's natural spatial advantages and his governmental designs for exploiting them. Madison did recognize that "the propertied class also included those [engaged] in commerce and manufacturing. Over time, the balance, he thought, would shift toward these two forms of economic activity. If that were to occur," his design with landed property holders as the social basis of the regime would be "significantly weakened" (Elkin 2006, 322n122). Madison thus worried almost constantly that America would eventually become a complex, decadent, and less peaceful society, with an economy centered on large industrial manufacturing. The wealth that such an economy would generate could lead to a society riven by party conflict as different interests vied to gain control of the government, enabling a faction that did gain control to manipulate the economy by granting incorporation privileges to favored businesses that would in turn support the faction and its effort to stay in power. Madison's regime design, with special political privileges for landed property holders that would make them disproportionately represented in the national legislature, was meant to delay and cushion the impact of this worrisome future reality.

Unlike Madison, Alexander Hamilton's "vision of the future was not clouded by the traditional republican fears that continued to plague Madison and much of agrarian America" (McCoy 1980, 133–134). While Madison remained to some extent "caught between the conflicting claims of classical republicanism and modern commercial society, struggling to define and implement a viable synthesis that was relevant to the American experience," Hamilton "had stepped confidently and unequivocally into modernity" (134). For Hamilton, time was not the enemy if only America would embrace an alternative political economy with a different social basis for the regime.

HAMILTON: CAPITAL, AMBITION, AND A MODERN COMMERCIAL REPUBLIC

The mutually reinforcing concepts and analyses in the Hamilton and Madison *Federalist* essays mask several theoretical differences in the regime designs of the two erstwhile allies, of which two are key. First, Hamilton did not regard Madison's design for regulating majority faction through interest diversification—through representation and extension of the republic across space—as adequate for the challenge. Second, Hamilton sought a more limited role for public opinion in the governance process despite his emphatic pronouncement in *The Federalist Papers*, no. 22, that the "fabric of American empire ought to rest on the solid basis of *the consent of the people*." The distinction rests on Hamilton's serious doubts that Madison's reliance on at least some virtue in the citizenry was realistic given the essence of human nature and the long-run prospects for the regime.

Hamilton's wariness about the effectiveness of representation and the extended republic to regulate the threat of majority faction centered on his contention that representation from larger districts required in the extended republic would not sufficiently broaden the interests of representatives. It might often be the case that "a small portion of a large district carries an election," resulting in representatives with quite narrow interests. Moreover, "representatives of an extensive nation still meet in one room and are liable to the same influences of those in a small country, including the charm of a powerful demagogue" (Sheehan 2004, 410). Factions could still form on narrow geographic and economic factors in an extended republic and seize control of the popular chamber through demagogic leadership. In an important sense, then, Hamilton did not regard the separation of powers and the distinctive design bases for other governmental institutions to be mere "auxiliary precautions" or "parchment barriers." Instead, "Hamilton contended that the problem of majority tyranny necessitates the establishment of a 'permanent barrier' in government that would counteract the passionate demands of the many, particularly their covetousness toward the property of others" (410).

Hamilton thus thought of representation in broader terms, with each institution playing a representative role. Together, they would create the centripetal, or unifying, representation of the nation's permanent interests. Hamilton saw the Constitution's design as creating "successive layers of direct and indirect election in the legislative and executive branches and then through participation in appointments of judges and subordinate administrative officials by those elected officials" (Green 2019, 29–30). It is through its coordinated parts, "including the subordinate public administration," that the Constitution "bolsters the representative principle" (30).

With respect to the role of the public, "Madison and Hamilton did not differ about the need to filter the interests, passions, and opinions of the citizens or about the need to achieve a reasonable, impartial, and durable will in government, but they did very much disagree about who or what legitimately gives voice to this will and whether the process involves modifying the actual views of the citizens" (Sheehan 2004, 422). Hamilton sought to address the challenge by "establishing a system of institutional counterbalances within the government of a diversified, commercial nation" (422). This reflects again his broader conception of representation through multiple government institutions. If the system operated properly, it would build confidence in the people that the government would protect their rights and they would enjoy a reasonable level of material well-being not undermined by factional manipulation of the economy for narrow economic and political advantage. For Hamilton, the role of public opinion was, therefore, generally limited to the expression of confidence in the government. For Madison, however, representatives would "stand before the bar of public opinion," and "an equilibrium of passions and interests in the society" would "reduce the likelihood of majority faction as well as . . . shape an environment conducive to the formation of a public will tempered and modified by the commerce of ideas" (422–423).

Both men "relied significantly on an educated elite to accomplish their ends." Hamilton aimed for "a type of statesmanship that sought to inspire respect and confidence more than to teach." Madison sought "a kind of civic leadership that aspired to cultivate civic understanding, refine mores and manners, and educate the people for their indispensable role in a self-governing republic" (Sheehan 2004, 423). Although this may sound illiberally intrusive, it is important again to stress that Madison envisioned this refinement and education to happen not through government but through the experiences of living in an agrarian commercial republic. In any case, the contrasting Madison and Hamilton conceptions of public leadership reflect their contrasting notions of representation and the role of public opinion. These contrasting views in turn point to their divergent conceptions of the pathway to diversifying interests, the social basis for the regime, and the process by which particular interests would be broadened toward taking account of more permanent national interests.

Madison and Hamilton agreed that expanding the diversity of interests was one critical feature of a republic that would increase the chances of inhibiting the emergence of factional rather than civic majorities. For Madison, the goal of a stronger central government—one that was vigorous enough to push other nations toward an international system of free trade ensuring relatively unimpeded markets for the agricultural surplus that American farmers would produce—precipitated the very problem of regulating faction that he had to address. A government strong enough to engage foreign nations on equal terms and compel them into agreement on trade was also a government that a faction would be motivated to commandeer for purposes "adversed to the rights of other citizens, or to the permanent and aggregate interests of the community" (*The Federalist Papers*, no. 10). Madison saw a diversity of interests already well formed in the United States, across the states and even within individual states. Hence, "increasing the area of land over which the national government exercises control does not produce diversity: it embraces the greater diversity which already exists" (Gibson 1993, 506). Bringing them together in the extended republic, backed by the auxiliary precautions of the Constitution's governmental design, would greatly reduce the risk of a majority faction forming, or if nevertheless formed, of its seizing control of all the powers of the new, more powerful government.

Hamilton and Madison also shared a general conception of virtue in a modern liberal state. "A modern liberal regime focuses and limits the aims of government on the material conditions and virtues required to ensure a peaceful and orderly society," where individuals freely choose "their way in life through social institutions of their choosing or on their own" (Green 2019, 20). Citizens, no matter what their social station, could, and would, pursue their own interests. Because Madison sought the creation of a particular kind of commercial republic, one with a sufficient base of virtue that could be further cultivated and expanded, interests should be advanced "only to the degree they were compatible with the public good, that obedience be given to laws and policies made collectively, and that deference be shown for established elites" (Gibson 1993, 524). For Madison, land and virtue were mutually reinforcing. Hence, the sort of American virtue that Madison identified and endeavored to foster, which he associated with both the spirit of the Revolution and the agrarian way of life, was the basis of his regime design's giving special political advantage to the holders of landed property.

To a considerable extent Hamilton regarded Madison's theorizing to create and sustain an agrarian commercial republic as misplaced romanticism. Hamilton thought it best to seize the opportunity presented by the economic instabilities of the 1780s to make the United States a modern commercial republic. As committed as any other founder to the republican form, Hamilton therefore had to find his own versions of the key elements of the design for a whole regime. He sought to weave those alternative elements together in a way that would fulfill a different vision of the American republic—not a virtuous agrarian idyll but a modern commercial and industrial empire. Yet Hamilton's designs for this alternative vision also had weaknesses rooted in an aim to preserve narrow elite control of commerce, industry, and finance.

Hamilton's departures from Madison's thinking with respect to representation and the role of public opinion were serious enough. Yet Hamilton's conception of a social basis of the regime, and how to tie the interests of the propertied—or in his case, the "monied men"—to the regime was the most dramatic contrast to Madisonian thinking about the regime's design. It was also the most threatening to Madison, Jefferson, and their allies. For them, "Hamiltonian policies would create a class struggle, a war of the poor against the rich" (Gibson 1993, 514). Yet it was precisely Hamilton's aim to get past such long-standing, deep-seated social divisions. "By multiplying and diversifying occupations and interests in America the age-old battle between the haves and the have-nots would be replaced by a new and much less dangerous rivalry in society" (Sheehan 2004, 412), namely, entrepreneurialism and economic competition.

Hamilton recognized the critical role of America's agricultural richness to the nation's long-run political-economic success. His focus, however, was on accelerating the development of a primarily industrial and commercial American political economy. This would lead to a multiplication and diversification of occupations and interests that would sideline, if not entirely extinguish, the most dangerous divisions in American society. Such divisions were not just between the propertied and the unpropertied, but also "between northern and southern interests, i.e., between industry and agriculture, between free and slave-holding states" (Sheehan 2004, 411). This diminution of more dangerous rivalries would also follow from the prosperity that accelerated economic activity and greater economic diversification would produce. Yet Hamilton's design was not simply aimed at unleashing a frenzied acquisitiveness. His primary objects were far more political than economic. Increased prosperity would increase public confidence in the regime and stabilize the republic. Economic diversity and greater prosperity would lessen the dangers of faction. All this would ensure that a modern American republic would have the capacity to develop itself further and effectively defend against external threats. A different social basis for the regime was thus required.

In contrast to Madison's design, fusing the force of public opinion with political advantages enabling a landed property elite to rule, Alexander Hamilton's ideas about what political economy was best for an American commercial republic reflected what he thought was more realistic for a republic that was already much larger in population and expanse than ever previously contemplated, and one destined to grow even more. Against Madison, Hamilton thought that trying to delay or suppress industrialization and commercial trade in finished goods "for the sake of preserving a rural agrarian republic would favor only a small, elite portion of the population that would continue to bank its prosperity on the backs of slaves" (Green 2019, 38). He "believed that only a complex political economy" consisting of "manufacturing, commercial trade, and agriculture would be able to provide the range of opportunities needed for Americans to better themselves" (37–38). Hamilton learned firsthand that the supposedly virtuous parsimony of agrarian life "often stemmed from severe want, punctuated by long periods of indolence due to crop cycles" (38). Local manufacturing would be a productive use of that otherwise wasted time. It would "complement the agrarian way of life and bring about a more mature and vibrant commercial and manufacturing base in northern states that lacked sufficient arable land" (38). Hamilton also saw that "the depreciated condition of landed property in America resulted from the scarcity of money. The increased quantity and circulation of capital would contribute to improve the state of agriculture. Further, it would unclog the wheels of commerce, thereby promoting commerce and manufacturing as well" (Sheehan 2004, 409).

To create a modern nation with a mixed, unified political economy (Brown 2017) that was more than a republic in name only, Hamilton accepted many of the key structural elements of Madison's design, particularly those "auxiliary precautions" that would help to regulate the worst hazards of factional tendencies, through the mechanism of "partial agency" (Green 2019, 44–52). Partial agency took the form primarily of separate institutions sharing powers, including further division within the legislature. Because he saw no realistic future for a commercial republican regime with a social basis tied to the interests and fortunes of a small agrarian elite, however, Hamilton had to find ways to tie the interests of a different class to the interests of the nation. This alternative hub of interest centered on bankers and financiers—those with an investment mindset—whom Hamilton regarded as far more likely to endure than a small, land-holding elite. He saw them also as nimbler and more adaptable and thus far more reliable an engine for the diversification of interests, economic growth, and long-run prosperity of the American nation.

Hamilton probably did not regard this collection of interests as comprising a distinct class comparable to the small landed elite. They were distributed more widely across the population, Hamilton presumed, because, far more than Madison, he accepted that self-interest, especially "the passion for material aggrandizement" (Sheehan 2004, 412) dominated human motivation. He was also wary of such men, whether as a class or not, for he "had had enough experience with bankers to know it was hardly safe to leave public finance at their mercy" (McDonald 1958, 193). Hamilton thus envisioned the broadening process to be anchored in their vices and ambitions and subject to proper institutional constraints and careful management.

One might say that Madison designed into the regime political advantages for landed property holders because he expected them to be motivated to defend the way of life that would anchor the politics and economics necessary to sustain the virtuous republic. Their interests would be the regime's interests, or at least they were more likely to become an acceptable approximation of the same thing when these men of equal standing faced one another and deliberated on national questions in the national forum designed for that purpose. In contrast, Hamilton believed that in the long run the basis of any modern economy was capital, not land. He thus aimed to make the social basis of the regime men who cared about money and investment, so as to harness money's productive potential. Although he participated in the constitutional convention, and even more so in the ratification debates, it was in practice that Hamilton fully fleshed out his design ideas with respect to the social basis of the regime. He seized the opportunities provided by the constitutional provisions reflecting the special political advantages for the propertied—the property-rights protections, the contract clause, the currency and public-debt provisions—to entice investment in a republic not defined by one special way of life but many ways of life. No matter what those ways of life might be, Hamilton surmised, the lifeblood of the pursuit was money and credit (Green 2019, 183). The nascent republic's government needed money, too, so Hamilton sought to harness for the regime's stability the motivations of those men whose principal interest was investment in money itself.

Hamilton's opportunities to elaborate on his regime design ideas and test them in practice came primarily through his appointment as the first treasury secretary and secondarily through his law practice in New York. Using the tools available in the new Constitution, along with the authority and discretion granted to the treasury secretary when Congress created the treasury department in 1789, Hamilton created the structures and processes for managing the republic's finances that in turn nudged the nation toward his version of a republican political economy. In doing so, he succeeded spectacularly in tying the interests of the holders of capital to the needs and interests of the regime. Through negotiation and logrolling with Madison and other opponents in Congress, and a final compromise on the location of a new seat of the government that gave Virginia a "favorable accounting of its sums due upon assumption" (Green 2019, 136) and satisfied the interests of Virginians involved in land speculation along the Potomac River, Hamilton gained congressional authorization for federal government assumption of the states' Revolutionary War debt. By monetizing the national debt, Hamilton turned a horrendous burden into the foundation of national faith and trust in the government and "tied the fortunes of many to the future of the country" (131; see also O'Connor 2014, 13–18). The immediate effect was also a powerful injection of cash into the struggling American economy. The creation of a national bank, privately managed so as to limit politicization, served complementary purposes by attracting as subscribers those whose financial "transactions reached amounts significant enough for an initial spur to the economy," but more importantly, "their investment in the bank would amount to an investment in the country" (Green 2019, 141).

For Hamilton, then, capital was the pathway for channeling Americans' "entrepreneurial disposition." The success of that channeling, however, required "both spur and rein" (Green 2019, 149). Recognizing "that free markets could break down or conduce to monopoly through unrestrained avarice" (152), Hamilton "factored such problems, especially the avarice of speculators, into his financial and economic designs" (151). Hamilton thus sought to ensure that the "stimulative and regulative functions of government [would] work to improve competition in general, not retard it," because "markets left to themselves" would not secure productive competition "over the long run" (153).

Although Hamilton "conceded that his program benefited the monied men of America, he denied that it created a special monied interest adverse to other citizens" (Sheehan 2004, 409). The "encouragement of manufactures in America would be disadvantageous to the other classes of society and to consumers in the short term," but "Hamilton argued that the long-term, permanent effect would be to the benefit of all classes of society and the nation as a whole" (410). Hamilton was convinced of this because he was confident that although people of every social rank or class had their vices, the vices of the rich "are probably more favorable to the prosperity of the state" (Green 2019, 115, quoting Hamilton). Those vices could be more readily harnessed to serve the common interest in greater prosperity for all by making public finance a sound and attractive investment, especially if some public investment would go toward supporting and protecting new economic endeavors. But it would also come about because a peculiar vice of those with means, Hamilton thought, was ambition for distinction in public honors.

Hamilton allowed that "where the qualifications of the electors are the same, whether they have to choose a small or a large number, their votes will fall upon those in whom they have most confidence; whether these happen to be men of large fortunes, or of moderate property, or of no property at all." Yet he concluded that "the representative body, with too few exceptions to have any influence on the spirit of the government, will be composed of landholders, merchants, and men of the learned professions" (*The Federalist Papers*, no. 35). They would be responsive to the interests of the people at large because their ambitions for public distinction that spur them to seek and secure public office would be kept within bounds by their desires for public honors and reputation.

A key distinction between Madison and Hamilton was thus their thinking about the composition of the representative body and how the connection between the interests of representatives and the public interest would emerge. Madison's design for representation aimed to bring the landed elite into the legislature because their interests overlapped considerably with the broader, more permanent interests of the agrarian commercial republic that he sought to preserve and strengthen. They would thus be more likely to deliberate with an eye toward the public interest because they would face one another as equals. The impact of local prejudices would be muted by the formation of more impartial majorities. Although Hamilton admitted that a propertied elite, albeit broader than Madison envisioned, would be most prominent in the legislative area, he sought "the broadest possible representation because he believed that the multiplicity of interests and the extended geographical sphere of the American republic would make compromise necessary and lessen the inclinations of local prejudice and faction" (Green 2019, 29).

In his efforts to develop the commercial republic by stabilizing and strengthening its fiscal foundations, Hamilton sought to harness the regime's design advantages for a propertied elite and to add to them so as to advantage more specifically a capital-holding interest. The aim was to bring the energy of those nascent capitalists, or at least their money, into the government. Either way, it would harness their interests to serve the public interest. Some of them would certainly show up in government, and their personal interests in wealth would push them toward a concern for a stable prosperity, which was among the permanent interests of the regime. Although the wealthy of any age seem to welcome the public adulation, or at least respect, that comes with the wealth they have attained, Hamilton expected that those who sought public office were even more likely to have ambitions for public honors, which combined with their interactions with other ambitious men of varying interests, would increase the chance that they would take the permanent interests of the regime into account in lawmaking. Also for Hamilton, the permanent interests of the regime would not simply, or even primarily, be served by deliberation in the legislature. Deliberation would arise throughout the constitutional system, by way of the interconnections and interactions of the various components. This was important for Hamilton, as it would keep the legislature in particular in check, preventing a return to "the enervating legislative vortex experienced under the Articles of Confederation" (Green 2019, 29).

Restraining Capitalist Ambition: A Middle Class and Administration

Reflecting his multifaceted approach to identifying and securing the permanent interests of the regime, Hamilton promoted two additional ways in which the interests of monied men might be aligned with the public interest and their ambitions harnessed for the good of the nation. First, he envisioned the "men of the learned professions" highlighted in his essay on taxation and representation as playing a pivotal role in ameliorating the risks of strongly connecting the fortunes of the republic to the combined interests of holders of land and capital. He suggested that the learned professions would form a distinct political class, at least with respect to the rivalries between rich and poor and between agriculture and manufacturing that would show up in debates over national policy. Those representatives, elected from among the learned professions, would "feel a neutrality to the rivalships between the different branches of industry, [and] be likely to prove an impartial arbiter between them, ready to promote either, so far as it shall appear . . . conducive to the general interests of the society" (*The Federalist Papers*, no. 35). By "industry" Hamilton meant something more like economic sectors than different manufacturing specialties, and specifically the rivalry between manufacturing and agriculture (Sheehan 2004, 411). Hence, in addition to the structural elements in the Constitution that would provide the institutional means for the rich and the poor to defend themselves against one another and also reduce the risk of the government being dominated by a minority capital-holding interest enjoying the political advantages that Hamilton's design afforded them, something like a separate middle class of professionals would both buffer the main and highly contentious rivalries in society and lend its weight to one or another of the contending classes as those professionals independently judged what would best serve the common interest.

In a later twist, Hamilton's "hierarchical method of pursuing economic diversification" (Shankman 2003, 331) and his similarly structured taxation and credit policies, all benefiting the then-dominant eastern commercial and financial elite, pushed an emerging generation of entrepreneurs, artisans, and merchants in the west and south to join the Jeffersonians, spurring policies for broader commercial development, including government subsidies and expanded banking and credit. Whether such policies were consistent with Madison and Jefferson's founding vision for a virtuous agrarian republic would prove a source of continuing contention (see O'Connor 2014, 30–47), but one effect was to facilitate the emergence of a small-business sector also with interests distinct from the rich and the poor. With some affinities evident between Hamilton's distinctive professional class and these commercial entrepreneurs, the two would later come to form two not entirely complementary pillars of an American middle class.

The second way that Hamilton envisioned containing the risks of tying the interests and ambitions of the holders of capital to the interests of the nation was embedded in his designs for national administration. It is unclear whether anything resembling a theory of administration was part of Madison's thinking about the design of the regime. In *The Federalist Papers*, no. 46, he highlighted the power of "a better administration" to bind citizens to the regime. Such a formative effect would come about by limiting to "a certain sphere" what can be "advantageously administered." In a sense, then, Madison's notion of constitutional government as active government operating within specified limits was a theory of administration. The administrative power, to be harnessed effectively, must be limited by enumeration and scope, and divided across and subordinated to specific functional spheres politically legitimated by popular sovereignty of varying form and strength.

It is most likely, however, that Madison incorporated no theory of administration into his regime design beyond accepting Hamilton's articulation of it as an extension of the executive power through executive unity and subordination of those responsible to the "chief magistrate" for "immediate management" of governmental operations (*The Federalist Papers*, no. 72). Madison's defense of a presidential removal power in the Decision of 1789 (Mashaw 2012, 38–40; Cook 2014, 43–50; see the expanded analysis in chapter 6) adds weight to this supposition, and it suggests that any concern Madison had that administrators would be directly vested with legal authority and thus responsible for exercising that authority in some way independent of instructions from the president were diminished by the power to remove officers on executive authority alone.

Hamilton did articulate a theory of administration, and it was far more expansive and detailed than his *Federalist* essays convey (Caldwell 1988, part 1; Green 2019, chap. 4). Most important, it envisioned the administration making a crucial contribution regarding the social basis of the regime. Hamilton not only expected but tried to plan for an experienced and professionally oriented cadre of administrators. A competent and professional public administration would serve as an additional buffer against the threat of faction wherever such a threat might appear in the general government. It would "participate in representation by protecting and tempering it through the rule of law and by extending it through the administrative ranks" and embodying "a temperament appropriate to governing in a republic" (Green 2019, 30). Not being of the country party persuasion of many of his contemporaries, Hamilton did not fear the dangers of a designing ministry using the powers of administration to manipulate monied interests to maintain its rule. Even if he did harbor such fears, however, the design of the executive in the Constitution and his well-developed design ideas for effective administration diminished those dangers considerably.

Three imperatives of Hamilton's administrative design and practice undergirded the importance he placed on this role for administration in his regime design. First, although subordinate to the constitutional branches, administrators had to have substantial, legally sanctioned autonomy that would enable them to exercise independent judgment. Hamilton stressed that administrators at all levels were officers of the Constitution, to which they gave their oath. This "clearly implied . . . the possibility that bureaucrats may have to resist or even disobey the demands of superiors for the sake of protecting the public's interest in preserving the rule of law, as well as for preventing perversion of the public good for private gain" (Green 2019, 97). Administrators would "balance subordinate status with autonomy," and "exercise 'a firm and virtuous independence' of judgment because, ultimately, they are beholden to 'the people through the government'" (101). Their independence of judgment would be tied to their professionalism and reinforced by following the principle of "rule by reason under law" (101).

Second, administrators had to be afforded extended tenures in office in order to develop the training and expertise in their areas of responsibility and apply their expertise in guiding the republic's extended national endeavors. Long tenure, as well as various accoutrements of public office that Hamilton promoted, such as reasonable compensation and the symbols and honors of office, would attract those most likely to possess a "public-spirited professionalism" (Green 2019, 100). With these characteristics of national administration, civil servants would be much more likely to "invest their time and develop a sense of ownership in their duties. Without that, the temptation to abuse the office for private gain" would be "enhanced rather than diminished." Extended tenure would also increase "permanence and stability in administration" (Green 2019, 103–104). Hamilton's ambitious designs "for industry regulation and promotion, financial policy and management, a diplomatic corps, and professional naval and military organizations would require stable, expert-based government" across an "array of offices staffed by a career service, both military and civil" (105).

Third, and most relevant to Hamilton's designs for the social basis of the regime, "he intended his measures" for administrative design and development and the character of the public service "to serve as at least a modest bulwark against both state encroachment and the inevitably oligarchic tendencies of capitalism" (Green 2019, 107). Intending his designs to attract men of modest means but of a professional bearing and a commitment to the public interest, an adequately paid public service open to all classes would check the influence of the rich in the halls of government and, in the long run, expand and fortify a distinctive social class that could continue to modulate the clashes between rich and poor.

Especially given Hamilton's conviction that building and sustaining a modern republican political economy required complex structures and processes of public-private interactions, a cadre of long-tenured, expert, professional administrators all the way down to the front lines of those interactions was essential to "the national government's role to both stimulate and restrain [the] wealth-creating dynamic" of Hamilton's regime design. Administration would restrain "wanton speculation and resulting boom-and-bust cycles that would destroy confidence." National government, well administered through robust structures and practices, Hamilton regarded as "best suited" to develop "carefully adapted regulation and consistency from a source outside the markets themselves" (Green 2019, 115). In short, a properly designed and executed public administration would have to be at the forefront of regulating the influences of a capital-holding class given special political advantages so that their ambitions and interests could be harnessed to serve the public interest in stable growth and broadly distributed prosperity. Thus national administration would, to the extent that Hamilton had his way, play a critical role in guiding the evolution of market-state relations and the constitution of the commercial republic in practice.

A COMPOSITE REGIME DESIGN

Madison's worry about a future in which the republic's agrarian character-sustaining expansion across space would no longer be possible, bringing the inevitable turn toward an urbanizing, industrializing society with its accompanying decline in stable republican social relations, norms, and virtues, had a parallel in Hamilton's vision of the republic's future. Hamilton's worry, or expectation, was about the eventual degradation of any republic, even one as wisely devised as the American variant. "As riches increase and accumulate in few hands; as luxury prevails in society; virtue will be in greater degree considered as only a graceful appendage of wealth, and the tendency of things will be to depart from the republican standard. This is the real disposition of human nature" (quoted in Green 2019,

116). Hence, the "ongoing challenge of a commercial republic is to stave off the oligarchic tendencies of wealth for as long as possible and to find ways to mitigate its effects as it ensues. And yet, Hamilton's realism convinced him of Aristotle's aphorism that regimes tend to die from an excess of their own virtues. For a commercial republic the accumulation of wealth would gradually take its toll" (Green 2019, 116; also see Elkin 2006, 91).

The formal design and early working constitution of the American commercial republic emerged as a combination of the ideas, worries, and contradictions of James Madison and Alexander Hamilton. If Madison deserves pride of place by delivering to his countrymen "an account of a whole political regime" (Elkin 2006, 49), his commercial republic might have been moribund in short order without the overlay of Hamilton's own regime design theory and practices. Beyond stabilizing and monetizing the debt, creating an effective revenue system and more general administrative structures and processes, Hamilton conceived of and put into place a design for bonding the interests of manufacturing and financial capital to the regime and keeping their ambitions in check. Even if not entirely complementary, it was the combination of Madison's and Hamilton's thinking about the social basis of the regime that addressed the problem of "how to get the propertied to serve in a government that would not be an exercise in class rule, while at the same time getting the propertyless to accept a regime that was not constructed with the express intent of relieving their distress" (Elkin 2006, 44). Neither man was deaf to the distresses of the poor, but they both concluded that doing something for the have-littles required harnessing the energy and the self-interests of those of great means. Albeit imperfectly, their combined designs show how to "distinguish between the value of private property and a commercial society, on the one hand," and the advantages of making "the propertied class" the "foundation of a republican regime on the other." While approaching this challenge from different perspectives, both men arrived at the realization that it "might thus be possible to construct a constitutional design that would allow us to defend private property and promote a commercial society while working to create a favored but limited role for the propertied class" (49) and thereby realize a greater prosperity and a stable politics.

Likewise, it is the combination of Madison's and Hamilton's ideas that give us a fuller design for limited yet vigorous government. Together, their thinking conveys that "good government is not first and foremost democratic government, one that maximizes popular control of government. It is instead popular government that secures rights, aggregates private interests, and serves the permanent interests of the community." Thus, government "must be both popular and limited," however imperfect such a combination might be (Elkin 2006, 45–46). For Madison, the core question was how to shape and sustain a sufficiently virtuous public capable of self-rule. Hamilton thought the key challenge was to ensure a sufficiently competent, active government to appeal to the self-interests of citizens and win their confidence and support for the regime. Both regarded popular opinion as a source of energy in the system. Madison was centrally concerned with cultivating the public spirit of a citizenry for the popular role through the formation of civic rather than factional majorities, while Hamilton was more focused on cultivating what one might call the entrepreneurial spirit (Green 2019, 145–146), as well as attending to the structures and functions that would channel and restrain popular energy.

The civic majorities that Madison sought to encourage would define the public interest in terms of the special agrarian republic that even he regarded as doomed in the long run. Nevertheless, hoping at least that the long run would be very long indeed, Madison concentrated his energies on neutralizing the factional dangers he saw in Hamilton's designs, which he expressed much later in his well-known recollection to Nicholas Trist: "I deserted Colonel Hamilton, or rather Colonel H. deserted me; in a word, the divergence between us took place—from his wishing to *administration*, or rather to administer the Government . . . into what he thought it ought to be; while, on my part, I endeavored to make it conform to the Constitution as understood by the Convention that produced and recommended it, and particularly by the State conventions that *adopted* it" (Farrand 1911, 534, emphasis in original). Thus Madison joined with Jefferson to help stoke and then capitalize on growing popular disaffection with Federalist rule by forming the first identifiable American political party, pushing aside any residual fears he may have retained about the dangers of party spirit to popular self-government. The party became the critical intermediary between popular opinion and representatives, the necessary vehicle for forming and sustaining civic majorities that could beat back the threat of minority factional government whenever it arose. Under the Jacksonians the party would also provide one kind of answer to a problem to which Madison gave little thought: how a public-spirited citizenry would relate to national administration given the likelihood that at least some citizens would come into direct contact with federal administrators despite the limited sphere of national responsibilities.

More than the opinion-party-administration nexus, however, a more critical contrast is that between Hamilton's vision of the commercial republic and Madison's with respect to whether administration was legitimately a constitutive institution of the regime. It was a question of whether the regime would in part be constituted by administration, especially through the character of particular administrative units, by their actions, and by their own unfolding understandings of their aims, efforts, and responsibilities. Although ever wary of the prejudice against administration in the ideology of the revolution, Hamilton considered it inconceivable that a commercial republic of continental extent could exist and function as envisioned without a robust administration. Administration would thus unavoidably contribute to the evolving character of the regime, including the evolving nature of business-state relations. It may be too extreme to claim that Madison and Jefferson were willing to countenance effective administration only on the least operative scope possible to give the national government a minimal level of functional competence. Madison was nevertheless emphatic that the regime should be constituted by politics outside of administration. To admit more than this was to savage the accomplishment of the revolution and condemn the republic to something less than self-government.

Undoubtedly Madison, Jefferson, and their successors sought to keep administration severely constrained in strength and scope—and instrumentally subordinate. Their rhetoric and some of their actions after vanquishing the Federalists in national politics—dismantling some administrative units, curtailing budgetary support—confirm as much. Yet all presidents at least through the Jackson presidency accepted that they could not completely dismantle the structures and processes that Hamilton had put in place—a national bank being the principal but not the only exception—and these presidents believed in and exercised robust executive power. Moreover, except perhaps for Jackson, they all enabled and relied on the development of legally sound, professional administrative units granted considerable discretion within their spheres of responsibility. This was unavoidable if the nation was to develop and expand as the leaders in business and politics, and the public at large, expected.

Hamilton's vision of the future development of the American republic, not only its expansion through space but also its development over time toward a more complex and diverse commercial nation, combined with his energetic, multifaceted effort to bring reality to his vision, stand in considerable contrast with respect to administration. Hamilton and Madison shared with their generation of political leaders an understanding of political economy as a highly integrated, and regulated, system of market and state. It was far more Hamilton, however, along with several other political leaders of the time, who recognized that even the Madisonian imperative of spatial expansion to preserve the virtuous agrarian republic would bring commercial development as well, and both had to be carefully managed through administrative entities. Madison was astute enough to recognize that policies for enforcing American penetration of international agricultural commodity trading markets would not be self-enforcing. That is why he accepted, and promoted, the extensive powers of the national government, the executive especially, in international affairs, including trade. When it came to internal development, however, he regarded the national government's role as far more limited, insisting that this was primarily a matter for the states, a position he held relatively consistently even as his thinking and actions evolved toward greater acceptance of a role for the national government in internal development.

At the time of Hamilton's departure from the Treasury in 1795, therefore, the American commercial republic was an uneasy but not entirely unstable combination of Madisonian and Hamiltonian regime design elements. Popular opinion exercised increasingly greater influence than perhaps Hamilton would have preferred, and it would develop much farther in that direction than most of the founders, including Madison, with his preference for property-based voting qualifications, might have found tolerable. Yet Hamilton's designs in practice to tie monied men to the regime alongside Madison's landed property holders and to develop a robust national administration with the beginnings of a professional cadre of competent administrators, remained largely in place. The combined regime design unfolding in practice was thus the first version of a working constitution aimed at addressing the essential liberal-democratic challenge of the division of labor between market and state. It reflected a common acceptance of the mutual dependence between public officials and the holders of productive assets, yet it was internally conflicted regarding which property-holding elites would have pride of place and how best to shape and further guide the behavior of public officials and privileged property holders with respect to the commercial public interest.

Hamilton had, moreover, constitutionalized critical components of his design with the help of John Marshall's Supreme Court. Crucial elements of Hamilton's design for national administration remained vulnerable, however, especially such features as legally supported autonomy, extended tenure, expertise, and the proper accoutrements of public office, all of which were important if public administration was to help keep within reasonable bounds the effects of the designed-in political privileges for a capital-holding class serving as the social basis of the regime. These features were vulnerable to the latent Whig fear that a corrupt ministry would use administrative power to manipulate financial interests and perpetuate minority factional rule. Thus they became the prime target of Jeffersonians claiming commitment to "a wise and frugal government" (Jefferson 1801) and "drudgery and subsistence only to those entrusted with its administration" (Jefferson 1795).

CONCLUSION

As the initial working constitution confronted political and economic reality in the young nation, the tensions in the Madison-Hamilton composite commercial republican regime design generated increasing stress within the body politic, stemming in no small part from the persistent conflicts over the nature of property and what productive uses of property most deserved political privileges and protections. In other words, the shaping and reshaping of the working constitution became a quest to structure and manage the American commercial republic so as to harness the class that formed the social basis of the regime. "Harness" has two meanings: first, to funnel the self-interest and energy of the class into government and encourage the broadening of its interest orientation toward the public interest; second, to restrain that class energy so that it does not stretch the institutional reins to the breaking point, such that the politically advantaged class can substitute its own interests for the public interest. In addition, the working constitution became a dynamic exercise in balancing the energy of the class forming the social basis of the regime with popular energy, a complex and volatile undertaking in even the most benign circumstances.

Prominent characteristics of the fashioning and refashioning of the working constitution over the course of the nineteenth century reveal how public officials coped with the essential features of the composite regime design. They fashioned a distinctive set of arrangements to harness, and sometimes rethink, the social basis of the regime and the class interests and energy that had to be directed toward defining and realizing the peculiar sense of justice and the general good of the American commercial republic. What comes into view is the distinctiveness of the nineteenth century political economy with respect to the scope and role of administration in defining, and sometimes reshaping, market-state relations, as well as the evolution in conceptions of property and the structure and operations of business enterprises. While all of these features of the nineteenth-century political economy stand apart in many ways from what Americans know today, they also paved the way for a successor arrangement of market-state relations with a central role for administration. Troubling consequences for the commercial republic and its particular sense of the public interest and liberal justice followed the far-reaching changes in the working constitution that eventually took hold.

2. Nation Building, the Public Economy, and the First Administrative State

The United States became a continent-spanning nation over the course of the nineteenth century. That hazardous, coercive, often violent enterprise, which almost failed in the moral, political, and economic strife over the treatment of some human beings as property, was also an endeavor in thinking and rethinking, constructing and reconstructing, a commercial republic. The shifting policy and administrative choices and counterchoices of successive generations of public officials reflected their struggles to confront and cope with the essential dynamic of market-state relations. Indeed, especially in the first several decades, elected officials, judges, and public administrators engaged in vigorous market creation and business development. This was a special imperative of national government leaders seeking to increase national unity and commercial might. Historical antecedents and ideological commitments, existing institutional designs, new forms for channeling popular energy, and the appeals and demands of emerging and increasingly influential business interests, energized and complicated the enterprise.

Nation building intertwined the imperatives of commercial development and expansion across space. Securing the Louisiana Purchase meant not just expansion into the land between the Appalachians and the Mississippi River, but everything west of the Mississippi, all the way to the Pacific coast. For many, this was not just a powerful commitment, but "destiny" (Stephanson 1995), even though the nation did not immediately possess all the requisite territory. Much of it was already well populated by self-governing peoples, many of whom were determined to resist becoming part of the United States. The imperative of westward expansion was rooted in the Madisonian-Jeffersonian ideal of the virtuous agrarian republic and the desire to forestall the nation's inevitable transformation into a decadent urban-industrial society. Jefferson modified the agrarian imperative, however, through his embrace of commercial and eventually industrial development as a way to prevent domination of commerce and trade, including the money and credit essential for it, by an eastern, urban, transnational elite.

Most of the familiar markers of nineteenth-century nation building and American political development—Thomas Jefferson's "revolution" of 1800, the rise of National Republicans, Henry Clay's "American System" and battles over the tariff and internal improvements, the rise of Jacksonian democracy, the Nullification

Crisis, every clash over the possible extension of slavery, secession and the Civil War, Reconstruction, and finally industrialization and the so-called Gilded Age—were also episodes of conflict over the meaning of the commercial public interest and the proper ordering of market-state relations, especially the status and organization of business, the facilitation of its development, and the nature and extent of its political privileges as the primary holder of economically productive property. Similar dynamics also pervaded governance and development at the state and local levels. The working constitution that evolved across the republic's first century was the expression of the internal deliberations and conflicts of legislatures, elected executives, and courts, as well as their complex interactions with one another. By implementing the law, responding to executive pronouncements and instructions, bringing cases to court, complying with court decisions, and taking their own initiative, administrators and administrative agencies also gave form and substance to the working constitution, the character of the mutual dependence of government and business, and thus the tangible, experienced meaning of the commercial public interest.

This chapter and the next present an account of the working constitution of the American commercial republic as it progressed from the Madison-Hamilton composite design and early practice, reflecting in that progression the struggle with the liberal-democratic challenge of governance defined by the division of labor between market and state. This account is neither a chronicle nor a detailed historical analysis of critical junctures in American political development. Instead, it is an interpretive portrayal of how critical characteristics of the founding regime design examined in the previous chapter, further developed and modified in the working constitution, combined to produce problematic effects for the political constitution of the American commercial republic. The critical characteristics and their development over time concern the nature and disposition of property, the structure of business operations, and the character, status, and role of an identifiable administrative state. The present chapter begins the account by first describing the nature of the political economy and the administrative state of the nineteenth century. The chapter then identifies key ideas and practices regarding public land, property rights, and the organization and operation of business and assesses their impacts. In total, the chapter illuminates the distinctive character of the working constitution and administrative state of the commercial republic's first century, as well as key elements of its transformation into a second political economy and administrative state. These elements combine with further developments in the twentieth century to produce a political economy that works against the commercial public interest to an extent that requires the fundamental law corrective of a fourth administrative branch, as presented and defended in part II.

THE POLITICAL ECONOMY AND THE ADMINISTRATIVE STATE OF THE COMMERCIAL REPUBLIC'S FIRST CENTURY

The American political economy in the nation's first century developed and operated in two distinct spheres, reflecting a new national state layered atop deep-seated, primarily state-based traditions, forms, and functions. The more prominent sphere consisted of the legal rules, societal norms, and governing practices constituting a "well-regulated society" (Novak 1996) primarily at the state and local levels. This sphere featured the widely accepted and practiced notions of a public economy and local regulation of the market, including a host of constraints on private property and profit-making enterprises and the privileging of general community welfare over private rights. It also featured organized private-citizen action to regulate social behavior and market activity—and even private-citizen policing to apprehend perpetrators and bring them to justice (Szymanski 2008). All this was rooted in common law but increasingly influenced by emerging constitutional law and constantly tended to and carefully reshaped by judges and other public officials.

The second sphere was nation building in the form of expansion across space and development of an increasingly complex capitalist economy over time. The conquest of a continent, the augmentation of transportation and communications networks, experiments in government finance, and changing connections with international finance and trade networks were prominent features. Although distinct in many ways, the two spheres were never completely separate structurally, and certainly not in terms of governing philosophy, with both marking few sharp distinctions between public and private, or economy, society, and government, and both animated by enduring interest in the science of government and practical statecraft (Novak 1996; Novak 2008). Both spheres continued to evolve as the nineteenth century progressed, with shifting orientations to governance emerging, especially after the 1870s.

Administration was prominent in both spheres, although notably different in form and function from what Americans generally recognize today. Overall, however, the presence, reach, and influence of administration across the two spheres comprised an administrative state with a pivotal role as setting for and shaper of the actual experiences of state-society, especially market-state relations, and their continued evolution.

Regulated Society and Public Economy

As the American colonies reconstructed themselves into states during and after the Revolutionary War, they had to take on all the tasks of colonial administration, and more, as independent, sovereign governments. Most of the state governments before 1787 had weak chief executives and diverse, decentralized administrative entities primarily subordinate to their legislatures. Much administration concerned public finance, including revenue collection, currency control, and the management of state militias, and also a considerable range of commercial and internal trade regulation. Some states administered public education and poor relief, as well such functions as land surveying and land management in the considerable territory that several of the states acquired after colonial dissolution. Although prebureaucratic in most respects, administrative functions and offices were identifiably public and authoritative. In some cases state administrative entities resembled executive departments, "technically oriented" and with "a specified mission and single head" (Beach et al. 1997, 518). With features encompassing "salaried, full-time officials and staff; public missions rooted in statutory authority; permanent agencies with ongoing histories; long-serving executives and managers; internally graded authority; internally produced rules and procedures; a concept of personal responsibility articulated in an oath of office; written records and annual reports; requirements for external accountability and disclosure; and independent monitoring of administrative discretion" (526–527), the states provided valuable guides for the construction of robust republican administrative structures and authority subject to law.

The framers of the new national constitution, most of whom had direct experience with these efforts in the states, thus understood that in reconstructing the national governmental scheme to rescue a union from dissolution and empower it militarily, diplomatically, politically, and commercially on a continental and international scale, they had to rely on and refrain from doing serious damage to those existing structures, legal frameworks, and practices of self-government, including market-government relations. The Second Amendment's "well-regulated militia" clause and the Tenth Amendment's reserved powers clause are manifestations of the recognition of the philosophies, structures, and practices already in place. Alexander Hamilton's recognition that the constitutional, statutory, and administrative law that would emanate from the Constitution had to be carefully interwoven with existing common law prominent in the theory and practice of governance in the states is instructive. He engineered that interweaving for national purposes by pursuing close interaction and collaboration between public administration and the courts (Brown 2017, chap. 1–2; Green 2019, chap. 3). His efforts undoubtedly helped reduce points of friction between the states and the new, more powerful national government (Balogh 2009, 238–240).

Those existing philosophies, structures, and practices of governance and administration in states, counties, cities, and towns had distinct attributes, specifically "four distinguishing principles of positive governance: public spirit, local self-government, civil liberty, and law" (Novak 1996, 24). These four principles defined a "well-regulated society" and "public economy" that comprised a distinctive working constitution. The first principle, public spirit, was an orientation to the welfare of the whole, individuals and community together. It reflected the Madisonian conception of a virtuous republican citizenry, and it provided the grounding for the other three principles.

In form and application, governance in the sphere of the developing commercial republic was detailed and far-reaching, often in ways Americans might regard as overly intrusive today, such as restricting or dictating religious practice and the rules of public morality. Enforcement of such norms and rules, often but not always codified in ordinances, occurred through a complex mix of loosely organized public authorities and private-citizen associations that burgeoned as the 1800s progressed. The public good, however defined—and again, it might be defined in ways we would object to today—was also superior to private interest. Private rights, no matter how clearly established, had to yield to the public interest as determined by local authorities and prominent private citizens. The structures of local government familiar to Americans today, with the exception of professional county, city, and town management, were also the structures of local self-government that constituted most of what nineteenth century Americans experienced as self-government. There was a fierce determination to preserve the autonomy of local self-government even as the new constitution laid claim to ultimate legal supremacy. That autonomy, along with the legitimacy imparted by local elections for nearly every local government post, enabled local government to exercise, through administrative agents, citizen associations, and especially the courts, the "open-ended local regulatory power" that was regarded as a "necessary attribute of any truly popular sovereignty" (Novak 1996, 23).

On the facade of the old Worcester County, Massachusetts, courthouse is the phrase "Obedience to Law is Liberty." This declaration perfectly captures the third principle, civil liberty, in the well-regulated society of the nineteenth century. Liberty was a function of a well-ordered society. People enjoyed only the liberties that were consistent with the health, safety, and tranquility of the community as a whole. What is notable about the old Worcester courthouse inscription is that although the courthouse was originally constructed in 1845, the phrase was not added until a major renovation and expansion in 1897 (Strahan 2016). The commitment to this particular kind of civil liberty, which was a kind of associational liberty often focused on ensuring obedience to law (Szymanski 2008), thus remained vigorous even near the close of the century, when the nation was on the cusp of a transformation that would usher in new ideas, structures, and practices about the economy, social obligation, rights, law, and administration.

That the phrase was placed on a courthouse also highlights the anchoring place of law in the public economy and well-regulated society. This is the law of municipal ordinance and the common law, with its deep Anglo-American roots. This was public law outside the structure of the Constitution, where in important respects "the boundaries between law and government were indecipherable" (Novak 1996, 24). This was also law that the Constitution recognized and incorporated into its enumerated powers and prohibitions. It did not have to define such terms as bills of attainder, ex post facto laws, and due process, as they were familiar to the common law tradition and the people's experience with it. Although under the Constitution the Supreme Court would, going forward, determine what such terms, and others like "impairing the Obligation of Contracts" (Article I, Section 10), would mean in concrete circumstances, the cases they would consider would arrive after having worked their way up from local and state courts, legislatures, administrators steeped in the common law, and statutory law and ordinance that hewed to the common law (see Novak 1996, chap. 1; also see Balogh 2009, 240–276).

The lived experience of the well-regulated society defined by the four principles did not evoke strong public sentiment that there was a distinctive entity in the form of "the state" looming over people's lives nor any sense of a big bureaucracy impinging on their lives and pushing them around. Yes, people would sometimes find some officials overbearing or excessively punitive, but for those holding the franchise at least, the next election offered opportunity for relief. Moreover, a wide variety of citizen associations exercised a notable portion of social and economic regulatory action and the application of prevailing norms and standards.

The distinction between public and private in social life also was different, with one's home the private domain and everything outside the home comprising public life. Citizens generally accepted that they would be governed by local authorities from the sheriff and justice of the peace to the fire warden, building inspector, tax collector, and town clerk, as well as local citizen groups. Of course there was crime and violence, and legal challenges to official action, as well as political dissent and conflict, and citizens formally organizing to seek change. All these were recognized as the products of social friction emanating from humans as naturally social beings. It was the intent of an extensive structure of social and economic regulation to address that friction, for the peace and security of the community as a whole first, with individual welfare secondary and individual rights yielding where and when deemed necessary.

Acceptance of economic activity as in the public realm and subject to regulation by a self-governing community through its public officials and organized citizens, ultimately subject to judicial supervision, was a particularly distinctive aspect of the well-regulated society. It reflected acceptance of the economy as "intertwined with public safety, morals, health, and welfare and subject to the same kinds of legal controls." A "host of particular rules and prosecutions solicitous of public goods over individual interests" defined that public economy (Novak 1996, 96–97).

The establishment of public spaces in cities and towns as the exclusive places where market exchange, primarily of foodstuffs and related essential provisions, was allowed and the rules effectively communicated and enforced embodied the most prominent characteristics of a public economy organized by government and civil society and controlled through extensive directives and prohibitions. Vestiges of this particular institutionalization of the public economy exist today in many US cities, with central markets still operating in places like Boston, Philadelphia, and Seattle.

Of course, the economy of the developing nation did not exist only in urban public markets nor in the market exchange of food, fuel, and other necessities. The economy was dynamic and growing, albeit relatively slowly until significant advances in technology and business organization emerged, some of which government facilitated. Still, "growth over the entire antebellum period was close to 1 percent per year; for the period 1800 to 1840 it was slightly lower (0.7 percent per year). Even with this modest increase the economy of 1840 had clearly surpassed" the growth achieved "just prior to the Revolution" (Weiss 1992, 35). Such growth produced an impressive number and array of new goods and forms of trade. Also impressive was how well local and state governments adapted to this economic dynamism with new requirements and restrictions, primarily in the form of product laws and licensing regulations (Novak 1996, 101–107). These amounted to a "mass of economic rules, controls, customs, and regulations" intended to protect and enhance the health, safety, and general welfare of the populace (100).

Most communities formulated and legitimated these market rules and controls based on the long-established state police power, a sweeping but somewhat ill-defined doctrine that granted public authorities broad power to protect the community as a whole from harm and to encourage its harmony and prosperity. The extent and limits of its application were ultimately determined by local and state courts, and it thus operated outside the penumbra of constitutional law for much of the nineteenth century, at which point federal courts began to narrow its meaning and incorporate it into the edifice of constitutional law (Novak 1996, 13–15, 245–248). Over most of the 1800s, however, the police power was central to positioning market regulations squarely in favor of concerns for the public welfare ahead of the protection of private rights and the opportunity to make a profit. When challenged legally on either count, courts more often than not upheld such local controls on the market as constitutionally valid exercises of that police power, even to the point in significant instances of overriding the provisions of corporate charters recognized as valid contracts (120–124).

The idea and practice of a public economy was clearly a very specific and highly developed solution to the problem of the division of labor between market and state, carried forward from tradition and deep-rooted legal practice and applied to challenges of combining those traditions and practices with the dominant commitment to republican governance newly crystallized in a written constitution. The public economy substantially blurred but did not completely obliterate the market-state division of labor. Large commercial and industrial endeavors that could in combination take on the lion's share of the burden of generating sufficient income and wealth to provide for the general prosperity of the community were only beginning to emerge in the early decades of the republic. Until they came on the scene more prominently, governments did not create and operate businesses, but both states and some localities incorporated a chosen few, and licensed, permitted, regulated, and in some instances prohibited the rest so as to ensure that the community as a whole gained from the ambitions of entrepreneurs and from the uses of private property, which, especially in the form of land, vastly exceeded what was in the public domain.

Life was still coarse in many respects, especially in antebellum America, but the remarkable expanse and detail of the well-regulated society softened the rough edges somewhat, especially for those in increasingly urbanized areas. The trade-off was that the sweep and detail of societal order and regulation in the economy was also repressive in many ways, at least when seen through modern eyes. One reason American politics and culture looks as though it took so long to shake off most, but not all, of its backwardness and reactionary tendencies was the sustenance that the well-regulated society and common-law tradition gave to the continued cultural, structural, and legal subjugation of women and the many and diverse people of color. Slavery, Indian removal, and patriarchy were exercised through the coercive power of the state and elements of civil society, often in very localized ways that, while hewing to well-recognized legal principles, were made even worse by the frequent arbitrariness of those practices. That arbitrariness often came at the hands of administrative officials, and it is the lack of both more robust legal constraints on their behavior and a professional ethos among them that also colors a modern sense of the backwardness of the era.

Another form of subjugation, of proprietor over worker, or capital over labor, was more ill-formed throughout most of the nineteenth century and would only gain further definition and strength as the well-regulated society gave way to the corporate-liberal capitalist state (O'Connor 2014, chap. 4). That change would arise in part from a tension in this period between industrial capitalism trying to break out and gain ascendance and the continued resilience in law and governing practice of a public economy controlling the exercise of property rights and entrepreneurial initiative through the primacy of public welfare over private rights, including the pursuit of profit and wealth.

The political economy was hardly static in the sphere of the well-regulated society, however. Innovation, profit, and wealth generation happened through both the encouragement of the state and within constraining rules of the state. Many people's lives improved materially, and some got rich (Lindert and Williamson 2012). Government at this time was neither hidden nor puny, although it was often loosely ordered and amateurish. Neither was it a mere tool for laissez-faire nor the epiphenomenon of emerging capitalist interests. Exercise of the police power to shape and restrain market activity continued well into the late nineteenth century. It also reached beyond the aims of protecting the local public from threats to safety and health, and from many of the vicissitudes of market exchange, to the establishment and control of public space and public property, including transportation infrastructure, that offered further pathways for regulating the market and controlling economic development. Single administrative officials, as well as groups of administrators increasingly organized into structurally coherent entities, with citizen associations working alongside, all embodied and actively applied the police power in all these areas. A particularly prominent area, again involving public finance, was state chartering and regulation of banks. At the local level, fire wardens and fire departments, building inspectors and code departments, and commissions and boards of considerable variety and significant authority, not to mention judges and marshals and clerks of the courts, gave concrete shape to the actions and interactions of state and market defined on paper in statutes, ordinances, and rulebooks. Indeed, even more so than local elected legislatures and executives, the combination of and cooperative interactions between administrative officials and the courts constituted the well-regulated society in its most concrete form, sustaining it over time and modifying it as the national government's presence and influence grew.

The national government's presence especially grew primarily in the form of administrative entities, expanding in number, authority, and organizational sophistication as the century progressed. These agencies of the national government operated primarily in places and with responsibilities and authority outside where local self-government and the authority of the states were most firmly established. Nevertheless, the two spheres connected with one another. They operated on a similar basis of "personal organization" common in law and business (Crenson 1975, chap. 3). More important, they connected through the shared aims and cooperative facilitation of spatial expansion and commercial development, especially in transportation and communications, in ways that reflected the agitation in and reshaping of market-state relations at the hands of both public officials and business as the nation's growth progressed.

Nation Building and National Administration

The Constitution's text is infamous for providing only fragments of guidance on how to organize administration to carry out the day-to-day operations of the national government. As noted, from the perspective of the framers there was little need to add detail to the general governmental structure spelled out in the first three articles. Many of the powers of the national government enumerated in Articles I and II were and remain administrative functions, and there were solid analogues available in the states and from former colonial rule for structuring the administrative entities that would carry them out. Many of those who would serve in the new government also shared a general set of expectations about basic government structures and functions. They knew that while Congress might "lay" taxes, determining what would be taxed and by how much, it would not directly "collect" them. Nor would it actually coin money for which it had set the value, or directly collect duties or imposts. Hence, the "national government of the United States was an administrative government from the very beginning of the Republic" (Mashaw 2010, 1366; see also Emerson 2021). The Constitution, like almost all modern constitutional schemes, is thus "a typical administrative-era enactment" (Rubin 2005b, 224–225; also see Rohr 1986, chap. 1).

Still, a national state had to be elaborated from both existing elements and practices and new structures and processes, and new posts had to be filled. Country party fears about tyrannical administration remained prominent in public opinion after the Revolutionary War. Political divisions stemming in part from those fears remained after ratification, and new ones stemming from suspicions about motives among the founding generation would emerge and quickly deepen. Nevertheless, the Federalists, the Jeffersonians, and their successors recognized and accepted that nation building was the essential task, and this meant constructing an administratively functional national state. Successive generations of political leaders would concentrate on contesting its cost and ambit of authority. President Washington and his appointees and the first two Congresses cooperated more often than not to install essential administrative foundations and set policy directions that activated a recognizable national state of extraordinary, and untested, authority, aims, and aspirations (White 1948, 11–12). To frame the qualities and impact of national administration that developed from the starting foundations, it is helpful first to consider briefly, with some comparison to the present, the simple quantitative growth and structural expansion of national administration up to the republic's centennial (see Short 1923; White 1948, 1951, 1954, 1958; Van Riper 1958 for greater detail and comparative analysis).

National Administrative Expansion

If any Americans today give much thought at all to the past structure and character of their national government, especially all the way back to the beginning of the republic, they are unlikely to think of it as bureaucratic. Peering into the misty past, and perhaps with a certain romantic inclination, they would hardly think that the government under the first six presidents and the first twenty Congresses looked anything like the massive, sprawling, complex, bureaucratic behemoth of a federal government they see today. Certainly at the very beginning the national government in total was small. The largest component of it, the executive branch, amounted to about 3,000 civil servants by 1800 (Van Riper 1958, 19). Those civil servants were also widely dispersed, with only about 10 percent in the national capital (derived from US Congress 1793).

In contrast, the national administration today is almost 800 times larger, depending on who is counted (e.g., including or excluding employees of the US Postal Service and civilian employees of the armed services), and the proportion serving in or nearby the nation's capital may be twice as high, about 21 percent (derived from US OPM 2017). Furthermore, national administration in the early republic did less and pursued some distinctive aims through very different means compared with today. It also had to exercise what authority it had, and provide what functions and services it was responsible for, over a proportionally larger land area: roughly one civil servant for every 288 square miles in 1800 versus one for every two square miles today (derived from U-S-History.org, n.d. and Wallis 2006). The states primarily governed day to day the existing settled land and people of the United States as they do to a considerable extent today. However, the old northwest territories, west of Pennsylvania and north of the Ohio river, which comprised over 30 percent of the land area of 1800, were governed by US territorial governors and secretaries. Territorial governance remained a major and active administrative arm of the national state well into the nineteenth century.

Peering into the past more discerningly, and with an appreciation for context, brings more prominent forms, actions, and implications into view. The national administration of about 3,000 persons in 1800 still seems remarkably puny. Yet, to "keep perspective . . . , one must remember that there were few other organizations even approaching this size, the [states] being the principal competitors" (Van Riper 1958, 19). Although the British government of the time had "twice the number of civil servants per capita and cost annually at least three times as much to maintain" (19), it had been around a while longer and was a bit more adventurous. The federal administrative establishment at even this early time was, moreover, not an undifferentiated lump or a mere collection of clerks scattered across the countryside. It had about thirty units and subunits, depending on how one counts, excluding the president and vice president (derived from US Congress 1793). The three original executive departments—State, War, and Treasury—all featured basic structural divisions of labor. The Department of State had a foreign and a domestic branch, and the Treasury Department included the office of the secretary, the controller's office, commissioner of revenue, auditor's office, and treasurer's office.

The secretary of war oversaw a pay office and an ordinance department, as well as the basic operational and command structures of the army and navy. There was the mint, the office of the governors and secretaries of the Northwestern Territories, district attorneys, US marshals, commissioners of loans, collectors *and* surveyors of customs, supervisors *and* inspectors of revenue, revenue cutters, and superintendents and keepers of lighthouses.

By 1817 the national administration had expanded to about 4,500 civil servants and about forty administrative units, again not counting the president or vice president, but including expansion in military organization (derived from US Official Register 1818). Such expansion reflected in part responses to the embarrassments of the War of 1812, but far more important was the enlargement in civil administrative responsibilities of the army in national expansion and economic development (Rockwell 2010; Bergmann 2012). Most of this administrative expansion by the beginning of the Monroe administration happened within established executive departments, such as the addition in the State Department of the Patent Office, and the General Land Office in Treasury, both by way of statute. Other notable additions were a commissioner of claims, a superintendent of Indian trade, commissioners of borderlands necessitated by the Treaty of Ghent following the War of 1812, and administrative elaboration in customs, revenue collection, and the postal services.

By the 1840s and 1850s, the federal establishment was remarkably elaborated. It was still small in total personnel in 1851, about 25,000 in the executive branch, more than 21,000 of whom were in the Post Office (derived from Wallis 2006). In 1845 the State Department had a diplomatic bureau, a consular bureau, a home bureau, the patent office, and a surprisingly far-flung foreign service cadre reaching across the globe. The War Department had a dozen staff in the secretary's office, and the rest of the department structure included a sizable Indian department, a pension office, an elaborate quartermaster's department, engineer department, topographical engineers department, ordinance office, sustenance department, pay department, medical department, and the much-expanded and professionalized organizational structures of the uniformed services. Amateurs did not win the war of conquest with Mexico. The Treasury Department was also more organizationally differentiated, with a much-expanded land office and a bigger and more far-reaching customs service (derived from US Official Register 1845).

Bypassing the structure and size of the federal government during the Civil War, with its rapid, temporary military administrative expansion and mass mobilization and then demobilization, executive branch personnel grew to just over 50,000 in 1871 (derived from Wallis 2006). The average increase per decade was nearly 50 percent to that point. In contrast, the US population grew from about 8.3 million in 1816 to just over 44 million in 1871, an average increase per decade of about 28 percent (derived from Haines 2006; see also Mashaw 2010, 1366). Much of the national administrative growth over this period was still concentrated in the post office department, which was involved in far more than just delivering letters and selling stamps (John 1995; Carpenter 2001, chap. 3–4). Nevertheless, while personnel outside the postal system constituted an average of 27 percent of all national administrative personnel per decade over the period 1816–1871, this category of personnel grew more than 54 percent on average per decade over this period (derived from Wallis 2006). Not counting the military and its administrative units—or the postal system with its vast array of deputy postmasters, postal clerks, mail contractors, and the emergence of railway service—there were about seventy-five national administrative units in the early 1870s (derived from US Official Register 1874). Among the additional units were the Department of the Interior, the Civil Service Commission, an executive office within the presidency, and numerous additional new or much larger existing subunits of the cabinet departments.

National administrative growth over the nation's first century was thus considerable—and necessarily so because both state and national leaders of whatever party or persuasion were committed to national growth. Just as important, however, national administrative expansion was neither haphazard nor a mere epiphenomenon of the forces of nature, history, economy, or society. Certainly all these factors were drivers of administrative growth in some way. A modern society, which the United States was in conception from the beginning and in fact by the 1830s (Johnson 1991), is dynamic and complex. Especially in a liberal democracy, people engage in a wide variety of pursuits, creating pressures and demands to which government must respond. Nevertheless, the nineteenth-century growth of the American state, and especially its largest component, administration, was strategic as well as reactive. The expansion in size, and the addition of organizational units of particular types, internal structures, and missions, reflected the successive policy designs of elected officials and administrators aimed toward expanding farther into the continental expanse of the west, and toward developing, connecting, and expanding markets with the intent to cultivate the commercial energy and boost the commercial prowess of the nation.

None of this is to say that all the various entities comprising the first administrative state were models of careful design, clean and efficient operation, and nimbleness in adjusting to changing conditions. There were numerous policy and administrative design flaws and errors, legal gaps and contradictions, and plenty of instances of fraud, corruption, and incompetence. With the emergence of a more robust party system, giving parties greater control over the practice of rotation in office, administration became a greater resource for and more active influence on the financial sustenance and operation of political parties in a distributive party state. The chances of maladministration thus increased further (Arnold 2003).

How much political patronage in hiring contributed to administrative failure despite the compensating value of greater responsiveness to public opinion is open to debate, however (Rockwell 2010, 167–173, 316–319; see also Bearfield 2009). In any case, among a number of administrative leaders, and some of their elected overseers, there was commitment to improvements in structures, processes, and administrative technologies. There was also sufficient stability in the middle ranks of some agencies that such advances could be sustained beyond the next election. Moreover, what might have appeared as administrative incoherence and failure—or was touted as such by those with particular agendas—might in some instances have been reflections of particular organizational cultures and modes of operation that proved effective for the missions pursued (Rockwell 2010, chap. 4). Despite the many political and administrative deficiencies of national civil and military administration, by mid-century the national state was thus able to fashion and execute successfully the first modern, industrialized total war strategy (Bensel 1990, chap. 3). It was an enterprise requiring new and expanded interdependencies of market and state realized almost entirely through administrative action, in particular the US Army's Quartermaster Department, "the largest economic organization in the industrializing world to that date" (Wilson 2003, 605).

Despite chronic underfunding and understaffing, frequent revamping of policy, and expressions of alarm about the looming threat of "bureaucracy," (Hoffer 2007, 165, 197), governing coalitions at every step forward up to and including the Republican Party ascendancy late in the century developed a national administration distinguished far less by its limitations and far more by its embodiment and active pursuit of the era's ambitions for national expansion and commercial progress. The notable public administrative presence in the well-regulated society and public economy of state and local governance, combined with a national state principally administrative in orientation and expanding in size, form, and complexity, thus comprised a distinctive administrative state for the commercial republic's first century. It was the republic's leading institutional actor in giving concrete meaning to and frequent rethinking of the commercial public interest.

Nature, Function, and Impacts of the First Administrative State

The administrative state of the nineteenth century was surprisingly complex and influential. It was the primary organizational manifestation of an American state that "was agile, formidable, and potent" (Rao 2014, 1017). Anchored in law, it extensively deployed in many forms "infrastructural power," the "actual power of state policies in action to have real effects" on society (Novak 2008, 763). Among its distinctive characteristics, the following are most relevant for illuminating its role in shaping and reshaping market-state relations and thus defining the commercial public interest in the working constitution of the commercial republic in this initial era of its development. First and foremost, the first administrative state had both regulatory and developmental, or distributive, functions. Second, the regulatory function was primarily aimed at developing, detailing, and enforcing standards of behavior, especially for property owners and market actors. Third, the distributive function, although certainly a form of business inducement, was principally aimed at facilitating the emergence and expansion of markets, trade relations, and new lines of business. The combination of the first three features comprised a boundary between state and market, public and private, that was both philosophically and practically ill-defined and, although subject to legal monitoring and occasional attack by market actors, was largely accepted by both business and government and reaffirmed by the courts. The first administrative state was steward of this boundary at every level of government, but it was at the national level that the boundary was subject to more active definition and redefinition as agency missions and operations required. Finally, the first administrative state's forms, processes, and operations at all levels reflected in the early decades considerable experimentation and adaptation, often with loose internal structures. At the national level concern about the separation of powers and lines of supervision and accountability was remarkably constrained. Front-line operators exercised considerable discretion in many areas of policy.

Also of note, policy specificity varied widely, giving some administrative entities considerable autonomy to interpret and even further develop policy and law. Administrators nevertheless recognized the imperative of anchoring their actions in law. They were often called to account for their efforts by elected officials, although the extent and care of the monitoring and supervision varied considerably. As the century progressed, forms, processes, and structures became more complex and elaborated, again at all levels but especially in national administration. At the national level the expansion and increasing sophistication of administration aggravated the underlying regime tension between the fear of administrative power and the inescapable need to rely on it to govern. These tensions sparked efforts to keep administrative power under legal and political control and to ensure that administrative entities remained subordinate to the principal institutions of the regime.

Regulatory and Developmental Functions

Dual developmental/distributive and regulatory functions are the most obvious feature of the first administrative state. National administration was also engaged in international relations, including diplomacy and defense, but between the War of 1812 and the 1890s these functions were primarily directed inward and became part of the spatial expansion and developmental drive. This lasted until the nation had spanned the continent and had industrialized to the point that its spatial, commercial, and defense and security horizons were situated beyond its two coasts.

The regulatory function was primary at the state and local level given the particular prominence at those levels of the philosophy, law, and practice of the well-regulated society and public economy. The dual functions did not divide neatly between state/local and national administration, however. States and localities engaged in developmental projects through various administrative devices, including wholly public entities as well as public-private arrangements established through corporate charters, contracts, and franchises to build roads, bridges, canals, and various public spaces and community facilities. This state and local spatial development and the commercial expansion it facilitated accelerated while national political conflicts raged over a national government role in internal improvements and the increasingly divisive question of slavery's place in territorial expansion. Yet none of the developmental endeavors of states and localities would have been possible without national administrative management of territorial acquisition and initial development through diplomacy and occasional armed conflict with Indian tribes and other nations, as well as surveying and mapping, trail clearing and road construction, and organization and distribution of public lands.

Although the distributive function of the nineteenth-century American state at the national level was primary—development being essentially the distribution of benefits to various interests through the deployment of resources and organizational power—there was an important regulatory dimension to national governance and to national administration. Indeed, the distributive and regulatory functions went hand in hand, there being both a regulatory aspect to the distribution of benefits such as the sale of public lands and the delivery of the mail, as well as other areas of market-state relations. These included trade, particularly both international trade and internal trade with the periphery through the customs system, the trading system with Indian tribes, as well as the varying, frequently stumbling efforts to manage credit and the money supply in the economy. Health and safety protections, as well as social welfare and education programs, were also distributive and regulatory—and well within the administrative state's ambit of authority and responsibility at all levels.

After the Civil War, with financiers deeply connected to and influential in government as a result of the necessities of war financing (Bensel 1990, chap. 4–5) and the developmental/distributive functions of the national state expanding rapidly as a result of both war necessities and the westward expansion drive after the war, established regulatory functions at the national level continued and expanded further. As hard as it is to see in many historical accounts dominated by the narrative of Gilded Age robber barons and the battles over the spoils system and civil-service reform, new types of regulation and accompanying administrative organization—information gathering, standardization, supervision—in such substantive areas as education, agriculture, and labor emerged from the keystone distributive function of sponsorship (Hoffer 2007, chap. 1–3). These constituted a "second state" philosophy and structure of administration that emerged despite the resistance of "first state" republicanism rooted in the old Whig fears (Hoffer 2007). Included in these developments was the emergence of administrative units increasingly professionalized and differentiated in internal structure and capable of developing a distinctive form of "bureaucratic" autonomy (Carpenter 2001).

Regulating Behavior

The distinguishing character of the regulatory function in the first administrative state was its focus on directing and restraining the behavior of people and organizations, including market actors in various guises. In contrast, little effort was directed toward improving the general function, efficiency, and performance of markets and businesses. The behavioral orientation was most evident in the world of the well-regulated society, with its remarkably detailed state and local statutes and ordinances, and its combination of public administrative and civic association monitoring and enforcement, aimed at defining the acceptable behavior of market actors, as well as the social, cultural, and moral behavior of individuals and organizations more generally (Novak 1996, chap. 2–6). Yet a similar orientation permeated the regulatory functions of national administrative entities.

Behavioral controls came in the form of information gathering, product and process standards, directives and prohibitions, and direct and indirect monitoring and supervision of exchange relations and other forms of market and social relations. The detailed regulation of trade with Indians during the years of the "factory system" up to about 1820 is emblematic in this regard and remarkable as largely an administrative creation of the Indian Office in the War Department (Rockwell 2010, chap. 3). It is additionally notable that the factory system came under pressure from growing populations of white settlers and businesses increasingly resistant to the government regulation under which they had profited. The most successful and influential of the latter was the American Fur Company, established by John Jacob Astor, generally regarded as America's first millionaire. Once population growth, commercial and business development, territorial expansion, military strength, and civil administrative capacity was sufficient, the nation shifted from a policy of relatively peaceful Indian trade to a policy of forced Indian removal and eventual banishment to far-flung reservations (Rockwell 2010, chap. 6–10).

A similar regulatory orientation and the administrative structures to carry it out were prominent in the postal system (Carpenter 2001, chap. 3–5), national revenue collection and control of trade through customs and internal taxation

(Rao 2016), in public-lands distribution (Rohrbough 1968), pension administration (Weber 1923), and in early forms of public health and safety regulation, like that for steamboats (Mashaw 2012, chap. 11). Certainly a behavioral focus in regulatory policy and the administrative structures for its implementation and further elaboration are a significant aspect of the political economy and administrative state that are in place today. These are most evident is so-called social regulation, in such areas as public health, safety, and environmental protection and civil rights. Yet this more recent form of behavioral regulation is primarily aimed at correcting market externalities and other market failures and thus is intended to supplement and refine the dominant regulatory orientation and structure—managing a highly administered national economy to ensure economic efficiency and growth—of a successor political economy and administrative state.

Expanding Space and Commerce

The distributive function of the first administrative state, especially at the national level, was principally aimed at guiding spatial expansion and market and business development. Land—what the young nation already had and what it sought to acquire to the west across the continent—was the central object and engine of the commercial republic's development across most of its first century. Spatial expansion and land development presented several major policy and administrative problems. First, some of the land was still under the dominion of other nations even after the Louisiana Purchase, and some boundaries were ill defined and unsecured. Second, much of the land seen as open to settlement was already populated by roughly a million native people of diverse cultures, settlement patterns, governance structures, and forms of livelihood, including already established trade with Americans and traders and explorers of other nations. Third, once acquired and controlled, the land had to be distributed in ways that would provide revenue to the national government and support settlement and commercial development. Fourth, for land distribution to meet its multiple goals, the land had to be surveyed and mapped, means of access developed and improved, and connections to developing transportation and communications networks established. Finally, in the antebellum period national decisions about the extent and direction of the expansion of slavery had to be implemented. Several national administrative entities took on these far-reaching, and at times oppressive and violent, responsibilities.

Perhaps most administratively central, especially in the early decades, were several units within in the War Department. The department's military arm pursuing its traditional war-fighting mission certainly had a role as expansion created conflict with Indian tribes and tribal federations occupying agriculturally rich land, land full of timber and mineral resources or simply land attractive as a speculative investment. The army was a poor match for Indian warriors early on, however. Moreover, the army had to divert some of its men and arms to prevent white settlers from occupying treaty lands and to remove squatters and others with questionable land claims (Rockwell 2010, 91–92; see also Bergmann 2012, chap. 1). Even as it gained effectiveness in armed conflict and grew in size, organizational sophistication, and professionalism, the army's contributions in westward expansion and commercial development were primarily in civil administration (Rockwell 2010). Its forts and outposts became centers of trade, and eventually central suppliers for settlers heading further west. The military roads connecting outposts provided initial access to new territory.

The army would eventually be involved centrally in the far more repugnant episodes of conflict with the many Indian tribes through its roles in Indian removal and establishment and enforcement of the reservation system. Most of these endeavors remained primarily civil administrative endeavors with armed forces serving mostly in a back-up role. In territorial expansion through Indian removal, the Mexican-American War, conflicts with Great Britain over the Oregon territory, and the considerable extent to which the army was deployed to protect slavery's expansion (Ericson 2017), however, the deployment of arms of necessity came before the Army's civil administrative elements could take over.

With the establishment of the military academy at West Point, the army became the primary source of professional expertise in engineering and land surveying for much of the antebellum and immediate postbellum periods. Its engineering corps and topographical engineers operated semiautonomously for several decades (Adler 2012). Complementing the coast survey and the lighthouse system operating not just along the Atlantic and Gulf coasts but in the interior across the Great Lakes, the army's engineers and topographical engineers conducted surveys and effectively mapped the growing western interior, including potential routes for a transcontinental railroad. The army's engineers built roads and bridges, helped connect the canal system developing at the state level, and surveyed and improved navigation on interior waterways.

Once the army had done its work, the land, "the most sought-after commodity in the first half-century of the republic" (Rohrbough 1968, xii), had to be organized for distribution. The administration of public lands evolved through several forms, with Congress first attempting to administer public lands by statute but eventually conceding the need for an administrative structure. Lawmakers settled on a combination of a decentralized network of land offices and a General Land Office in Washington, first established in the Treasury Department but eventually moved to the Department of Interior. The increasingly complex surveying, claim processing, and adjudication of disputed claims forced the development of an administrative adjudication process when federal and territorial courts could not handle the claims' demands and complexities (Mashaw 2007, 1708–1723).

Through subsequent reorganizations and statutory reforms up to the point of the diminishing importance of public-land distribution in the early twentieth century (Conover 1923), "public lands law was developed largely through administration" (Mashaw 2007, 1727). That placed in administrative hands perhaps the most crucial dimension of market-state relations in the commercial republic's first century (Rohrbough 1968). The pervasive historical and normative sense of the American nation as one uniquely tied to the land, so essential to the Madison-Jefferson vision of the virtuous republic, was constituted administratively.

Beyond spatial expansion and public-land distribution and development, the first administrative state was engaged in other developmental-distributive endeavors centered on creating and developing markets and businesses. The most prominent of these endeavors was the creation and stimulation of financial markets to attract investment and provide liquidity to the economy and, especially at the national level, to meet the government's needs for revenue, credit, and debt management.

The states had already been in the game for a considerable time, and they facilitated a variety of financial institutions even as they limited competition and regulated the institutions extensively. Consistent with the well-regulated society and public economy, public officials "wanted banks and other financial institutions to serve their communities in ways that were transparent and trustworthy, and that would prevent them from becoming too powerful" (Green 2014, 26).

At the national level, the Treasury Department, through the considerable authority granted the treasury secretary from the start with respect to public debt management, trade regulation, revenue collection and management, and banking supervision structures and functions, succeeded in stabilizing the nation's finances while expanding the economy's cash and credit resources and stimulating economic growth. A quasi-public administrative entity, the First Bank of the United States was not only instrumental to the nation's early financial stabilization and economic expansion, it was central to constituting early business-state relations with respect to finance, expanding the financial market, attracting investment, and tying the interests and ambitions of those with capital to the security and success of the republic.

As already noted, for the nation's long-term commercial development, incorporating investors and money managers into the social basis of the regime alongside landed property holders from Madison's design may have been Hamilton's most essential but also his most controversial move. Madison's vision of a vigorous agricultural trading nation would not have succeeded without stable national credit and access to financial markets. Nevertheless, the moneyed class remained suspect among the Jeffersonians and their successors because of its ties to international financial markets controlled by Great Britain, its concentration among the eastern seaboard elite, and its control of money and credit, so vital to the growth of agricultural as well as commercial markets. Hence governance of national finances may have been the most unstable, or most contested, responsibility of the first administrative state.

The inability of national financial administration to head off or better respond to financial panics and regulate the emerging business cycle is the most obvious evidence of its limitations. Despite the considerable mutability of fiscal and monetary policy across much of the nineteenth century—the lapse of the First Bank's charter, scandals in the customs houses, chartering of a stronger and more effective Second Bank of the United States, Andrew Jackson's destruction of the Second Bank and the removal of government deposits to so-called "pet banks" in the states, and the creation of the subtreasury system—the reach and influence of the financial arm of the first administrative state in shaping and reshaping market-state relations in the evolving commercial republic was significant. It managed the integration of the merchant class into the regime through the customs system (Rao 2016), coordinated Jefferson's embargo (White 1951, chap. 29; Mashaw 2012, chap. 6), largely designed and managed public-land sales, modestly supported and regulated a banking system, cobbled together financing of a total war, and through that effort initiated the process by which a new class of financiers would become an even more prominent part of the social basis of the regime (Bensel 1990, chap. 4–5). It is hardly hyperbole to state that Wall Street would not exist without the need of a national government for financing and managing its debt (Geisst 1997, chap. 1). The design and activation of an administrative structure that created the necessary financial instruments, established a market for them, and provided the requisite safety to attract investment in those instruments followed. Such investment then provided the liquidity necessary for an economy of farmers, merchants, traders, and manufacturers to grow.

Flexibility, Autonomy, and Emerging Administrative Law

States and localities deployed a diverse array of administrators to carry out statutes and ordinances and thereby shape market relations, and social relations more generally, in the well-regulated society and public economy. Individual agents, boards, commissions, and increasingly over time, well-defined administrative units of general government distributed benefits and regulated behaviors in ways that gave active meaning to the idea of a commercial republic. Particularly before the Civil War, national administration also exhibited structural diversity and flexibility, as well as the ability and freedom to adapt and innovate in many instances. This reflected in part the willingness of Congress to try different organizational forms, mix and reconfigure those forms for different problems, respond to changing conditions, and cope with its own varying capacity and motivation to maintain oversight (Mashaw 2012, chap. 2–4).

The structural flexibility, adaptation, and innovation also reflected the considerable authority and operational autonomy that Congress granted administrators. Congress did insist on a constant stream of reports and statistics, having little in the way of direct monitoring and analysis capabilities itself. It also set and reset appropriations levels and ordered and reordered agency structures. These are all experiences in dealing with Congress to which current federal administrators can well relate. And like their current counterparts, in many instances Congress gave administrators wide latitude for putting the law into effect. In turn, top administrators ceded to middle managers and frontline operators significant discretion in many instances, a necessity especially early on as travel and communications were arduous and slow. As the US attorney corps expanded, it was increasingly involved in field administration as well.

From the very start, exemplified by the circular letters that Alexander Hamilton employed and his successors continued to use and expand upon, national administrators and their organizations produced formal rules and processes, norms of practice, and record-keeping protocols that, through interaction and collaboration with the courts, developed the first vestiges of administrative law. Attorneys general became increasingly involved in these developments, especially in advising agencies and the president regarding the legality of procedures and administrative rules.

More importantly, from there very early national administration developed "a culture of governance whose guiding ideal was of government according to law" (Mashaw 2006, 1344). Alexander Hamilton was surely the initiator of that culture (Brown 2017; Green 2019). His contributions to the design of the regime required positioning administration as a bulwark against the overreach of the capital-holding class he had successfully integrated into the social basis of the regime. Just as important and remarkable, however, is that even at the height of the anti-statism proclaimed by Jeffersonians and their successors, including most virulently politicians from the slave-holding states, national administration continued to expand and develop organizationally, taking on more functions and responsibilities and fashioning more elaborate sets of organizational rules, structures, processes, and forms of communication. State and local administration developed along similar lines, giving the administrative state increasing structural definition, regularity, stability, and constitutional and legal validity. The first administrative state's "internal" administrative law grew more elaborate procedurally and substantively over time, incorporating such norms as due process long before they became universally required in the twentieth century (Mashaw 2012, 309–312). This internal rationalization and legal elaboration also gave national administration an increasingly hierarchal and functionally bureaucratic cast while laying the groundwork for controlling it through the constitutionalization of administrative law, including its internal organizational and process rules. Thus, like the constitutionalization of the police power that was the legal backbone of the well-regulated society and public economy, the administrative law that developed in the first administrative state was adjusted and adapted as part of the reconception of state and market that eventually produced a new political economy and second administrative state.

Before turning to that transformation of market-state relations and its consequences for the political constitution of the commercial republic, it is important to examine more closely two key aspects of the American political economy and its development over the course of the nineteenth century: the nature and treatment of public space, public land, and evolving notions of private property, and the evolving legal and political status of corporations. Tracing the changes in these areas, of central importance in the composite Madison-Hamilton commercial republican regime design, and the object of much political and economic conflict across the nineteenth century, illuminates the procession of adjustments in market-state relations in the working constitution that presaged the rise of that new political economy and new administrative state.

PROPERTY, CORPORATIONS, AND CHANGING MARKET-STATE RELATIONS

The "takings" clause of the Fifth Amendment to the Constitution was an important addition to the property protections in Madison's regime design privileging private holders of productive assets. This constitutional constraint was not applicable to the states until the late nineteenth century, however. Thus, as the American political economy developed after 1789, private-property dominance in the states and the common law gave way to the exercise of public authority to acquire land and adjacent waterways for public use and control in the form of roads, ports, canals, and eventually railroads (Novak 1996, chap. 4), along with the establishment of public markets and other public spaces. The public rights that developed in law and practice even extended to prohibitions on government actions allowing public space to be used for private purposes and private gain (158–161). In a sense, then, the compound Madison-Hamilton regime design anchored in a set of political privileges for landed property holders was subject to slow but deliberate restriction outside the Constitution's original reach. This was so even as important Supreme Court decisions would reinforce private-property protections important for shaping the development of the economy. However, the more important question regarding the status of land as property, particularly for the viability of Madison's vision for the American commercial republic, was the disposition of the land outside any existing state. Such land was not unsettled, of course, occupied instead by peoples with very different interests as well as varying notions about land possession and land rights and titles (Rockwell 2010, 10–14). An account of the evolution of property and property rights under the commercial republic's first working constitution best begins by tracing the unfolding disposition of these vast "public" lands.

Public-Land Disposition and Land Holding as Anchors for the Commercial Republic

It is important to recall that for Madison specifically, tangible property in the form of land was the center of gravity for his virtuous agrarian republic. First and foremost, "justice was defined largely in terms of defending property rights" (McCoy 1989, 193), and that remained Madison's view long past his primary service to the nation. He regarded "permanent public good and immutable standards of justice" as "linked to the rules of property that stabilized social relationships" (41). Land was also the foundation for a prosperous commercial republic because productive land was the primary source of both private and public wealth and the driver and source of strength for the republic's engagement with other nations. Making land productive, moreover, was constitutive of republican virtue. That relationship could not be sustained over the long run, however, without the availability of much open land that would accommodate a growing population. The growth of the nation and its people and the expansion of land with respect to both quantity and productivity were intimately connected.

Even more important, making agricultural land productive predisposed large holders of such land to a broadening of their interests toward a concern for the public interest. Or, perhaps more accurately, given his conception of justice, Madison saw the interests of large landholders as substantially overlapping with the public interest in the virtuous agrarian republic. They would easily see the necessity of sustaining and defending the core elements of the public interest in the form of commercial strength and republican virtue because defending such general interests served their particular interests as well.

Madison seems initially to have expected that those with substantial land holdings would remain a minority. A landless majority posed the threat of factional majority rule, and industrialization would only increase their relative numbers and the intensity of their ire directed at the propertied minority that controlled the nation's economic prospects through the extent of their success in producing goods and gaining access to markets for those goods beyond America's shores. Hence it was essential to grant property holders particular political privileges, including significant rights regarding private property, not just to protect their particular interests, but the public interest and that special kind of republican justice tied to landed property rights.

Madison's vision of the interconnections among landholding, the nature of the republic, property rights, and the public interest faced two especially tricky challenges, however. First, how would westward expansion and the distribution of public lands for settlement affect the social basis of the regime centered on a minority landholding class? Second, given Madison's own experience dabbling in land speculation to build an independent fortune (McCoy 1989, 232–233), what would actually happen to land and its value to the republic with the realization of his sought-after spatial expansion? Land value was multifaceted, after all. The obvious risk was that land speculation, rather than preservation and cultivation, might be a more attractive source of investment and wealth for landed property holders.

With respect to the first question, Madison's vision for the regime would appear to have been internally contradictory. The vast tracks of public land made available for westward expansion—an expansion critical to retaining the virtuous agrarian character of the republic—would either have to be primarily owned or controlled by a relatively small, landholding elite or widely distributed to keep most citizens tied to the land and the benefits that would derive therefrom. It would be difficult for both to be the reality simultaneously. The nation would also have to gain possession of that land and allow settlers access to it. This would necessitate a significant exercise of federal government authority largely through administration robust enough to stably secure the land. In short, the maintenance of republican virtue would have to be an administrative undertaking about which Madison should have been wary but to which he gave little thought.

Certainly a relatively small number of landowners already possessed from colonial times, or acquired in the early years of the republic, significant tracts of land in the trans-Appalachian west. This initial reality was largely overwhelmed, however, by the considerable broadening of land ownership through public-lands distribution. As Alexander Hamilton recognized and early governance in the republic dictated, public lands served dual purposes. The sale of public land raised revenue, already a practice under colonial governments and which the states and national government continued under both the Articles of Confederation and the new constitutional system. Land sales displaced direct tax and fee revenue, reducing the burden on citizens and commercial transactions. Hamilton pursued this aim in his legal and administrative organization of the newly refashioned republic's finances, and it served the aims of the Jeffersonians as well, although its revenue yield proved disappointing (Mashaw 2007, 1697–1698n253; Green 2019, 146–147).

Just as important for the Jeffersonians, however, public lands offered the open space needed to accommodate "eastern farmers, who had exhausted the fertility of their lands, and recently arrived immigrants" wanting "to move west," as well as "veterans who had been promised substantial land bounties that had never been received. Men of means and influence were also eager to speculate in western lands" (Mashaw 2007, 1698). Hence, the "sale of western lands . . . would provide a counterweight to the mercantile interest of the eastern seaboard" (1735). Although "land sales fueled massive speculation and colossal instances of corruption" (1735), westward expansion through the partition and sale of public lands, especially when supercharged by the Louisiana Purchase, helped cement Jeffersonian ambitions to democratize the republic.

This expansion in the population of landholders is consistent with several dimensions of Madison's thinking about a social basis for the regime tied to landed property holders. First, with his conception of republican justice tightly connected to the protection of property rights, combined with his ingrained concern that periods of social instability and chaos created opportunities for oppression and injustice, expansion of land ownership would expand the portion of the population directly concerned with the features of the regime that would protect their interests, including social stability. Conceptions of justice and the public interest tied to stable property rights also served as a brake on the momentary passions of majorities. Hence, a wider distribution of landed property holding would incline a larger portion of the population—maybe even a majority—toward the conception of justice and the general good that Madison regarded as foundational to republican government.

Second, even if these new property holders were quite self-interested, their interest in protecting their property naturally opened them to a concern for the general interest because their self-interest overlapped with what Madison regarded as the heart of republican public interest. To state it even more broadly, because "the character of the new regime would significantly affect the value of [landed] property," the new property holders, like the old landed elite, "might be supposed to take a particular interest in the fate of the country and to have a broad view of the country's interests" (Elkin 2006, 39). This view would at least be broad enough to support policies that would preserve the value of their land in the longer run, and thus at least indirectly "secure stable government" (40), which served everyone's interests, a point that Madison made twice in *The Federalist Papers*, in no. 10 and no. 62.

Third, the same design forces that Madison might have expected to further spur the broadening of the self-interests of a landed propertied elite should also work on an expanded population of property-holding citizens. The majoritarian nature of elections would force those among the new property holders who decided to stand for election to articulate a version of the public interest that would go beyond just serving the pecuniary interests and property protections of their own and those like them. Even if a majority of the electors in any given locale were of the same class, which Madison's design for large electoral districts was meant to inhibit, the other features of his design might nudge them toward a broader conception of the public interest. The extended republic would still bring a diversity of interests into the halls of government.

In the legislature, representatives from this broader class would be forced to deliberate and form coalitions with others not sharing exactly the same conception of the public interest because the separation of powers might draw property holders of somewhat different interests into the different branches because of the different manner of election or selection. Hence the separation of powers would actually push men of somewhat differing interests into cooperation in order to overcome the institutional divisions and get things done. Again, an expansion of landed property holding might increase the chances that civic or publicly spirited, majorities would form, at least on the basis of the formulation that Madison considered central: protection of property rights that reinforced social stability, which in turn cemented a commitment to preserving republican government. An expanded class of landed property holders might therefore be nearly as susceptible to a broadening of their interests and in turn committed to maintaining republican government. Such an effect—a stable pathway to civic majorities and the durability of republican government—should in turn serve the interests of the whole citizenry, even those who might at any point in time still be suffering from prejudice, social oppression, and other degradations. Apart from overthrowing the regime, their best path to greater liberty would lie through well-functioning republican institutions that would expand rights.

Whether all these possibilities became reality is a matter of interpretation of complex and ambiguous evidence. Land ownership, at least in the form of home ownership, only became a reality for a majority of US citizens in the 1940s. It has hovered relatively consistently in the 60–70 percent range since the 1960s. That sounds impressive, and it is reinforced by the higher home-ownership rate in rural versus urban areas—81 percent versus 60 percent (Mazur 2017). However, rural areas contain only one-fifth of the US population. Home ownership also varies considerably by income, age, and race (Ford 2017). Moreover, home ownership may be an inadequate proxy for landed property ownership. Land for single-family homes is divided into relatively small parcels in most housing subdivisions. On average, home ownership is restricted to one property, and even fewer own enough property to make it the primary income source. Home ownership thus serves only partially the anchoring and constituting functions that Madison envisioned. The NIMBY phenomenon and the property tax–limitation movement, largely phenomena restricted to white property owners, only muddy the picture further as they suggest a resistance to interest broadening (Lindsey and Teles 2017, chap. 6).

Owning a house and a modest parcel of land certainly generates a keen interest in protecting the associated rights, but it is unclear whether that particular form of self-interest tied to property is of a sort amenable to or sufficiently overlapping with the republican public interest in the way Madison had in mind. Although home ownership provides many advantages to the political economy of the commercial republic, that form of landed property holding does not itself provide the resources that sustain such landowners in pursuit of election to office, especially at the national level, nor even enough to support sustained engagement in public affairs in other ways.

Perhaps, then, most US homeowners fall into Madison's large basket of "those who are without property, or with but little" (McCoy 1989, 200). This would place them on the wrong side of Madison's equation regarding factions. Alternatively, homeownership might be a key pillar supporting a distinct middle class that might help form a better class politics for the regime. Yet it poses challenges even there (see Elkin 2006, 68, 225, 293). It bears repeating that both Hamilton and the Jeffersonians sensed the possibility of a middle class serving a pivotal role (278) in the political economy of the commercial republic.

Equally important, landed property ownership beyond home ownership is comparatively limited for nonwhites, which is also true of larger tracts of agricultural land. Furthermore, while by the end of the twentieth century 58 percent of agricultural land was in the hands of "owner-operators" and thus presumably regularly farmed as Madison and Jefferson might have hoped, the other 42 percent, or nearly 390 million acres, was owned by "non-operators," including corporations and owners renting the land for nonagricultural uses (Gilbert, Wood, and Sharp 2002, 58). While the United States remains primarily an agricultural nation by land-area uses, it is not so with respect to population. By 1900, less than 40 percent of the population lived on farms, and farms were receiving less than half their household income from farming by 1960 (Lusk 2016). Today, only about 2 percent, or 3.2 million people, are directly engaged in farming in the United States, of which about two million are those owner-operators. Are these Madison's landed property elite? Probably not, especially because the folks Madison had in mind all became holders primarily of a different kind of property—capital. Madison's landed property elite became capitalists, certainly in the North. In the South they remained throughout the antebellum period the sort that Madison had in mind, but their fortunes and power were tied to that "peculiar," i.e., hellish institution known as chattel slavery. Whatever Madison's own struggle with slavery might say about his views on that topic (McCoy 1989, 260–263), his conception of republican justice as centered on property rights made the political power of large slaveholders nearly unbreakable without an immensely destructive war that in the end still fell short of completely upending the conceptions of property and property relations (Bensel 1990, 437) at the heart of both the political economy of slavery and the republic's founding design.

Westward expansion, and the sale of public lands to facilitate it and help fill government coffers as well, served some aspects of Madison's design and the Madison-Jeffersonian shaping of the political economy. Yet it diffused landed property ownership in a way that watered down, if it did not completely neutralize, Madison's design for the social basis of the regime anchored in a landed property minority embodying republican public interest and therefore deserving special political protections and privileges. With landholding more widely distributed it became more fragmented—by the land act of 1820, a minimum purchase was as small as eighty acres at $1.25 per acre (Bien 1910). More land, more finely divided and widely distributed, made land less attractive as a durable source of wealth and social stability and more attractive as a commodity to be bought and sold for relatively immediate financial gain. Thus, without even considering Hamilton's push to transform the political economy of the republic to one with a commercial and industrial character, through their theoretical imperative to spur westward expansion and facilitate that expansion through the distribution of public lands, the Madison-Jefferson alliance and its heirs altered the political economy in ways that weakened the keystone of the Madisonian conception of the social basis of the regime.

It is not just the effect of the disposition of vast public lands that deserves attention, however. Land is a target of investment and source of wealth as a commodity. The practice of land speculation, that is, acquiring land not for agricultural production that would in turn produce a livelihood and reinforce republican virtues, but as an investment in an appreciating asset to be sold for profit, was already well established in colonial American and the early United States before the Constitution was ratified. Some citizens—at least those with sufficient wealth or access to credit—already regarded land primarily as a commodity or capital asset. It is not hard to see that the virtue-inducing qualities of land that Madison imagined were likely to be diminished as a result.

Certainly, even if the landed property–holding minority had mixed motives for investing in and holding land, those mixed motives might still serve the aims of Madison's design related to giving them special political privileges. Yet the characteristics of land as property already evident in Madison's time tended to undermine the effectiveness of this key aspect of his regime design. The stability of land values, vital for sustaining farm production at a profit and as a safe form of savings and inheritance, is highly dependent on factors that the owner or investor cannot control. These factors include not just the weather, and the locational decisions of fellow citizens, but also decisions by governments. This latter factor sharpens the incentives of landholders to use their special political privileges and access to serve their self-interest, including through means like manipulation of land-sale rules and processes. This time-honored form of rent seeking works against the broadening of landholder interests through interaction in the councils of government that Madison aimed to facilitate. Indeed, they might even form a faction that would seek to manipulate land ownership and tenure rules to serve their pecuniary interests, and worse, use those manipulated rules to perpetuate their hold on power by the control they gained over an economy dependent on land. If the Constitution included special protections for the kind of labor structure these landholders employed, and provided enhanced political representation based on that labor structure as well, that landholding minority might not only gain control of the national government but sustain that control for a very long time. That is exactly the control of all three branches of the federal government that the proslavery political coalition achieved and sustained until its violent destruction (Ericson 2017, 133–134).

Even as the republic was reforming under Madison's plan, therefore, savers and investors were shying away from land and toward other forms of more stable, more liquid assets. The "market value of financial instruments held up much better than real-estate prices . . . , because the value of a given instrument was uniform and not subject to degradation, local caprice, or the political atmosphere" (Wright 2002, 59–60). As much as land as tangible property was and remains a key pillar of the American republic, citizens with a desire to save and invest quite early on "gave up the age-old prejudice against intangible forms of property" because property in other forms was less susceptible to the uncontrollable "physical" risk to which land was subject. In addition, intangible property was more diverse in form and quality (52–53). Thus, in addition to the effects of the sale of public lands on Madison's particular social basis for the regime, the nature of property was already undergoing irreversible change, which Madison saw happening all around him, even in Virginia (McCoy 1989, 222–224). That transformation would have an even more profound effect on the organization of the political economy as the acceptance of intangible property, and especially its cousin intellectual property, would be one key to the transformation of the corporate form, the rise of the private-business corporation, and the sweeping changes in the political economy that began at the end of the century.

All this captures only a few dimensions of the evolution of land in theory and practice in the political economy of the American republic. Nothing about the developments in the nature and disposition of public land or the connection of land as private property and social and cultural icon, however, contradicts the essential point that land does not provide the anchor for a specific and limited property-holding social class that can serve as the social basis of the regime with a special potential to recognize the true public interest, and it has not done so for a very long time. Property-rights protections and the special political privileges that emanate from them, remain, however, with enormous implications.

Expanded Property Rights and the Transformation of the Corporation

The corporate form was from the beginning a creation of government, and corporations only exist within a legal framework that government maintains and refashions as necessary. The corporate form emerged, prominently but not exclusively in England, to extend the economic, geographic, and administrative reach of the state, as in the process of colonization and economic exploitation of faraway lands. In England and the American colonies corporations came into being through discrete legislative acts—special charters that defined the aims, scope, rights, privileges, and immunities of the corporations. This practice carried forward as the new nation came into existence, with the individual states having primary governing authority over the creation and regulation of corporations, eventually within a few specific constraints imposed by the Constitution, especially the contracts clause in Article I, Section 10.

Corporations served as a major organizational vehicle for state-sponsored and state-supervised economic management and development in the early republic. Banks were a key form of corporation for public and private financial management and the structuring and further development of the economy. Development-oriented corporations were created to undertake internal improvements—roads, canals, and eventually some railroads—and to maintain various other forms of infrastructure, including eventually public utilities like water supply and waste removal. Banks, of course, were essential to developing and sustaining a money economy and spurring economic expansion. "The number of state-chartered banks passed 200 in 1815 and nearly doubled, to 392, in the next three years" (Sellers 1991, 132).

Corporations were always suspect, however, and were often at the center of spirited debates about what constitutes the common or public interest and how these entities served it (Hilt 2017, 42, 44). As previously noted, among English Whigs corporations were regarded as part of the nexus of suspect institutions by which ruling factions could create and control interests in government and thus maintain their power. The central basis for this fear was that only certain members of society had the resources to seek legislative approval of a new corporation or to form and operate a corporation that a state might create to achieve public purposes. This resulted in first-mover advantages and the potential for a chartered corporation to monopolize an area of economic, and public service, activity. The combination of "entity benefits," or legal privileges and protections flowing to corporations as special legal entities and thus also to the owners of the entities, plus "corporate benefits," the rights to control particular areas of economic and public service activity, raised the specter of "systematic" corruption (Hennessey and Wallis 2017, 81). Through the management and control of economic resources, which corporations were specifically intended to facilitate, political factions could control the state, economy, and society and sustain electoral support. They could also cripple their political enemies by denying them legal access to economic and political resources.

The Whig fear of an institutional nexus, especially of the executive and corporations, was part of the motivation for a separation of powers scheme in American republican design. In a fused power or unitary government arrangement, gaining control of the legislature meant gaining control of the executive and judicial powers as well. This deep-seated worry about corporations was also behind Madison's objection to Hamilton's first Bank of the United States. Although Hamilton structured the bank to distance it from political manipulation, it was the connection between the treasury and the bank, and the considerable financial resources this arrangement commanded, along with the closer relationship between the treasury and Congress than was enjoyed by other executive departments, that Madison feared. Although neither the First nor the Second Bank of the United States survived, the more general problem the corporate form posed continued to complicate governance under a working constitution that directed market-state relations in substantial part toward both spatial and commercial expansion and development.

The drive for territorial development combined with a surging acquisitive spirit resulted in the corporate form and a national bank receiving a boost over the ten years after Jefferson left office. Although the National Republicans and Henry Clay's American System of tariffs and internal improvements had its time in the sun, the Panic of 1819, resulting in part from the politicized management of the Second Bank of the United States, spurred an antitax, antispending, antitariff, and anti-elite backlash fueled by the expansion of the franchise in many states (Sellers 1991, chap. 4–6; Baxter 1995, chap. 2; Shankman 2003). Growing sectional differences over the composition of the American political economy—the divergence of agricultural and industrial interests that proponents thought the American System would overcome by integrating the economy geographically—created further political fractures, as did an emerging North-South divide over the expansion of slavery. The Jacksonian Democrats emerged triumphant out of the wreckage. For a considerable time thereafter, up to the Civil War, initiative for economic development fell back to the states.

The story of the evolution of the corporation in the American political economy beginning roughly in the 1830s, therefore, is the story first of the generalization and privatization of the corporation by state initiative. From then on, in that new legal setting, the story continued with the co-evolution of industry and finance, supported and facilitated by corporate-friendly lawmaking, including critical judicial decisions. That legal evolution centered on a recognition of property rights in not only tangible but intangible property, eventually via the Fourteenth Amendment granting corporations the status of quasi-persons entitled to many of those new property rights. What is key in all this is the recognition, from the very beginning, of corporations as distinct entities, legally separate from, yet tethered for their rights protections to, those holding financial stakes in the corporation.

Andrew Jackson attacked corporations as organizations of moneyed interests capable of corrupting government. But the movement to transform the corporate form still hewed to the old Whig fear that corporations would be not the principal but the agent by which ruling factions could corrupt the economy to perpetuate their power through selective legislative chartering of corporations. Despite the many advantages to economic development of state chartered corporations, state political leaders found plenty of evidence of deleterious fiscal impacts, primarily because the states themselves often held most of the shares in the corporations they chartered, saddling them with serious debt problems when corporations failed. Broader corrupting effects were the most serious concern, however, specifically the control and manipulation for political ends of the considerable economic resources that state-chartered corporations controlled. Political factions with majority control of legislative seats also controlled the power to promote or squelch business development. Ruling factions could issue charters to their friends and fellow party members, denying their political opponents business-development opportunities and the accompanying economic and material resources. This was a prominent tactic, using state bank charters, that Martin Van Buren's Albany Regency deployed to maintain its grip on the New York state assembly (Hilt 2017, 66).

The growing alarm about this problem was a key impetus for the general incorporation movement, "an economic solution to a political problem, not a political solution to an economic problem" (Hennessey and Wallis 2017, 94). The economic solution was to open up business creation to all who desired it irrespective of their connections to party or faction. General incorporation statutes generalized entity benefits, shifting first-mover benefits from those with political connections to those who could convince investors that they had winning marketplace ideas. General incorporation statutes simplified the incorporation process and transferred it, along with the authority to apply any requirements or restrictions included in a given state's statute, to a state administrative official, often the secretary of state. State legislatures varied in the requirements and restrictions they imposed on corporations created under their statutes, and they could amend those statutes as they saw fit. Primarily, however, general incorporation laws helped elected officials in the states extricate themselves from the fiscal trap they had set through special corporate chartering, as well as the normative problem of corporate chartering seeming to undermine core republican principles by facilitating factional rule. State lawmakers also unburdened themselves of difficult and increasingly complex decisions regarding the appropriate design of economic entities to organize the economy and facilitate economic growth.

This sort of political self-restraint can be seen as quite admirable. By simplifying hard decisions and delegating them to administrative entities, it offered such significant benefits that the idea of general laws spread to other areas of law and policy where the legal structuring of formal organizations was prominent, particularly municipal incorporation (Hennessey and Wallis 2017, 88). The decision of the US Congress eventually to shift the process of public-land claims and appeals to an administrative process might be seen as in a similar vein of self-restraint and acknowledgment of the need for specialized experience and expertise.

Whether this broadening of legislative restraint to reduce special-interest corruption improved the tendency and ability of state legislatures to deliberate about the public interest with respect to economic management or other areas of public policy is an open question. It did solve the key political problem, however, and beyond that the general incorporation movement had two significant consequences. First, general incorporation essentially privatized business formation. Although the state still set the general ground rules and could change them, at least until many states amended their constitutions to mandate general incorporation, the decision to create a business became almost entirely a private choice and a function of entrepreneurial vision influenced by market and social forces. General incorporation did not itself lead to significant increases in rates of incorporation, but it did boost an already advantageous legal environment that, when combined with subsequent shifts in the economy and society, made the corporation the most attractive solution to the economic, political, and social problems that became critical by the late nineteenth century.

Second, general incorporation transformed a significant category of political decision making from a legislative to an administrative process. The process was pro forma in many ways, yet it thereby expanded public administration involvement in the organization and management of the market in a manner different from the first administrative state's behavioral regulatory orientation in the public economy and first administrative state. General incorporation also expanded the points of contact between business and the state. Business did not stop approaching and attempting to influence legislatures with the spread of general incorporation. But business did expand its interactions with administration, especially to the extent that general incorporation statutes granted regulatory authority in some form to secretaries of state or other administrative entities created for that purpose, as was the case in New York when it liberalized banking incorporation and set up a co-insurance fund and regulations to stabilize the state banking system (Hilt 2017, 69).

All twenty-seven states that had joined the union by the end of Reconstruction had enacted statutes or constitutional amendments for general incorporation of private business corporations by that time (Hennessey and Wallis 2017, table 2.1). Although corporations did not amount to even one-third of the manufacturing establishments counted in the census of 1900, that ratio is deceiving because shortly after 1900 acceptance of the economic and political advantages of the corporate form as the solution to the most serious economic problem the nation faced after the Civil War—rapid industrialization combined with unrestrained market competition—spread rapidly.

In addition to the privatization of the corporation through general incorporation, the great development in the evolution and eventual triumph of the corporation was its financialization. In important ways the Civil War was the critical spark. The demands the United States faced to wage total war, smash the Confederate rebellion, and reunify the country, stimulated significant advances along a number of fronts, especially in industrial production and transportation. Most far-reaching were the developments in national finance.

Although there was plenty of fervor among northern industrialists for a war to reunite the nation, they had no intention of freely supplying the government with the tools of war. The government would have to buy their help, and it would need the financing to do so. In waging the first truly industrialized war, the United States transformed the structure of government finance, stimulated the rise of a new breed of "finance capitalists" (Bensel 1990, 118), and further tightened the interlacing of state and market through the vehicle of money and finance. Among the most significant changes were, first, a much expanded internal revenue system tapping "a much wider array of revenue sources" and the "administrative apparatus" for collecting it (303). Second, the government floated substantial new debt as the chief way to finance the war. This proceeded almost simultaneously with the retreat of European investment that essentially weaned the United States and private financiers from primary dependence on foreign capital for domestic financial markets. Third, lawmakers and executive officials replaced the inefficient subtreasury system that emerged after the destruction of the Second Bank of the United States with something closely resembling a national banking system, including the creation of the comptroller of the currency. The new system was key to creating the market for the new government debt. Finally, the government authorized a new national currency designated as legal tender and backed not by gold but by the full faith and credit of the United States.

In the war's aftermath, during Reconstruction and beyond, the American political economy was permanently transformed—but in peculiar ways. Or rather, it was refashioned into a form that looks familiar in retrospect but that emerged out of the particular political and economic dynamics of the Civil War and Reconstruction (Bensel 1990, chap. 5–6). The new breed of financiers, who partnered with the federal government to finance the war and keep the Northern industrial economy functioning stably and productively, foresaw serious repercussions from the most radical plans for Reconstruction. Property and class relations would be radically upended; the Southern planter class would be destroyed and with it the stability of cotton production while cotton was still a major component of American international trade and the source of hard currency. Controlling the conquered South effectively, on top of the other national developmental aims in the Republican Party platform, would have required continued massive government expenditures, relatively high taxes, and the administrative capacity and competence to manage the financial system, oversee Reconstruction, and otherwise administer the rest of the national government, including control of its increasingly far-flung boundaries. The administrative and managerial requirements seemed especially unlikely to be met so long as civil administration remained deeply enmeshed in the party patronage system; civil servants who had remained loyal to the Union were also few in number in the conquered South. The demands of finance capital thus included civil service reform and a merit system, at least for governmental financial management, as well as budget retrenchment and "rigid economy" in bureau and department operations, simplification of the tax system, and gradual but steady return to the gold standard (338). In this interpretation finance capitalists were among the primary forces that drove the bargain to terminate Reconstruction and begin liberalizing and privatizing the national economy and reducing national government primacy over the market. The exception was in the operation of the financial system, where the national state would have to intervene enough to regulate the banking system, impose the gold standard, and continue some "countercyclical operations in the money market" (338). As representatives of the readmitted Southern states and the Democratic Party they revitalized regained power, they pushed to counteract these developments by advocating broader civil-service reform and enhanced central state power and authority to regulate the new, more economically powerful corporations, first the railroads and then the other large commercial, industrial, and financial combinations that began to appear in the 1880s.

Why did these large corporate combinations begin to emerge in the late nineteenth century? In one sense the answer is simple. A classical liberal philosophy of political economy emerged out of the termination of Reconstruction and coincided with accelerating industrialization spurred in part by the war and by the renewed national developmental drive. Between 1870 and 1896, manufacturing production tripled. With increasing efficiency through standardization and mass production, the technological, commercial, and managerial advances of emerging industrial capitalism tapped the abundant raw resources of the continental United States and transformed the American economy from relative scarcity to relative abundance in a surprisingly short time (Atkinson, Hake, and Paschall 2019, 4–5). The economy had the vices of its virtues, however. Cutthroat competition drove prices down. Wholesale prices dropped 40 percent over the same period that production tripled. Despite increasing production and widening markets, owners and investors could not secure stable revenues and profits from the accelerating economy. With large fixed costs, the temptation to increase output to stabilize revenue per unit at the expense of profit was irresistible. In the search for ways out of the vicious cycle by restraining output, industrialists and investors first turned to collusive arrangements. However, the "temptations to breach the agreements and the difficulty of enforcing such agreements made consolidation more effective than price restraint agreements in battling ruinous price competition" (7).

The corporate form became the structure of choice to achieve consolidation through vertical and horizontal integration. The merger wave that swept the national economy in the period 1895–1904 was made possible in part by the US Supreme Court's blunting of the impact of the Sherman Antitrust Act of 1890 through its so-called "rule of reason"—that a large industrial combination was not by definition an illegal restraint of trade. More critical to facilitating the merger wave and the consequent transformation of the economy, however, was the "co-evolution" of industrial organization and finance.

The traditional notion was that the owners of a "going concern" invested their wealth in the business's property and thus had a direct and substantial stake in its productive success. That also meant, however, that their wealth was tied up in the business. Consolidation led to the transition from active to passive ownership, in which investors bought and sold securities representing the projected future performance of the company—its intangible property. Control of industrial enterprises transitioned from active owners to professional executives and managers. With the help of emerging property-rights protections for intangible property, over the subsequent decades the orientation of the economy shifted from investment in business enterprises to pursuit of liquidity. Financiers increasingly exerted control over how businesses operated, seeking to influence business operations with an eye toward liquidity rather than toward production and sales.

In addition, corporate rights expanded in other ways, particularly with respect to speech rights and political engagement. The idea that corporations have rights is deeply embedded in American constitutional jurisprudence, originating in the Dartmouth College case [17 U.S. (4 Wheat.) 518 (1819)] and related cases. The idea that corporations are artificial persons deserving the Fourteenth Amendment's due process and privileges and immunities protections began to emerge in the late 1880s, just as the great corporate-merger wave was looming. The general logic at the center of the judicial expansion of corporations as artificial persons was the associational model—that corporations were associations of real persons who came together, as owners or shareholders, to create a corporation for their collective benefit (Blair and Pollman 2017, 251). Rights flowing to the corporation were thus a derivation of rights already held by the natural persons who made up the corporation. The courts also recognized that there were limits to the rights that could be extended to corporations. Rights that could only be associated with or exercised by individual natural persons—such as citizenship, voting, and protection against self-incrimination—could not be extended to corporations. The notion of corporations as associations nevertheless remained powerful, rooted as it was in the rich associational life of American social and political culture and tied to the speech and assembly provisions of the First Amendment.

Since the 1920s modern business corporations with their separation of ownership and control, "branded identities, professional management, . . . anonymous shareholders who traded in and out of stock," and highly bureaucratized structure, have looked very little like an association of like-minded citizens (253). Nevertheless, the associational doctrine has continued to hold sway in constitutional jurisprudence regarding the corporation. Eventually it would have profound effects on the ability of the regime to serve the commercial public interest when its design is predicated in part on providing special political privileges to a specific class that forms the social basis of the regime. Before moving to a deeper examination of these developments, their subsequent effects including the emergence of a second administrative state, and the changes in fundamental law and governmental structure that the effects necessitate, the nature and impact of the first administrative state must be given its due.

CONCLUSION: ADMINISTRATION BETWEEN STATE AND MARKET

Through its far-reaching developmental/distributive and regulatory functions, the administrative state of the American commercial republic's first century filled the role that all liberal democracies demand of administration, a role that Woodrow Wilson described about as well as anyone before or since: "*Administration*, therefore, sees *government in contact with the people*. It rests its whole front along the line which is drawn in each State between *Interference* and *Laissez faire*. It thus touches, directly or indirectly, the whole practical side of social endeavour" (Link

1969, 116, emphasis in original). That line was blurred for much of the nineteenth century, especially at the state and local levels and nationally during the early decades of national development. This was so despite the old Whig fears of a ruling faction using administrative power to enlist corporations as a tool to remain in power and the efforts of the Jacksonians to execute a hard "divorce" between market and state (O'Connor 2014, chap. 2; McCormick 1981, 253–255). The first administrative state significantly shaped the blurred boundary line, managed its particulars, and adapted it to changing dynamics by executing the instructions of its political and judicial superiors, developing its own strategies and internal operations and processes, and designing new policy for adoption. Despite the subordination of administration to political parties, the first administrative state was actively involved in managing party politics and the relations of the citizenry to the state (Zavodnyik 2007, chap. 4). As the century progressed, a number of agencies developed their own constituencies, and in some cases adept agency leaders developed and managed substantial networks of interests that provided them with sustained political influence and policy autonomy (Carpenter 2001; Wilson 2006; Adler 2012).

This is the answer to the theoretical and practical question of the proper place of an administrative state in liberal-democratic governance that the working constitution of the commercial republic in its first century provided: administration spanning and overseeing a relatively porous boundary between market and state, one that grew less porous in important respects as the century wore on. It is important, of course, not to overemphasize the scope or strength of this first administrative state; it remained far less organized and conceptually coherent, less professionalized and adequately staffed and resourced, and more limited in structural and functional scope than its successor. The first administrative state, while being well anchored in law, also remained well subordinated to its elective and judicial masters, in rhetoric and ideology certainly, but in practical ways as well, and increasingly so in both respects as it grew in size, capabilities, and policy responsibilities, especially after the Civil War. It also served as a vehicle for the rise of more coherent national parties and additional links between market and state (John 2003; Polsky 2000). While the assessment system of patronage politics restrained and distorted administrative competence, moreover, party patronage also enabled national administrators to engage in the effort to fashion civic majorities for national governance.

The administrative state of the nineteenth century was the primary organizational and institutional setting in which national elected officials, and both political and professional administrators, identified and examined the problems of the central liberal-democratic challenge of governing market-state relations. Those most involved conceived the challenge primarily in terms of the two imperatives of expansion across space and commercial development across time and with increasingly complexity. National administration and what it would do was both the primary object of and an active participant in the ideological and instrumental conflicts over spatial expansion and the difficult questions regarding how to organize markets and facilitate business development. The policies, administrative structures, and frontline operations designed and redesigned in response to the conflicts and underlying imperatives of national development constituted much of the working constitution of the commercial republic. As "agents of change" (John 1997), administrative agencies and their leaders, managers, and frontline officials did much to constitute the working constitution and thus the commercial republic in practice and effect.

Despite the horrific travails of nation building with the many instances of coercion, repression, marginalization, and violence that are so disturbing in retrospect, the nineteenth-century working constitution's formula for the problem posed by the division of labor between market and state in liberal-democratic governance succeeded in constructing an increasingly robust commercial republic. Government cultivated, and where necessary created, the private entities that could carry some of the burden of governance during the developmental drive of nineteenth-century nation building. As the development of markets and business succeeded, government needed to do less cultivation and creation, and could, through contracting and other vehicles, increasingly rely on existing and relatively effectively performing private entities to take on specific tasks and continue spatial and commercial expansion more generally.

This was the character of market-state relations in the working constitution that enabled the emergence, for a favored but not insignificant portion of the population, of a reasonable approximation of the liberal justice to which the commercial republic aspires. A considerable number of citizens enjoyed opportunities to be seriously engaged in self-government through selection of their political representatives and other avenues of political influence. Their representatives seemed sincerely concerned with maintaining the capacity and integrity of the major governmental institutions, although there was increasing worry that the most prominent extraconstitutional institution, the political party, was more and more serving its own interests rather than the larger public interest in sustaining self-government. Finally, many of these citizens enjoyed considerable freedom to pursue their entrepreneurial predilections, offering products and services that gave them a comfortable income and a decent living for some of those they employed; a few such entrepreneurs gained considerable wealth.

Undercurrents of trouble were rising to the surface as the century neared its end, however. The successes of the nineteenth-century working constitution exposed flaws in or generated conflicts with key elements of the founding regime design that began to generate economic consequences threatening both business performance and the relatively equitable prosperity that the formula seemed to promise, at least for the favored part of the population. Portions of the population ignored or treated unjustly by the working constitution, by being denied the economic benefits and state protections of the nineteenth-century's formula for the commercial republic, increasingly organized for recognition and a share of the promised prosperity and just governance. The old Whig fear of administrative power, never completely absent, resurfaced as the power and reach of both the national state and business increased. These forces coalesced to pave the way for what would eventually be dramatic change in the working constitution—in the relations between market and state, in the administrative state, and thus in the design and practice of the commercial republic.

The characteristics of the working constitution of the commercial republic in its first century, and the first administrative state that was a key part of it, do not by themselves provide an adequate basis for fashioning an understanding of how an administrative state can be reconciled in the political constitution of the American commercial republic. Yet these characteristics deserve to be highlighted because they show the dynamic nature of thinking about the commercial public interest that has occurred within the established traditions of American law and governance in theory and practice, as well as the possibilities for a more fully articulated theory of the administrative state as a constitutive institution in the political constitution of the American commercial republic.

3. Corporate Consolidation, the Privatized Economy, and the Second Administrative State

The newly created US Bureau of Labor issued its first annual report in 1886. The subject was industrial depressions. The bureau's first commissioner, Carroll D. Wright, highlighted overproduction as a critical problem plaguing industrial economies, along with underconsumption, speculative investment, and labor displacement from technological transition. The "persistent depression of the early 1890s" (Goldberg and Moye 1985, 24), punctuated by the Panic of 1893, spurred Wright to investigate the overproduction problem further. He published a two-part study in late 1897 and early 1898. By then the phenomenon had become "an established fact," of American economics and politics (Sklar 1988, 56), precipitating "the avalanche of corporate reorganization in industrial enterprise" (45). By 1904 "about 300 industrial consolidations with a market capitalization of $7 billion" (46) had occurred. The total value of the property involved in the transactions amounted to about "one-fifth of the nation's gross national product in 1900" (47). This relatively sudden punctuation in the existing economic equilibrium marked the transition from an economy of "proprietary-competitive" capitalism to "corporate-bureaucratic" capitalism (27), as well as the rise of the "administrator-investor" and the decline of the "entrepreneur-debtor" as the primary business actor.

Industrial consolidations creating vertically and horizontally integrated corporate trusts represented the market solution to the ruinous competition of an economy of small and numerous competitors made possible by general incorporation laws. This was an economy in which revenue and profit were hard to secure because of cutthroat pricing, resulting in the futile pursuit of greater production as the way to secure a stable flow of revenue. Financiers came to the rescue, in a sense, by restructuring ownership of industrial enterprises through incorporation, replacing the proprietor-owner with shareholder-investors and professional corporate managers. Investors imposed production constraints on the hired managers, and consolidations enabled control of prices. Along with labor unrest and the growth of the labor movement, agitation from social reformers, especially about the living conditions of the poor and working class, and the reactions of small producers to consolidation, considerable political turbulence and conflict ensued as a wide spectrum of political actors engaged in an effort to redefine market-state relations and the commercial public interest on satisfactory terms. The market-side solution of corporate consolidation required a corresponding solution on the side of the state. A "corporate-liberal" consensus eventually emerged out of competing models for reconstructing market-state relations (Sklar 1988). By about 1920 a transformed political economy matching a market dominated by bureaucratized corporations with a bigger, more nationalized, more bureaucratic administrative state was on its evolutionary way. Although the market side was dominant for a time because of the continuing influence of the laissez faire ideology, the New Deal and World War II helped boost the state side of the relationship so that market and state faced one another on relatively equal terms. They became increasingly intertwined through a variety of quasi-public structures commingling public and business officials and through a growing complex of business associations. A bureaucratized market and state would together carry the burden of administering prosperity. The advantages that a second, more bureaucratized administrative state provided for disciplining popular rule and protecting rights further solidified the legitimacy of the corporate-liberal working constitution.

Continuing the previous chapter's account of the ongoing development of the American commercial republic, this chapter begins by reviewing some of the major areas of conflict that arose in response to the corporate consolidation of the national economy, as well as other intensifying social and political conflicts carried forward from the state-building era. The chapter then considers key elements of the corporate-liberal reconstruction of the political economy, with particular attention to the nature, scope, and role of the second administrative state fashioned as a part of that reconstruction. From there, the chapter briefly traces further developments in the political economy and the second administrative state that have empowered the bureaucratic-corporate market relative to the administrative state. Whether these developments have produced a new kind of market and corresponding administrative state is open for debate, but features of a neoliberal regime are increasingly prominent, signaling the degraded condition of the commercial republic with respect to its ability to find the concrete meaning of the public interest and serve liberal justice. The chapters of part II then present the case that a major change in the regime's institutional design is necessary to renew the republic's capacity to discern the political value of a commercial society.

PROPERTY RIGHTS, CORPORATIONS, AND THE CORPORATE-LIBERAL CONSENSUS

The second administrative state, which emerged in the first decades of the twentieth century and settled firmly into place by about 1950, resolved, or at least ameliorated for a time, a tangled nest of late-nineteenth-century economic and political problems. The failure of the Civil War and Reconstruction to resolve the original American sin of slavery and racism—and the moral, social, and property relations that went with it—precipitated some of these problems. The other major source of problems for the working constitution was the acceleration of industrialization, with its social disruptions and economic confusion and instability. Coursing through many of these problems were serious questions about the viability of James Madison's "republican principle"—majority rule—especially with respect to the threats that majoritarian democracy seemed to pose to minorities and their rights and the seemingly frequent ignorance and irrationality of majority policy preferences. Political and social leaders eventually saw "bureaucratic authority structures" (Nelson 2006, chap. 5) and bureaucratized regulatory agencies (DeCanio 2015) as answers to these perceived problems of majority rule. The question about popular majorities was not a separate concern, moreover, but part of the larger and ongoing conundrum of how to sustain a commercial republic. Hence, the combination of an administered market and a second administrative state represented a solution to multiple social, economic, and political problems as well as the most fundamental problem of finding the necessary adjustments to market-state relations in response to the late developmental stages of the nineteenth-century working constitution.

The most prominent features of the second administrative state as it took stable shape—more nationalized, greater in scope and authority, more technically expert and professionalized, and thus more fully bureaucratic than its nineteenth-century predecessor, reflected the most acute demands arising from the problems of the late-nineteenth-century political economy, as well as the competing ideas proffered to address them. The competing ideas addressed how to assemble existing, and if necessary new, state and market institutional components to address the most acute economic and political problems and demands in a way that would motivate and enable public officials to give concrete meaning to the public interest. Questions about the nature of property and property rights, and about how to actuate the opportunities for mass economic well-being that industrial capitalism seemed to offer, prominently shaped the process by which a transformed working constitution, including a second administrative state, took shape.

It bears repeating that the protection of property rights is fundamental to conceptions of liberal justice and the design of liberal-democratic regimes. Nothing more clearly distinguishes the evolutionary path of the American commercial republic than its shifting conceptions of property and property rights. In confronting the corporate consolidation of the industrial economy, American political and business leaders focused on the need to protect property rights—and by extension to serve the commercial public interest—not only from concentrated power but also from destructive competition (Sklar 1988, 19). The evolving redefinition of property, giving primacy to intangible property and its exchange value, was central to the corporate reorganization of industrial-property ownership. In particular, the protection of property rights in the exchange value of intangible property enabled the fluidity of industrial ownership and the capital mobility of the individual capitalist. This stood in contrast to the relatively immobile capital of industrial owner-operators, whose capital was tied up in the large investments in fixed assets required of industrial concerns. The corporatization and financialization of industrial firms enabled by the protection of property rights in intangible property and its exchange value thus facilitated both successful investment in long-term, fixed assets and the multiplication and mobility of capital for further investment and wealth expansion (50).

With the emergence of marginal-utility theory, which enabled price setting to be separated from production costs and empowered industrial producers to be price makers rather than price takers (Sklar 1988, 69–70), the protection of property rights in intangible property and its exchange value freed the industrial economy from the deleterious effects of the unrestricted competition among atomized units (53). It also accelerated the capital mobilization and wealth expansion effects of corporate consolidation of the industrial economy. The chances of securing and even expanding mass economic well-being thus increased as well. In combination, these developments were what made the trust problem so confounding. The power of trusts such as Standard Oil to set prices irrespective of their production costs and to get customers to pay those prices enabled the trusts to generate substantial revenue, which could be used for further acquisition and consolidation. The market value of these companies, not the value of their physical assets, became the primary form of property needing the protection of property rights. The great wealth of owners and shareholders and the legal protections tied to property rights combined to make the trusts serious economic and political threats to the commercial republic. Yet the efficiencies of the trusts and the consequent expansion and mobility of the wealth of the trusts also meant that those with the requisite skills, know-how, and ambition could be far better compensated than under the old producer-competitive economy. The nation as a whole could be wealthier. No one wanted to return to the old days of cutthroat competition.

The corporate consolidation of the economy offered other advantages to various elements of American society. Corporations reduced the principal-agent and information asymmetry problems of owner-operator industrial concerns because investor leverage spurred greater transparency regarding business operations, including internal management and governance (Wright 2002). This expanded the possibilities for relatively safe investment for a larger segment of the population. Corporations were also comparatively more integrating and democratizing organizations, reaching across social, class, and sectional divisions to staff corporate bureaucracies. With the closing of the west, corporations offered a new "frontier of opportunity" and a "new bourgeois freedom" in the form of upward mobility via the ladders of the corporate bureaucracy, thus helping to constitute and sustain a growing urban, and eventually also rural, middle class (Sklar 1988, 26).

Reformers seeking to finish the job of freeing government from the corruptions of party patronage and establishing merit-based, professional, and technically expert public administration gained the support of the politically active leadership of major corporations, who advocated the adoption of the new business principles of corporate bureaucracy for government as well. Both groups sought to reinforce the legal anchors of government as "conducive to a favorable investment environment, techno-economic progress, inter-class cooperation, and social stability" (Sklar 1988, 31). Even small producers, disillusioned with the many adverse effects of the competitive market of debtor entrepreneurs, welcomed corporate consolidation as more likely to draw government action to force competition among large corporations. This would help "curtail competition among themselves," and thus realize "stability and fair play" in the market (33, 28).

Finally, with increasing consistency courts ruled that even large corporations, with valuations far greater on paper than in physical assets, could nevertheless be tied to the deep American traditions of liberty of association and contract. From this perspective, administrator-investor capitalism was still simply a matter of like-minded individuals coming together for their individual and collective benefit (see Blair and Pollman 2017).

Despite the attractive qualities of corporate consolidation, the new corporate entities were nevertheless unprecedented in size and market power in their respective sectors of the economy. Yet business as a whole was hardly monolithic (Sklar 1988, 32). The challenges thus remained the same, in a sense, as in past developments in the corporate form, in the nature of property and property rights, and in the struggles of the working constitution to contend with both these prominent strands in the weave of the commercial republic. The first challenge was to determine how to induce large controllers of productive assets to perform at a level that would generate reasonably widespread prosperity. The second challenge was to determine what special political privileges to grant to asset controllers that might enhance the chances that their interests would be broadened beyond very narrow concerns while preventing those special privileges from going too far, and otherwise limiting concentrated power in both market and state (34). Even under corporate consolidation, business interests were more diverse and fragmented because of the expanding complexity and specialization of industrialization.

Once firmly settled into place, the solution in the form of the corporate-liberal consensus was a far-reaching reconception of the public interest of the commercial republic. It was a philosophical reconception of the meaning of private and public and a major reordering of market-state relations through expansion and redirection of the state's "regulative and distributive functions," still firmly anchored in law, "in a manner consistent with the greatest possible preservation of private initiative and private-property ownership" (Sklar 1988, 38–39). It drew a striking new version of Woodrow Wilson's line "between *Interference* and *Laissez faire*." Paradoxically, redrawing that line resulted in a closer integration of public and private, albeit in a far more nationalized form (Balogh 2009, chap. 9). That form was an economy extensively administered—and increasingly so as the twentieth century progressed—by a combination of large market, state, and increasingly diverse hybrid organizations created to avoid at least the appearance of "state direction and state ownership" (Sklar 1988, 39). For a time, roughly between 1940 and 1970, the new corporate-liberal working constitution generated a remarkable level of prosperity that was more equitably distributed than at any other time in the nation's history (Saez and Zucman 2019, 37–39). As a result, it stimulated demands for even more economic equity and other forms of social justice. The working constitution forged in the progressive and New Deal periods has unraveled substantially, however. Further exposition of key facets of the corporate-liberal working constitution and their effects provide the necessary markers for tracing how the unraveling has happened to the point that radical regime redesign now deserves serious consideration.

THE PRIVATE MARKET AND THE SECOND ADMINISTRATIVE STATE

It bears repeating that the move to general incorporation statues in the states had the effect of privatizing the corporate form. Although corporations were not completely freed from state scrutiny and regulation, general incorporation released the business corporation from most of its obligations to serve the public welfare. Conceptions of corporations as public utilities and their operations as freighted with the public interest (Novak 2017) hardly disappeared. With the financialization and bureaucratization of the corporation and consequent corporate consolidation of the economy, however, the acceptance of the corporation as a private entity created almost entirely for the benefit of its shareholders fully took hold. A corporate-administered economy would bring more efficiency, innovation, and stability in the market, meaning the functions of the market could rest more safely and fully in private hands. This meant even more discretion for large controllers of productive assets to allocate those assets as they saw fit to serve the private interests of corporate investors by ensuring productive investment—controlling output and prices, maintaining market share, and preserving an attractive rate of return. The wealth-generating and wealth-distributing advantages of corporate consolidation would follow. Even with the attractive advantages, however, the large and commanding economic entities could not be left to their own devices. To ensure that a market dominated by the pursuit of private gain functioned in ways that served public ends—sufficient general economic efficiency, equitable distribution of wealth, stability and fair play—required a bigger, more powerful administrative state that would exercise its power through the tax system and various forms of regulation. Yet this more powerful administrative state was, paradoxically, more restrained in critical ways than in the era of the public economy and well-regulated society. Progressive reformers would also pursue nonadministrative changes to enhance the capacity of an engaged public to counterbalance the political weight of a corporate economy, but a managerial-administrative strategy on the side of the state was central to corporate-liberal consensus (Rahman 2017, chap. 2–3).

Government's scope, legal backbone, and administrative capacity had grown substantially at both the state and national levels by the end of the nineteenth century, including with respect to monitoring the market and inquiring into business operations (Novak 2010). As corporate consolidation of the economy emerged and rapidly took hold, the state could not ignore the rising chorus of demands for action in response. Because government was already deeply involved in the transformation of the political economy—through such actions as railroad regulation and early antitrust law—the question was what more should be done, if anything, to bolster the state in a way that would best counterbalance the corporate consolidation of American capitalism. Two models for a more administratively robust state character and role vis-à-vis the market—a role that would be more coherent and comprehensive while still falling well short of direct state ownership and control—were prominent.

The first, federal incorporation or registration of corporations, envisioned the national state overseeing a corporate-trust–dominated economy by directly creating and structuring the corporate form, essentially returning to the idea of corporations as special creatures of the state guided and restrained by the incorporation provisions of the state's contract with the incorporated entity (Crane 2017, 103). The model never gained sufficient traction to endure beyond the limited realm of government corporations because it ran afoul of the history and legal precedent of corporate creation and oversight power divided between the federal government and the states and because of political conflicts over the legal status of the labor movement resulting from the courts applying antitrust law far more vigorously to labor unions than to corporate trusts (Crane 2017, 104; see also Sklar 1988, 223–226).

The second, the public-utility model, emanating from the theory and practice of the police power in common law and constitutional law, was far more legally robust and administratively enduring. Although generally associated now with natural monopolies in such areas as transportation, communications, and power and water generation, the "overarching goal of the public utility idea was an enlarged police power—an expansive conception of state (and, ultimately, federal) regulatory power over corporations, business, and the American economy more generally" (Novak 2017, 135). The public-utility model was centered on "a more generalized and autonomous conception of the public interest . . . as the basis for increased state and governmental regulation" (149). Although for multiple decades afterward the US Supreme Court sustained the constitutionality of "a wide variety of extensive economic regulations" (164) anchored in the public-utility model, the model was never as generalized in law and administration as its most ardent advocates envisioned. It did, however, help facilitate the corporate-liberal consensus by providing the administrative and legal structures around which a reconception of the nature and role of the state could form.

This new conception of the state, more executive-centered, contained a second administrative state that elected officials, judges, and public administrators constructed and expanded over several decades. This new administrative state, more nationalized, bigger, more bureaucratic, and more legally powerful in many ways, fulfilled both distributive and regulatory functions in some ways similar to, but in others quite distinct from, its nineteenth-century predecessor. Its substantial empowerment to confront the big, economically powerful, and politically active corporate consolidations also required political legitimation that entailed structural, legal, and philosophical constraints that would eventually prove problematic for the regime's ability to maintain a larger, political view of the value of a commercial society.

Functions and Legitimation of the Second Administrative State

Under the nineteenth-century working constitution, the first administrative state's regulative function was aimed at policing the behavior of market actors to enforce compliance with the norms and rules regarding the health, safety, and general community welfare of the well-regulated society. The regulative function of the second administrative state under the corporate-liberal working constitution was not only more nationalized, its responsibility shifted to ensuring that the conduct of corporations as rights-bearing "persons" enjoying a new form of "private sovereignty" (Novak 2010, 394) was properly competitive and thus did not impede or undermine the efficiency, stability, and wealth-generating potential of corporate capitalism. The second administrative state's regulative functions concerned not just conduct in the marketplace, including the circulation and multiplication of capital but also, eventually, public and workplace health and safety, environmental quality, and freedom of "natural" persons from violations of their civil and political rights. Still, the primary object of both economic and social regulation, and even to a considerable degree the expansion of civil rights protections, was to restrain conduct that was anticompetitive or that otherwise impeded market efficiency and the realization of broad-based economic well-being.

The distributive function of the second administrative state differed from its predecessor as well. It continued to encompass creating or encouraging new markets and business development, but in ways far more targeted than building a general infrastructure for commerce and international trade. Most business creation and market development or expansion was left to private entrepreneurship, and any remaining action by the state in this regard was subsumed under the general distributive function of inducing business performance. Hence, the distributive function of the second administrative state centered substantially on improving general market and business performance with respect to efficiency and fairness. Indeed, especially from the time of the New Deal onward, even the market-efficiency regulative function was essentially aimed at inducing business performance and thus increasing wealth and expanding mass economic well-being.

Generally speaking, the dangers of unbridled competition spurred business to seek certain forms of regulation at both the state and national levels. Regulations aimed at particular businesses or business sectors were in many instances tailored inducements for business performance. Not all businesses welcomed all regulation, but in general, "systematically" regulating "modern capitalism," resulting in the "legal and political reconstruction of business" and the economy (Novak 2010, 390) was the essence of the corporate-liberal consensus. All of this stemmed from the critical move that public officials made—to accept political responsibility for overall economic performance and the maintenance and expansion of mass economic well-being. This forced public officials to become more attuned than ever before to the need to induce business performance.

The agreement, manifested in the outpouring of regulatory statutes and the creation of new regulatory agencies over several decades, especially since the 1930s and at both the national and state levels, was unprecedented in almost all respects. The state—especially the national state—gained in size and policy scope, and in legal and exhortative power over the market. It also received acquiescence from corporate capitalism to use new, more powerful, and more rationally and precisely designed policies, such as the reporting and auditing requirements in securities and banking regulations, to monitor and police the market and correct detrimental conduct. Going even farther were such statutes as the Employment Act of 1946 and the Full Employment and Balanced Growth Act of 1978, in which the federal government took on greater responsibility for managing the national economy. Public officials in turn gained much greater power to claim political credit for the success of such policies and to defend them as being responsive to the public desire for expanding prosperity. Through subsequent social regulatory statutes they could lay claim to improving other aspects of social life. This cemented in the public mind the expectation that the state was responsible for, if it did not quite guarantee, prosperity and the quality of life. The mass electorate soon became practiced in rewarding and punishing political leaders for economic performance. The ability to claim credit for prosperity and quality of life also won elected officials, especially legislators, the kind of long-term political advantage that enabled them to have more stable and more lucrative careers in public service.

Through the corporate-liberal working constitution, business, primarily large corporations, gained greater leverage to demand more inducements to perform. The politically "privileged position" of business in the regime expanded considerably. In a burgeoning variety of forms developed as early as the 1940s, but especially since the 1980s, these inducements have come to include special regulatory protections, subsidies, favorable tax provisions, property-rights protections for more varieties of intangible property, and insurance programs and other forms of the socialization of entrepreneurial risk. Such inducements and the increased political leverage they reflect would be unpopular if exposed to sustained publicity and public scrutiny. Hence, a general shifting of risk emerged within the state as corporations demanded as inducements more offloading of entrepreneurial risk onto the state. Legislators shifted the authority to make policy choices that might sustain prosperity, and thus the responsibilities for and the consequences of policy failure, onto elected executives. The ultimate risk shifting, however, was toward the most politically insulated actors—the administrative state. This second-level shift included giving elected executives greater control and supervisory authority over the administrative state.

Most of these developments growing out of the corporate-liberal consensus and redefinition of the working constitution of the commercial republic took time to emerge and reflected frequent adjustments that business leaders and public officials felt compelled to make. Details on some of the key adjustments and developments that emerged in the later decades of the twentieth century follow below. Critical elements of the character, scope, and role of the second administrative state took shape early on, however, as the new working constitution gained definition.

The more extensive and explicit political legitimation of the more nationalized, more powerful and far-reaching second administrative state stemmed from the pairing of new and old factors. The new factor was the more definite line between public and private that was central to the public philosophy of the corporate-liberal consensus, including the market as exemplar of the private sphere. The old factor was the indefatigable Whig fear of a corrupt ministry using administrative power to control the economy and maintain power. Given these two phenomena, what could justify this new, more powerful administrative state, especially one that was more organizationally complex and bureaucratic?

The bureaucratic character of the second administrative state was its most worrisome feature, seemingly alien to American political practice, culture, and spirit. Although increasingly bureaucratized public entities had been growing nicely on American soil for some time, the message of bureaucracy as an alien threat struck a chord. Thus, Woodrow Wilson felt compelled to declare that to be safe, bureaucratic administration would have to be Americanized. It would be forced to "learn our constitutions by heart; . . . get the bureaucratic fever out of its veins; . . . [and] inhale much free American air" (Wilson 1887, 202). The manner in which political legitimation through Americanization proceeded was to instrumentalize public administration to a far greater extent than it had been under the first administrative state.

The primary dimension of this instrumentalization was to declare public administration politically neutral, to discount, at least rhetorically and philosophically, public administration as a political institution in its own right, with both instrumental (purpose-serving) and constitutive (purpose-shaping) qualities. The constitutiveness of administration under the system of political patronage and party assessments clearly had corrosive effects on the polity by equating the aims of parties and party leaders with the general interest and directing the use of public resources, especially the labor and earnings of civil servants, to serve party interests. Civil-service reform promoting nonpartisan merit as the basis for hiring and promotion began the hard push for politically neutralizing administration by purifying it of party corruption. As administrative entities gained more completely the features of bureaucracy—not just merit selection and promotion but also professionalization, rational and increasingly complex divisions of labor, increased technical and scientific expertise, and powerful information gathering and information processing capabilities—political neutralization had to be more comprehensive in order to ensure that the immense powers of the bureaucratic form, and the perceived threats it posed to self-government, were safely restrained. It took on the character and form of technocracy, and this became part of the developing study and practice of public administration. That was not enough, however. Hence, bureaucratic administration had to submit to greater control by those public officials constitutionally authorized to represent the people, formulate policy, and oversee the day-to-day work of government. All of this was essential to the political legitimacy of a more powerful second administrative state empowered to monitor, and if necessary reconstitute, the market.

Rhetorical legitimation through instrumentalization in the form of both the more complete and emphatic subordination of administration to political oversight and control and the conceptual separation of public administration from politics, did pose a conundrum. It was hardly a secret among the actors involved in constructing the corporate-liberal working constitution that even a nonpartisan administrative state would have formative effects on society, if for no other reason than politically neutral administration would not be value-neutral even if the aspiration to scientific administration and management suggested political impartiality. Technical and scientific experts have particular worldviews, and these would inform their decisions, including those decisions that would shape public aims even if only in very subtle ways. The technocratic veneer would also incompletely hide the reality that many experts would be coming from business and industry into the regulatory fold, a point of considerable contention as the corporate-liberal consensus was still forming.

The actors engaged in constructing the new working constitution also recognized that the constitutional design of separate institutions sharing powers would make political oversight messy, conflictual, and disjointed. This would open the door for other actors in the system—businesses and business associations and other organized interests—to fill gaps in the oversight space by monitoring, and if necessary raising alarms about, the conduct and performance of the administrative state. In subsequent decades, political overseers would come to rely on such interest-group monitoring and "fire alarm" activity (McCubbins and Schwartz 1984; Balla and Deering 2013). This would also, however, further encourage and enable administrative agencies to engage in bargaining and coalition building with organized interests, and to some extent with their institutional superiors, in processes of mutual adjustment and incremental change that would also preserve at least some administrative discretion and autonomy. The incentives created in this regard forced internal adjustments within the constitutional branches to enable them to more effectively oversee the new administrative state—reorganization of committee structures in Congress, expansion of presidential supervisory authority over administrative instruments and the accompanying expansion of a presidential supervisory bureaucracy, and new conceptions of administrative law and judicial supervision of administration (Arnold 1998; Cooper 1988; Rosenbloom 2000).

Rhetorical political legitimation of the second administrative state remained insufficient, however. It had to be accompanied by actual systemic and institutional change reflecting the rhetorical claims to politically neutral instrumentalization of administration. Politics became the realm of the "policy maker" (Heidelberg 2019), and the administrator or manager simply carried out the given policy. Such thinking had plenty of precedent in the regime, with Anglo-American law recognizing that purely ministerial duties could coexist with discretionary duties in a single position. For constitutional purposes *Marbury v. Madison* [5 U.S. (1 Cranch) 137 (1803)] and other jurisprudence drew a sharper distinction between ministerial duties and discretionary judgment, with the latter subject to the direction and ultimate control of the elected executive. Public policy and administrative action had become so much more far-reaching by the twentieth century, however, with greater authority and judgment unavoidably placed in the hands of administrators. Thus legitimation required a much more emphatic articulation of the separation of administration from politics and policy discretion. Any discretion placed in the hands of administrators would have to be more explicitly authorized, and how far that could go before exceeding constitutional limits proved to be a continuing source of contention as the working constitution evolved.

Over time mutual reinforcement of rhetoric, governing philosophy, and institutional adjustments developed. The struggles within the judiciary that began in the late 1800s over the formalization of judicial reasoning, applying the law as a quasi-scientific endeavor, rationally discovering the meaning of the law rather than creating law as in the common-law tradition, was a microcosm of the adjustment dynamics (Nelson 2006, 133–155). Within the administrative state itself, civil servants internalized the rhetoric, philosophy, and structural adjustments. This was not a hard transition. Professionalism has a similar orientation, and professionalization had already increased considerably as the first administrative state developed. Neutral competence to serve those politically chosen and constitutionally designated to rule was easily defended as consistent with self-government. Professional judgment and expertise were required to execute the law, certainly, but that was part of the agreement in which political institutions would exercise strategic vigilance in monitoring, and if necessary correcting, administrative action. Management precepts presumed to be neutral came to stand on equal terms with adherence to law in guiding administrative philosophy and practice. A serious problem persisted, however. The promotion of a politically neutral, wholly instrumental administrative state did not square with the reality of the constitutive, purpose- and value-shaping effects of administrative action that members of the general public observed and experienced. This contributed to the eventual erosion of public confidence and trust in government (Cook 2014).

The process of political legitimation in rhetoric, public philosophy, and structural change was also not sufficient to satisfy corporate capitalism's concern for the safe political restraint of the far more powerful and far-reaching administrative state. One of the key compromises of the corporate-liberal consensus was that regulatory policy and administration could not be fully centralized, generalized, and rationally comprehensive. Business was already segmented and specialized under corporate-consolidated capitalism, with varying industry and commercial interests having somewhat differing demands for inducements. Hence, regulation was "fragmented by administrative topic and institution rather than comprehensive and seamless" (Crane 2017, 103), as both federal incorporation and a generalized public-utility model had contemplated. Although the divided administrative "topics" reflected to some extent legal and policy legacies—antitrust distinct from fair trade, for example—the administrative and policy divisions aligned much more with the divisions in the market by industry sector and lines of business. Separate policies thus concerned securities regulation, banking regulation, electric power regulation, communications regulation, transportation regulation, and more. Different regulatory agencies with varying structures and more limited, specific missions and responsibilities were assigned these distinct policy specializations. The second administrative state would thus not be monolithic, and there was a certain advantage in the development of regulatory expertise that the fragmentation of policy and administration provided. The problem of convergence of the interests of the regulated with the specialized policy mission and expertise of the regulator—and the political overseer of the regulator for that matter—was an inherent risk, however, that would eventually plague the working constitution.

The absence in this bureaucratized but Americanized second administrative state of any institution for establishing and advancing a general administrative cadre at the national level was also a tacit part of the corporate-liberal consensus. There would be no *École nationale d'administration*, no centralized training ground for federal administrators and no centralized personnel system for the second administrative state nationally, at least until the second half of the twentieth century. American universities would fill some of the gap in various but limited ways, with some providing training in certain areas of substantive expertise such as the foreign service. A bifurcation in education and training for the second administrative state also emerged, with law schools teaching administrative law—essentially training regulators—and public administration and policy schools teaching general management. In both realms, education and training reinforced neutral competence as a guiding value orientation. Hence, no public institution was centrally and explicitly responsible for developing and disseminating theories and practices of statutory interpretation and judicial review, administrative processes, management techniques, and other critical skills and abilities—in short, administrative science—to make the second administrative state more capable and more coherent. Instead, because demand for ways to improve administration in both the market and the state was present from the very beginning, what emerged was an intermittent exchange of techniques, processes, and management theories—or at least fashions—between business administration and public administration, although business law and public administrative law remained separate domains.

THE DECLINE OF THE CORPORATE-LIBERAL COMMERCIAL REPUBLIC

From the standpoint of commercial republican regime design, the most far-reaching effect of the emergence and institutionalization of the corporate-bureaucratic capitalist economy was its completion of the transition to and legitimation of a capital-holding class as the primary social basis of the regime. One indicator of that reality is that since the advent of the federal income tax in 1913, the tax rate on realized capital gains has always been lower than on wages and business earnings (Saez and Zucman 2019, 48). Nevertheless, the special political privileges of the holders of capital, although substantial, were restrained in many ways while the corporate-liberal working constitution was well ensconced. The tax system was highly progressive, with high marginal tax rates on income, corporate earnings, and large estates essentially capping the legal income of the most affluent. Elected officials supported aggressive tax enforcement to rein in such conduct as exploiting loopholes or self-dealing through phony charities (37–50). Three wars in the span of forty years further restrained excessive self-interest among corporate CEOs and wealthy financiers by imposing strong expectations of shared sacrifice across the political and economic spectrums. More generally, the agencies of the second administrative state were empowered to such an extent as to approximate the vision of the state "not as an economic policeman or even as a countervailing force to private economic power, but as a full, interactive partner in a legal-economic vision of modern state capitalism" (Novak 2010, 395).

Whether the structures and incentives of this "social control of capitalism" (Novak 2010) at its peak of power succeeded in getting at least some in the capital-holding class to glimpse the larger public interest and appreciate the broader political meaning of a commercial society is an open question. Opposition to the entire corporate-liberal transformation of the political economy existed from the beginning, but business generally did not contest the cornerstones of the consensus, and initial adjustments in the public philosophy and the working constitution favored business in any case. Declining wealth inequality, one rough measure of the increase in mass economic well-being, was notable between 1940 and 1980. This at least suggests that business leaders saw the advantages to business, and to the general welfare, of a more equitable distribution of wealth. It is at least possible that this established sufficient affluence to move the regime toward liberal justice by enabling groups still marginalized on the basis of race, gender, and national origin to pursue greater political and civil equality, up to a point, without threatening general economic well-being. Liberal democracies are inherently dynamic, however, for better or worse. Thus, further developments in the corporate-liberal version of the commercial republic eventually paved the way for major expansion in the privileged position of business in the regime and a diminishing capacity to keep the public interest in view. This came about when economic conditions shifted and political coalitions reshuffled, reanimating old animosities and spurring new ideological claims.

Wars, Reorganization, and an Administrative Separation of Powers

Military structures and operations comprise a domain of especially extensive interdependence of market and state in liberal democracies. Indian policy and the Civil War exemplify this tendency in the American commercial republic's first century. While the corporate-liberal working constitution, including the second administrative state, was just beginning to take shape, the nation entered the First World War, with more than four million men and women eventually in uniform. The war presented an opportunity to consolidate the new political economy linking an administered economy and new administrative state, but military and societal mobilization on the scale required exceeded the actual administrative capacity of existing federal agencies. Congress and President Wilson authorized the creation of various war committees and boards, ostensibly attached to executive departments, to manage the mobilization on the home front, primarily by controlling the economy and shifting industrial resources toward mobilization. These entities brought businessmen and public officials into close working relationships. Their decentralized administrative structures, exemplified by Herbert Hoover's organization and leadership of the Food Administration, "afforded [business] privileged access to policy choices, enabling businesses to influence who has access and influence in the future" irrespective of political control of the responsible agencies (Durant 2014, 608). It was Wilson's own resistance to allowing more hierarchical, bureaucratic structures in order to diminish the threat to administrative legitimacy that enabled greater intertwining of state and market during the war (Cook 2007, 173–174, 222–223). It was a messy situation, however, because business was not all that well organized either, despite corporate consolidation. Hence, to impose further order on the market-state relationship within the context of the war, "the federal government encouraged the establishment of various associations of independent businesses to make it easier for government agencies to engage a growing number of interest groups" (Durant 2014, 609), and these organizations would continue to develop and represent business in the corridors of government even after the war concluded and rapid demobilization ensued. Typical calls for government retrenchment of both administrative authority and budgetary resources followed in the wake of demobilization, complicating the continued development of the second administrative state and its capacity to respond when fascism trampled the shaky peace engineered by the Treaty of Versailles.

The administrative development that accelerated in response to the Second World War spurred the same dynamic relationships of business and government on an even greater scale (Durant 2014, 615). Business was already better organized and represented, and the second administrative state was more fully developed in size and scope. In important respects a fully engaged market-state partnership in administering American industrial capitalism reached its peak. The significant element of antagonism toward the market that the New Deal had infused in the greatly expanded second administrative state had to be tamped down, however. Any further effort to control big business and reform corporations was suspended for the duration of the war (Crane 2017, 120), and much of that effort never reappeared. More significant, demobilization was far less extensive than after World War I. The Korean conflict, the nuclear arms race, and the Cold War heightened worries that crystalized in Dwight Eisenhower's farewell warning about a "military-industrial complex" (see Griffin 1992). More to the point, in the domain of military and national-security policy there has ever since been an extensive form of state-managed capitalism providing particular industries and specific corporations not only privileged access and favored inducements but significant coproduction of defense and national-security policy.

The "cold-war liberalism" that emerged with the rising spread of communism also rocked the stability of the corporate-liberal consensus supporting the legitimacy of the second administrative state. Although this anticommunist liberalism only modestly pulled back from the most ambitious social welfare aims of the late New Deal, it permitted the rise of a willingness to curtail civil liberties in pursuit of Soviet infiltrators and the more general communist threat (Grossman 2002). More insidiously, this "second Red Scare" prompted so-called loyalty investigations of federal civil servants that went far beyond the primary aim of ferreting out communist spies and sympathizers. Whatever residual wisdom there may have been in looking out for real Soviet infiltration, the perceived threat primarily empowered conservative public officials and institutional power players, enabling real purges of the federal civil-service ranks, diminishing the strength of the second administrative state vis-à-vis the market and the possibilities for expanding economic opportunity and constraining corporate capitalism (Storrs 2013).

It was not just wars hot or cold that eventually enhanced the privileged position of business as the corporate-liberal commercial republic continued to evolve.

Built into the working constitution was a serious tension between demands for transparency and the impulse to insulate governance from perceived irrationalities of popular reaction to governing decisions. On the market side, the privatization of the corporate form through general incorporation was an innovation in business transparency, resulting in the democratization of business governance of a certain sort. The information asymmetry at the heart of the principal-agent problem in business organization diminished with the power of shareholders to hire corporate administrators and through their employment contracts require the information on business performance that investors needed to make sound investment decisions. This increased transparency of the corporate form was eventually further bolstered by regulations requiring corporations to report on properties and operations, executive management, details about the stock or other securities they offered and to issue independently certified financial statements. This kind of regulatory authority reflected the influence of the public-utility idea and the push for the social control of capitalism more generally. The form that such regulation should take was widely debated before it was incorporated into the corporate-liberal consensus, and it continued to evolve. A secondary market offering analysis and investment advice based on regulatory requirements for corporate disclosures further magnified the corporate form's transparency advantages and made stock market investment attractive to a broader segment of the public.

Despite the increased transparency of the market under corporate capitalism, there remained strong tendencies toward information asymmetry and incentives for privileged access to corporate performance information. Legal restrictions on insider trading were critical to securities regulation and remain in place today. Yet early in the evolution of the corporate-liberal working constitution, the simplest and most far-reaching transparency requirement—public disclosure of corporate tax returns—ended less than two years after the creation of the corporate income tax in 1909. From then on, "the tax affairs of America's corporate giants have remained well-kept secrets" (Saez and Zucman 2019, 79).

Within the state, the development of a large, nationalized, and bureaucratized regulatory apparatus provided a kind of safety valve that reduced pressure on public officials from populist demands for far-reaching government economic intervention to address the wrenching effects of corporate consolidation (DeCanio 2015). The regulatory bureaucracy and the second administrative state more generally insulated elected officials from at least some public reaction to unpopular actions deemed necessary to solve the problem of competitive capitalism and to guide the shift to and the development of corporate-administered capitalism. Going forward, the second administrative state diminished popular scrutiny of and pressure to reduce the mutual interdependence between market and state in the corporate-liberal commercial republic. Alleviating at least some popular pressure made sense within the new working constitution. It allowed public officials to take responsibility for economic performance while lowering the risk of doing so by shifting that risk to an administrative state that stood at arm's length from the popular scrutiny and pressure that elected officials experienced. Without such insulation, popular pressure might force lawmakers into hasty and potentially damaging economic-policy decisions.

The greater opacity and insularity of the second administrative state, when combined with its fragmented structure and expanded regulatory authority and power, posed serious problems, however. The rights of businesses to fair hearings and fair decisions in the regulatory process seemed to require that regulatory agencies follow at least quasi-judicial procedures of due process and publication of a complete decision record, with the process and decisions being subject to judicial review. To the public, or at least to some elected officials and other interests claiming to speak for the public, the benefits of a powerful second administrative state were diminished by confusion about who supervised and controlled the vast array of new and powerful agencies, inconsistent and insufficient public information about the reasoning behind the decisions those agencies made, and the absence of a public voice in the regulatory process. Calls for reforms to address these gaps and weaknesses grew louder as the number of regulatory agencies and their scope and impact increased during the New Deal. The two reform responses—executive reorganization and the managerial presidency, and the creation of an "administrative separation of powers" (Michaels 2017)—did much to further cement the legitimacy of the second administrative state by addressing the transparency-insularity tension. Eventually, however, both reform responses opened up avenues for access to and influence in governance running through the administrative state that business could exploit, enhancing the privileged position of business and its leverage in the deeply interdependent relations between market and state.

Executive Reorganization and the Managerial Presidency

Franklin Roosevelt's ambitions for a top-to-bottom reorganization of the American state to establish an integrated system of rational resource planning, and his concerns about the haphazard additions to the second administrative state stemming from early New Deal actions, provided the primary impetus for a plan to reorganize the executive branch (Karl 1988, 188). The President's Committee on Administrative Management—the "Brownlow Committee"—focused considerable attention in its report on bringing under the president's direct supervision and control the many independent regulatory commissions that Congress had authorized as the topic-based structure of the second administrative state developed under the corporate-liberal working constitution. The reorganization legislation that emerged from the committee's recommendations sparked furious debate in Congress—including dire warnings about executive dictatorship and bureaucratic tyranny (Cook 2014, 148–156). As a result, the final version of the legislation delivered far less in structural changes than FDR had desired, ending for all intents and purposes any effort to install a strongly state-centered version of managed modern capitalism (Karl 1988). Nevertheless, and far more important, the legitimation argument and the governance rationale for executive reorganization articulated in the committee's report and in the congressional debate gained a permanent foothold and placed the lion's share of the supervision and direction of the second administrative state within the presidential sphere.

The legitimation argument and governance rationale were woven together in the concluding passage of the report's introduction. The committee declared "but one grand purpose, namely, to make democracy work today in our National Government." That required making "our Government an efficient, up-to-date, and effective instrument for carrying out the will of the Nation" (President's Committee 1937, 4). It was the will of the nation to expand and improve the modern ministrant functions for which the burgeoning administrative state was responsible, "the constant raising of the level of the happiness and dignity of human life, the steady sharing of the gains of our Nation, whether material or spiritual" (1). In short, placing the bigger, better, more "efficient" and "up-to-date" administrative state under presidential supervision and management would make it more democratic, or at least more responsive to some version of an articulated popular will. It would also deliver expanded, higher-quality services to make individual lives better and enhance societal well-being. It would be better coordinated and more rationally managed.

Well anchored in prior claims that the presidency is the only elected office representative of the whole polity and thus democratic in a unique way in the constitutional system, much of the normative and pragmatic logic of a "managerial presidency" (Arnold 1998) became mainstream by the end of World War II. Presidents from then on nevertheless continued to lament that they could not control the administrative state, and each president added control mechanisms of one sort or another, mostly with the support, or at least the acquiescence, of Congress. The effect has been to enable the "managerial presidency . . . [to] treat much of government as if it were an extended executive department" (Arnold 2007, 1038). This might not have been a problematic adaptation within the working constitution if presidents had a truly national orientation that made them more resistant to parochial or special-interest influence and, especially, to overreaching demands for inducements from business. Such claims are historically, constitutionally, and factually dubious, however (Nzelibe 2006).

Presidential influence on, direction of, and intervention in the processes of the second administrative state are far less the reflection of civic majorities formed during the course of presidential elections and far more a manifestation of the particular collection of interests of presidential electoral coalitions and the "parochial bias" of the electoral college (Nzelibe 2006, 1235–1243). More powerful still was the increasing pressure on presidents to respond to business demands for inducements so that they could claim to have delivered good economic performance as the presidency acquired increasing responsibility for management of the economy (Genovese 1987). Despite their claims of caring about the overall economy, moreover, presidential candidates and presidents generally favor particular business interests—those in their electoral coalition—through their policy actions (Nzelibe 2006, 1243–1246).

Taming the Second Administrative State

Even if presidents do articulate national interests in a way unique in the constitutional system—and as a result of their rhetorical powers and expanding legal authority are able to resist special-interest influence to some extent—congressional responses to the second administrative state and the managerial presidency sent additional pathways of business privilege and influence coursing through the second administrative state. Two key developments opened these avenues of business influence. First, the Administrative Procedure Act (APA) initiated the formalization and standardization of administrative rulemaking and the judicialization of administrative adjudication. Second, other congressional actions accumulated "to ensure that agency decisions accommodate legislative preferences" (Nzelibe 2006, 1262).

Serious worries about the fusion of legislative, executive, and judicial powers in agencies of the second administrative state, including the particular concern about fragmented, inconsistent property-rights protections in administrative procedures and adjudication, spurred parallel executive and legislative studies and actions that produced the Administrative Procedure Act of 1946. The APA required more due process protections in administrative adjudication and more standardized administrative rulemaking procedures, including opening up rulemaking to public input, increasing the transparency of agency decision making, and bolstering the legal rationales for administrative rules. Over time, judicial decisions and legislative refinements further strengthened and expanded these requirements.

The APA and its legal and practical refinements represented more than a set of procedural safeguards, however. In combination with other developments, such as the merit-based civil service, the APA created an "administrative separation of powers" that "refashioned" the second administrative state "to resemble the framers' tripartite scheme." The administrative separation of powers "triangulated" the combination of powers delegated to the second administrative state, lessening its internal structure and the normative tension between political insulation and popular control by buffering administrators from political pressure while at the same time enabling the "public writ large . . . to engage meaningfully and directly in most administrative matters" (Michaels 2017, 8). The development of the administrative separation of powers enhanced the "constitution-in-practice" and in effect generalized the constitutionalization of the second administrative state (64) and harmonized "leading, but conflicting, administrative values" (65).

For a generation the administrative separation of powers stabilized the corporate-liberal working constitution and reduced political conflict engendered by the bigger, more powerful, more far-reaching second administrative state. Yet the APA and the administrative separation of powers also enhanced business leverage and its privileged position in two significant ways. First, enhancing rights protections in rulemaking, and especially in administrative adjudication, originated from a concern that business rights be protected in the regulatory process. After all, business was the prime target of the greatly expanded regulatory state, and regulatory requirements could potentially affect the value of business property or even amount to a regulatory taking, completely depriving a business of any economic return from the use of its property. Business thus deserved to be heard in the rulemaking process, and in administrative adjudication business was entitled to a fair hearing and other due process protections. Other organized interests, and individuals for that matter, took advantage of the same protections, but corporations and trade associations had the greatest resources available to gain the benefits of due process protections. Second, as judicial review of administrative actions expanded and rulemaking procedures and adjudication protections thickened, it was again business that had the resources to take full advantage of notice and comment requirements, exploit opportunities to enter independent data and analysis into the rulemaking record, press claims of arbitrary and capricious administrative actions, and otherwise command the attention and responsiveness of regulators in increasingly complex and technically demanding regulatory actions.

The APA and administrative separation of powers were part of a larger set of developments in which Congress sought to "domesticate" (Michaels 2017, 65) the second administrative state by infusing it with legislative values and enhancing legislative oversight and supervision of administrative agencies. In this enterprise to create a "legislative-centered public administration" (Rosenbloom 2000), Congress reconstituted itself through such instruments as the Legislative Reorganization Acts of 1946 and 1970, reasserting its control over the shape and evolution of the second administrative state. Although Congress intended its efforts in part to counterbalance an expanding managerial presidency, some of its initiatives relating to improving management and performance in the second administrative state enhanced presidential managerial control. More important, congressional efforts to infuse legislative values into the actions of administrative agencies included, in addition to the process values of open participation and transparency reflected in the APA, the constituency-orientation and particularistic interests of legislators, harnessing administrative agencies for casework, as well as funneling agency labor and budgets and imposing new restraints and mandates on agencies, all to serve favored constituencies. These efforts reflected not only typical pork-barrel items such as appropriations earmarks but also moves to enhance business leverage in the regulatory process, such as reforming "informal rulemaking" by way of the Negotiated Rulemaking Act of 1990 and the Small Business Regulatory Enforcement Fairness Act of 1996 (Rosenbloom 2000).

The congressional enterprise to construct a legislative-centered public administration enhanced business leverage in its interactions with the second administrative state in more general ways. First, it proved a boon to congressional career aspirations through improved reelection chances by enhancing not only the delivery of tangible and intangible benefits to favored constituencies but also the claims of legislators to be able to do something about the sluggishness and errors of big government bureaucracy. This advantage led in turn to the benefits gained from employing a rhetorical and symbolic politics centered on denouncing the "Washington establishment" (Fiorina 1989) and trumpeting the need to "drain the swamp" (Garcia 2016). Over time, the rhetoric trended toward increasingly shrill attacks on alleged bureaucratic incompetence, wastefulness, intrusiveness, and threats to liberty, dovetailing with the development of a conservative billionaire-funded think tank and university complex and broader neoliberal ideology explored further below. The result has been damage to administrative effectiveness in the form of impediments to effective policy implementation and "recruitment, retention, and training difficulties" affecting the competency of both career administrators and the critical political appointee positions below the senior level (Garrett et al. 2006, 236).

Vastly improved opportunities for legislative careers attracted electoral competition, eventually generating increased demands for campaign funding. Between 1986 and 2016 the inflation-adjusted average cost of winning a US House seat nearly doubled, from about $800,000 to over $1.5 million (Campaign Finance Institute 2018). The combination of anti-Washington, antibureaucracy rhetoric and campaign funding demands strengthened the relative influence of business in interactions with the second administrative state by simultaneously weakening the public standing of administrative agencies and magnifying the influence of business on representatives and senators through the campaign cash that businesses could funnel directly into the financing of congressional campaigns, and indirectly through business political action committees (PACs) and so-called "independent" expenditures. Between 1979 and 2012, over 80 percent of individual corporate officers and directors at Fortune 500 companies donated to political campaigns, with an average lifetime total per individual of over $197,000 (Bonica 2016).

A second general effect of congressional pull on the second administrative state has been to place added restrictions on administrative action, imposing more reporting demands and expanding performance requirements. These have swelled and complicated internal bureaucratic structures and processes and diverted resources to support them, pulling material and managerial resources away from the substantive policy missions of agencies. Added to original restraints on the second administrative state from a fragmented structure, more procedural and structural constraints have increased business access and leverage in its close interactions with the second administrative state because of the resources that business can direct to scrutinizing the minutiae of agency adherence to the new processes and requirements.

Perhaps most profoundly, but far less tangibly, the growth of the managerial presidency and the congressional push to create a legislative-center public administration, as well as the development of a new administrative law centered on greatly expanded judicial scrutiny of agency actions and the crafting (Bremer 2015) or recrafting (Mashaw 2012, chap. 15) of an "administrative constitution," has been to reinforce the increasingly dominant instrumental conception of administration and its legal and political subjugation. Although conflict among the three constitutional branches in their efforts to influence the administrative state sometimes advantages agencies by giving them opportunities to pit one branch against another and secure a measure of autonomy, the far greater effect is to weaken administration by denouncing its alleged incompetence while also weaponizing it in partisan and ideological battles, further undermining its public standing and its competence and capacity. This further bolsters business political standing—business administration succeeds, public administration fails is a constant refrain—and strengthens its ability to get the inducements to performance it seeks.

The Demise of the Corporate-Liberal Working Constitution

Developments and refinements in corporate-liberal governance, defined by a working constitution with administered markets and administrative government at its core, did not only focus on restraining the second administrative state. New forms of social control of capitalism emerged as the second half of the twentieth century got underway. Much of this new "social" regulation was still aimed at improving markets by attempting to correct, or at least ameliorate, prominent varieties of market failure. Some of the new regulatory efforts were centrally concerned with regulating social and political relations, rather than only market relations, by expanding various forms of civil and political rights for still marginalized groups, including correctives to how the second administrative state treated those groups. Overall, however, reformers across the ideological spectrum directed much more of their energy toward pulling back on the reins of the second administrative state than on sustaining its capacity to function on equal terms with the market in fulfilling the corporate-liberal conception of the public interest. The institutional restructurings and political reorientations within the constitutional branches, and the various administrative reforms and control efforts those changes engendered, took some time to fully emerge, but they finally did so just as the ideological and institutional underpinnings of the corporate-liberal working constitution began to erode in the 1970s and came under full-blown assault in the 1980s.

As the 1970s dawned, the regulatory authority and power of the second administrative state remained substantial, and thus business and public officials of all sorts continued to negotiate the boundaries of corporate economic power and state regulatory power in the frame of a corporate-liberal understanding of the public interest. While imposing some new and significant constraints on business operations and measurably improving economic and social well-being for a broad swath of the general population, social regulation added to the second administrative state's structural and programmatic fragmentation, creating new opportunities for particular corporate interests to gain special attention, access, and responsiveness from agencies pursuing tailored regulatory missions. Social regulation's significant demands and constraints on business, taking such forms as pollution control, worker safety and health protections, consumer product safety, and transportation safety, also created a serious tension between social regulatory program objectives and the fundamental liberal-democratic imperative of inducing business performance. Social regulatory agencies eventually found themselves, if not captured by the businesses they regulated, then at least forced to respond to pressure from both business and elected officials to bend their regulatory programs toward sustaining, or at least not interfering with, inducements to business performance.

More important to the unraveling of the corporate-liberal working constitution than the friction generated by social regulation were key developments that undermined the ability of corporate-administered capitalism and the second administrative state to perform satisfactorily. On the market side, the financialization of corporate capitalism accelerated, industrial production stagnated, and upward pressure on prices from such factors as oil embargoes drove up unemployment and inflation simultaneously. Most significant, however, a new, international competition threat arose. These developments spurred business to expand demands for performance inducements and to alter the terms of the corporate-liberal working constitution.

This pressure from business received a boost from two developments in society. First, the successes of the civil-rights movement, and in particular the push for desegregation of public institutions, primarily schools, drove "white flight" (Kruse 2005)—white middle- and upper-middle–class abandonment of urban communities and urban economies. Second, ideological attacks on the social-welfare features of the corporate-liberal working constitution, which had roots at least as far back as the beginnings of the New Deal, blossomed into a powerfully influential conservative intellectual movement (Nash 2006), especially with the infusion of resources from a cadre of reactionary billionaires. Individually and occasionally in cooperation, these men and women—named Bradley, Koch, Mercer, Olin, Scaife, along with several others (see Page, Seawright, and Lacombe 2018)—created networks of institutions and activists to develop the economic and political theories and political strategies to dismantle as much as possible the core agreements underpinning the corporate-liberal political economy, especially the understanding that gave corporations domain over the market in exchange for state scrutiny of and involvement in how corporations behaved. The resulting political and economic disarray led to the transformation of a market of corporate-administered industrial and commercial capitalism into "rentier capitalism" (Standing 2016; see also Lindsey and Teles 2017) and an administrative state with significant neoliberal features.

Within the market, the economic power of financial capital accelerated in the 1970s and 1980s. The great transparency advantage of the corporate form for shareholder discipline of corporate managers proved something of a mirage as the shareholder rights movement, intended to further democratize the corporation, instead empowered wealthy investors and the legal and investment establishments that served them. Through financial deregulation, shares of most public corporations increasingly flowed into the hands of big investment banks, private equity firms, and large institutional investors such as pension funds and university endowments, the latter with boards of directors comprised of representatives of already financially powerful entities. In order to serve the interests of financial capital, corporate boards of directors constructed contracts with CEOs and other primary corporate officers to incentivize quarterly performance and short-term rates of return over long-term stability and steady growth. Such objectives do not necessarily reflect or serve the interests of small shareholders and certainly not those of workers (Winkler 2017, 361), supposedly the primary target of the shareholder rights movement. Indeed, one key means for boosting short-term earnings often "cheered on by Wall Street" (Long 2020) is to cut labor costs.

This further empowerment of financial capital and further distancing of ownership from corporate operations was reinforced by that strange judicial alchemy in which courts endorsed the doctrine that corporations were still nothing but associations of natural persons reflecting the construction of "a web of voluntary agreements among corporate stakeholders" (Winkler 2017, 360). The effect has been to expand the bundle of rights that corporations could exercise, derived from the natural persons entering into the agreements, including continued flaying of legal restrictions on corporate campaign contributions. These developments marked the rise of "money manager capitalism," the current stage of Minsky's (1992) theory of capitalist development, succeeding a "commercial capitalism" stage (Atkinson, Hake, and Paschall 2019, 15).

If these developments of shifting market control increasingly to money managers did not exactly turn corporations into giant slot machines for the economic and political ambitions of their largest stakeholders, they certainly eviscerated most of the remaining tenuous connections that corporations had to their public-chartering origins and the accompanying obligations to serve a larger public interest. Thus, for example, the dominant electric power utility in the Commonwealth of Virginia, Dominion Energy, has repeatedly succeeded in fending off efforts of public officials to increase competition in the power sector by threatening to seek higher rates, which its 2.6 million customers would have to pay. Dominion's reasoning is always that its ratepayers must "absorb the lost revenue" (Olivo 2019) from competition, because, although its customers depend on electric power for a minimally decent quality of life, it is always better to make those millions of customers pay more rather than to threaten the "reasonable" rate of return on investment promised to its shareholders.

Destructive competition being the great threat that spurred the crafting of the corporate-liberal consensus, any new form of it that emerged posed an existential peril for administered capitalism. Such a threat did finally appear on a global scale in the 1970s and 1980s, as money-manager capitalism was developing and expanding. The reconstructed global trade and financial system that structured the "globalization" response to that threat, was born out of the international version of the liberal-democratic nexus of market and state created after World War II. The competition threat grew in nations recovering from the devastation of the war and from American economic internationalism that was part of the nation's cold-war strategy. The rise of this new competition caught both American capitalism and American political leadership flat-footed, shattering confidence in the terms of the corporate-liberal working constitution among corporate CEOs, large corporate shareholders, and public officials.

The increasing financialization of the corporation and the economic power of the money manager, along with the rise of global competition, put a hard squeeze on corporate-administered capitalism. The corporate-liberal working constitution seemed incapable of the nimble adjustments needed to relieve the pressure, having been designed in response to a very different competition threat. One adjustment that did succeed was further liberalization of international trade, opening up new markets and spurring an advanced form of corporate consolidation—the rise to dominance of the multinational corporation (Wilkins 2001). This development made capital more mobile than ever, and in conjunction with money manager capitalism, the movement of manufacturing out of the United States battered communities with the loss of high-paying jobs.

The effects of accelerated capital mobility and the struggles to tame stagflation converged with other societal developments, especially white flight and white middle-class rejection of expanded social-welfare support for people of color, plus the construction of the network of shadow philanthropy designed to produce the economic, legal, and political doctrines, and political activism intended to delegitimize the second administrative state (Mayer 2016), to rescue the fortunes of American capitalism. A hold on the commercial public interest—recognition that the principal value of a commercial society is political—was largely sacrificed in the bargain. By the late 1980s these developments had pushed the philosophical, legal, and structural underpinnings of the corporate-liberal working constitution toward a state of accelerating collapse. The endeavor kept going—gaining strength in resources and ideological fervor through successfully polarizing Christian fundamentalism, stoking economic discontent and racial animosities, and seizing control of one of the major political parties—toward an attack on key tenets of the commercial republic, namely that the state is not a mere tool of elite wealth accumulation, and the Constitution is not simply a plan for oligarchy (Fishkin and Forbath 2014).

Out of the ruins of the corporate-liberal working constitution has arisen a new working constitution, if it can even be called that, with different conceptions of state and market and their interdependence. If the altered administrative state in this new political economy is not entirely new in form and function, it does have features that evince strong neoliberal tendencies. Across levels of government, its programmatic features center on austerity, privatization, deregulation, and tax cuts for the highest income earners (Hohle 2015, 8–14). Demands for these features are continuously reinforced by the billionaire-funded networks of think tanks, university departments and programs, training of political activists, preparation of "model" legislation by such entities as the American Legislative Exchange Council (ALEC), and funding of campaigns for political office at every government level.

The market in this transformed political economy retains many of the hallmarks of corporate-administered capitalism, but it is burdened by a heavy overlay of rentier capitalism that distorts the liberal-democratic division of labor between market and state. This distortion comes in the form of a shift in the attention of public officials away from the question of how much business inducement will be just enough to spur the necessary performance for broad-based prosperity and toward enabling the shift of public resources to private control and the redistribution of income and wealth upward from the less fortunate to the already most fortunate. Privatization exemplifies this distortion, as whatever gains in public-service delivery efficiency and effects it may produce (see Brown, Potoski, and Van Slyke 2018), it is essentially a form of "asset-stripping" of public resources by the private sector (Johnston and Kouzmin 1998). Additional features include the dramatic shift to a consumption-based economy with the offshoring of production, supported by inducements to business in the form of policies undermining organized labor, accelerating the de-skilling of the workforce, and the expansion of the service sector and part-time labor force.

Among the neoliberal features of the altered administrative state, deregulation and privatization have been the most successfully mainstreamed politically, largely by portraying them as nonpartisan, technocratic reforms in the public interest (Michaels 2017, chap. 5). Yet they have also served as the leading edge of the hollowing out and constitutional delegitimation of the administrative state, including substantial attacks on an independent, merit-based, professional civil service at all levels of government, but especially at the national level. However mainstream the strategies and the ideas behind them have become, there is no escaping the reality that the changes in public policy and government structures sought, and to a considerable extent achieved, have created a new political-economic dynamic that encompasses greatly reduced social control of capitalism. The strategies have included politicizing both economic and social regulatory programs, aggrandizing state powers that are deployed to shield business from risk at public expense, and expanding other inducements to business that enhance rent extraction. Within the state, control of the expanded powers, and their exercise through the weakened and subjugated administrative state (to the extent that public bureaucracies are even needed to implement them) is centralized in the presidency and backed by a judiciary far more receptive to expanded executive power (Michaels 2017, chap. 6).

At its core this debased working constitution redefines the public interest to be coterminous with the interests of financialized, multinational corporate capitalism, especially a corporate capitalism in which wealth accumulation is increasingly based on control of information and intellectual property. In addition to weakening the civil service through politicization and delegitimation and subjugating it to a "unitary executive" (Calabresi and Yoo 2008; Kovacs 2018; but see also Posner and Vermeule 2010), elected officials gained further distance from public scrutiny through the co-optation or marginalization of civil society (Michaels 2017, 99, 140), demobilization and even disenfranchisement of the electorate (Ferguson and Rogers 1986; Wang 2014), and the construction of a conservative-libertarian federal bench as the judiciary solidified its status as the final arbiter of what is constitutional (Hollis-Brusky 2015; also see Whittington 2007).

Whether public officials from the 1970s forward held onto some sense of the larger political value of a commercial society seems seriously in doubt. It is a dubious proposition that they sincerely regarded expanded property protections for a small minority with outsized control of capital and enhanced opportunities to extract rent as giving concrete meaning to the public interest. Perhaps they envisioned how to rearrange the other components of the regime to fit together in a way that would both broaden the interests of a rentier class as the social basis of the regime while also restraining its ambitions. The actual results from the transformation of the working constitution are cause for deep skepticism, however. How the interests of a propertied elite focused on the preservation and multiplication of capital and the extraction of rent in complex and varied ways are coterminous with the public interest is very hard to discern. The claims that their political privileges and advantages are necessary both to facilitate the exercise of their rights and induce them to use their discretionary control of productive assets to sustain a prosperous economy are no different from the claims that business has always made and are therefore largely meaningless. The question is whether the advantages obtained, combined with other regime design features, increase the chances that the interests of this small, extraordinarily wealthy minority might be broadened toward an appreciation of the wider political view of the value of a commercial society. Such a possibility seems extremely remote when quite a few members of this minority have recycled their gains from inducements and rent extraction into securing more of both by capturing and degrading the constitutive institutions of the regime. It is no coincidence that the most precipitous decline in trust in government (Pew Research Center 2017), and people's trust and confidence in societal institutions and in one another (Twenge, Campbell, and Carter 2014), occurred after the attacks on the corporate-liberal working constitution were underway. Institutional trust and confidence have remained low and have sometimes fallen further as the neoliberal features of the new working constitution and administrative state have become more prominent and deeply rooted.

CONCLUSION

From the founding through most of its first century, the working constitution of the American commercial republic constituted the commercial public interest as a combination of the well-regulated society—in which the welfare of the community took precedence over rights and regulations on commerce were substantial—plus the spatial expansion and commercial and industrial development of the nation. The social basis of the regime was an uneasy combination of landed property holders and holders of capital, although the former diminished in relative significance as the nation emerged from the Civil War. The administrative state in this first working constitution was loosely defined and organized at the start and operated interdependently across governmental levels and with other constitutive institutions, especially the courts. As the nation developed, the first administrative state increasingly carried the burden of both the regulative and developmental functions that the working constitution emphasized. Both business and public administration also remained largely prebureaucratic for many decades, but both took on the characteristics of modern bureaucracy in the latter decades of the nineteenth century.

The searing social, economic, and political effects of slavery and the Civil War, combined with the far-reaching disruptions of rapid industrialization, forced a reconstitution of the commercial republic and the assembly of a new political economy and administrative state. The corporate-liberal working constitution that emerged redefined the commercial public interest. The new conception cemented holders of capital assets as the sole social basis of the regime and balanced a far more autonomous market of corporate-administered capitalism with a far larger, more robustly structured, and authoritative administrative state. This second administrative state's regulative function, significantly fragmented across policy domains and agencies, was to ensure market efficiency in close cooperation with corporate bureaucracies, in part by keeping market competition within reasonable bounds. As this new arrangement developed, elected public officials increasingly subjugated the administrative state to political, and especially presidential, control and placed administration's regulative functions under tighter constraints, partly out a renewed fear of bureaucracy, but primarily to ensure that inducements to business performance would deliver on their promises.

It is difficult to contest the notion that the corporate-liberal working constitution, despite a period of considerable success in moving the commercial republic a few significant steps toward its aspirations to liberal justice and broad, sustained economic well-being, planted the seeds of its own demise. The business inducement process is in a very real sense addictive, which is exactly why there must be institutional bulwarks against its excesses in any liberal democracy. Over the past thirty to forty years in the United States, the newest versions of these design restraints have weakened or completely unraveled. Business and public officials have cooperated to go far beyond the accommodations to business that are necessary and reasonable in order for the commercial republic to realize its aspirations. The result is "an outcome that Madison found offensive: a republic in which, if it does not quite rule, a minority with narrow concerns is at least uncomfortably strong in the councils of government" (Elkin 2006, 72). If what Thorstein Veblen declared more than a century ago was not exactly true at that time, the current condition of the American commercial republic makes it very hard to dispute now.

> Representative government means, chiefly, representation of business interests. The government commonly works in the interest of the business men with a fairly consistent singleness of purpose. And in its solicitude for the business men's interests it is borne out by current public sentiment, for there is a naive, unquestioning persuasion abroad among the body of the people to the effect that, in some occult way, the material interests of the populace coincide with the pecuniary interests of those business men who live within the scope of the same set of governmental contrivances (Veblen 1904, 286).

Alexander Hamilton's design for the commercial republic sought to overlay capital holders onto Madison's landed property elite as the social basis of the regime. If Hamilton was not quite as visionary a designer of a whole regime as Madison, he nevertheless better appreciated that particular design elements had to be fitted together to harness the ambitions of what he was sure would become the dominant holders of productive assets. Unlike most of his contemporaries, moreover, Hamilton contended that something like an administrative state was central to the long-term viability of a modern commercial republic, especially because, if properly designed and maintained, administrative structures populated by a robust administrative service was the key institutional design feature for harnessing the interests and ambitions of capital holders as the sole social basis of the regime. The corporate-liberal working constitution resembled such a design and, whatever its flaws, it achieved a remarkable combination of economic prosperity and progress, however inadequate, toward liberal justice. Sadly, a common appreciation that an aspiration to liberal justice should be at the heart of the theory and practice of the American commercial republic now seems more elusive than ever. The administrative state in its current form is no friend of such a notion, as its capacity to function as an equal partner and counterbalance to business in the unavoidable interdependence between market and state has seriously diminished.

Given the American regime's degradation, the founding design of the American commercial republic and the evolution in practice require reconsideration, if not to immediately rescue the republic from its current sorry state, then at least to consider other possibilities for the design of a commercial republic that are consistent with its liberal-democratic aspirations. For a modern liberal democracy to function at all, it is virtually impossible to eliminate some form of an administrative state. That is so for the American commercial republic as well. Hence, an essential question for any rescue plan is how a reasonably substantial administrative state can best be made compatible with the commercial republic and the theory and practice of its political constitution.

PART II

Reconstructing the Commercial Republic and the Administrative State

4. The Case for a Fourth Branch

The American commercial republic is in trouble, and the administrative state in its current incarnation is a serious contributor to the difficulties. Administration as an institution has been twisted into an instrument serving the excessive political prerogatives of business, exacerbating distortions in the essential relationship between market and state that have weakened them both. This has generated considerable confusion in public understanding of the regime's essential design, and dented if not breached the armor of legitimacy surrounding the American conception of self-government.

The common responses to the problems that an administrative state poses for the commercial republic take two forms: either continued tinkering with the internal components and authorities of the administrative state itself, as well as its relationship with the other constitutive institutions of the regime, or demands that it be cast off entirely. The former frequently comes in the form of the continuing search for effective but as yet elusive reinforcements of the separation-of-powers scheme and the troubled project of accommodating the administrative state to it. The latter often comes in the form of schemes to cut the market and the state loose from one another, abandoning the policy scope of the modern state and freeing the market so that its supposedly self-correcting features can fully operate. A presumed effect is also the elimination of much of the incentive for rent seeking in either the market or the state realm, making control of the state an unattractive goal of the political faction that benefits handsomely from the continuing enrichment of inducements to business. A milder form of this strategy is rooted in the claim that recovery of a more robust federalism is needed. The strategy amounts to shrinking the policy and the administrative scope of the *national* state and handing those responsibilities (back) to the states.

The path of further tinkering and accommodation seems in important ways merely to add to the complexity of a system already rife with unintended consequences. That complexity stems in considerable part from past control and accommodation efforts, making yet further accommodation through tightened control and subjugation of administration to the allegedly more politically responsive constitutive institutions extremely difficult to fathom. Analyses of the threat of regulatory capture contend that evidence of the threat is unpersuasive (Scheffler 2020) or that regulatory agencies can adapt existing strategies or deploy new strategies to resist business influence (see Carpenter and Moss 2014). More strategies will only add complexity to an already incredibly complex system, however. In many respects, furthermore, even the honest efforts of the constitutional branches to rein in the elaborate political privileges of business in the new administrative state by constraining the public administration side of the equation merely cancel out one another. Beefing up the capacity of administrative agencies to counterbalance the political privileges of business only works until the next election that brings to power the political faction whose only aim is to enhance business political privilege and the financial gain that comes with it.

The path of separating market and state, and the accompanying hope of some for the destruction of the administrative state, seems equally improbable, since those vested in the current arrangements are unlikely simply to abandon their gains. Should it nevertheless be realized, the outcome could not be called a commercial republic because it would abandon the aspiration to marry market and state to serve a larger political purpose: the liberal justice of a regime in which an acquisitive people stand in political relation to one another as free and equal and join together to govern themselves as a nation. Moreover, as an institutional form for realizing liberal justice generally, and the equality side of the equation specifically, markets are seriously suspect (Dietsch 2010).

The milder form of an enhanced separation of the *national* state and the market solves nothing because business is even more likely to hold sway if much of what the national state does now is relegated to the states. Madison recognized this in his defense of the extended republic in *The Federalist Papers*, no. 51. The privileged position of business is even more starkly on display in state capitals, where mobile capital can exploit the competition among states to offer inducements to large employers so that state and local political leaders can demonstrate their bona fides in sustaining economic activity (Robertson and Judd 1989, 31–32, 45–49; Weiner 2014). The complete destruction of the administrative state is called for because the edifice of administrative law that undergirds it is "unlawful" since it is an expression of the "absolutist ideal of rule" that contravenes the "constitutional ideal of rule," which limits the realm of lawmaking to legislators and courts (Hamburger 2014, 12).The administrative state is thus "not merely unconstitutional; it is anticonstitutional" (Lawson 2010, 55). Such contentions are a complete dead end theoretically and practically, however. The republic has virtually never been without an administrative state, and it is incapable of functioning without one now. Hence, while offering a radical way to think about the problem of the administrative state, these closely related perspectives are looking in the wrong direction.

In contrast to the continuously recycled efforts just summarized, this chapter presents the normative case for a more fundamental rethinking of the theory and practice of the commercial republic in the form of a constitutional reconstruction to make administration an independent fourth branch. More precisely, the chapter presents the case that administration as a distinct constitutive institution is wholly consistent with the theory of political constitution of the American commercial republic and thus can and should be constitutionalized.

To present such a case, setting an evidentiary baseline is an essential starting point. This means supplementing the account of the developments in the working constitution and the administrative state offered in part I with more detailed evidence about the character and extent of the advantages and prerogatives that business realizes through its interactions with the administrative state. From there, the theoretical case for the creation of a fourth administrative branch and how such a move would not only address state-market relational distortions and the excesses of business privilege, but also how a fourth branch would improve constitutional politics in the commercial republic more generally, can proceed. To reiterate, the primary intention of this normative case is to advance the development of the theory of political constitution of the commercial republic. It is thus a venture in "thinking constitutionally," that is, contributing to the "practical political reasoning that takes account of how the world works and can be made to work" that is essential to "the business of creating, reforming, and maintaining" a political regime (Elkin 2006, 267, 268).

BUSINESS PRIVILEGE AND INFLUENCE IN THE ADMINISTRATIVE STATE

The inescapable reality of modern liberal-democratic governance is that it has its primary effect on people's day-to-day lives through an administrative state, especially in the social space where administered market and administered state meet and interact. The commercial republic is an "interactive republic" in which "government's relationship with its citizenry" is comprised of a "set of interactions across the boundary separating the government" from other regions of a networked society (Rubin 2005b, 121). The administrative state is at the center of these interactions (131–34). Under the successive forms of an administrative state that have unfolded as part of the evolution of a working constitution, a distinctive set of highly complex actions and relationships, arrayed along a continuum from highly informal to highly formalized, have developed and redeveloped for policy making, policy management, policy outcomes, and other dimensions of governance centered on administration.

Considering first the most formalized end of the continuum, administrative rulemaking, current patterns of business (and other organized professional interests) engagement in the legislative process often reappear in administrative policy making. These patterns center on stability, status quo bias, and an underlying structure of "professional communities, complex constellations of actors with different elements of concern," that "keep existing policies in place until pressures build for large numbers of them to change their positions" (Baumgartner et al. 2009, 25–26). Businesses and professional groups are not always the most engaged on every rulemaking that might affect them or at every stage of the process, but they are never completely absent, and they can shape administrative rules and policies to a considerable extent when sufficiently motivated and organized (Yackee 2014; Haeder and Yackee 2015). They also enjoy structural advantages that reduce the cost of engagement and particular influence efforts. Hence, the large set of supposedly facially neutral procedures for participation in formal rulemaking, as well as those intended to make rulemaking more transparent through such devices as the Freedom of Information Act, actually advantage narrow interests, particularly business (Bagley 2019). To a considerable extent this is to be expected in a regime designed to give political advantages to business because its control of productive assets must be nudged toward broadly distributed economic performance. Yet "business and professional interests have undue, if not inordinate, influence" in the administrative process (Kerwin, Furlong, and West 2010, 600). It's unclear what difference there is between "undue" and "inordinate" influence, but further evidence strongly supports the conclusion that business and professional interests influence the administrative process in ways that constitute a form of business political privilege well beyond a tempered effort to induce business to perform.

At both the federal and state levels, for instance, interest groups (Yackee 2006a), especially business (Yackee and Yackee 2006), exert a preponderance of the influence on agency final rules through the notice and comment process. This appears to be so even where researchers find little evidence of business *capture* of the rulemaking process (Scheffler 2020). Also, as interaction between what are predominantly business and professional interest groups and state agencies increases, business and professional group influence over agency decisions also increases (Kelleher and Yackee 2006). Furthermore, business and professional interests exert significant influence at early stages of the agency policy-making process (West and Raso 2013), including through ex parte contacts (Yackee 2012). Moreover, agencies tend to distill a central meaning from the messages conveyed by these interests, boosting the signal of business preference even if business groups do not coordinate their efforts at influence (Yackee 2006b). Any coordination, especially involving new group participants, increases influence further (Nelson and Yackee 2012).

Privatization, through its principal vehicle of contracting out, has opened a new and significant pathway for business and professional interest lobbying of administrative agencies that influences agency policy making (Kelleher and Yackee 2006; see also Arnold 2011). The push toward more business-like operations and more market-based regulatory designs has made agencies hypersensitive to business interests (Rosenbloom 2010). This hypersensitivity can be promoted further through the electoral process. Corporate political expenditures can successfully signal regulators regarding business demands for reductions in regulatory enforcement (Gordon and Hafer 2005), and business interests can influence the strength of underlying regulatory statutes and who is appointed and confirmed for leadership of regulatory agencies (Shapiro 2012).

Even under present conditions, however, administrators and their agencies are not simply marionettes with business pulling the strings. Agencies act strategically in acknowledging, processing, and responding to messages intended to influence agency policy (Yackee 2006b). For example, they may "balance or structure decision outputs so that they protect the weaker interests against the strong but accommodate politically or economically important interests whenever prudent to do so" (Schmidt 2002, 209). They also tend to split the difference between the contrasting demands of business interests and public interest groups regarding regulatory stringency (Scheffler 2020, 759–760). Even in an environment of hypersensitivity to business preferences, the administrative state retains some checks of various sorts, primarily structural, that reduce somewhat the otherwise dominant influence of business and professional interests on administrative policy making (Potoski and Woods 2001). Despite the advantages to business that facially neutral procedures provide, mechanisms like notice and comment requirements sometimes increase the capacity of outside entities to monitor agency policy making, diminishing the "comparative advantage" (Croley 2008, 144) that regulated interests would otherwise have in monitoring and reacting to agency actions.

The administrative state is, however, subject to both ex ante and ex post controls, the former primarily taking the form of agency design (Moe 2012). Ex ante controls represent the efforts of political coalitions, with the most well-organized interests as primary players, to insulate implementing agencies from attack and disruption when political fortunes change. Insulation could thus inhibit business influence on an agency if its design is intended to make the agency responsive to a broad cross-section of interests, including those citizens too resource poor to remain permanently mobilized. Unfortunately, "design choices that insulate the bureaucracy" structurally, "systematically advantage groups with greater organizational capacity" (Reenock and Gerber 2007, 433). Designs to insulate agencies from subsequent political manipulation can backfire, inducing "officials to ignore certain groups based upon perceptions of the informational value that they offer" (435). Generally speaking, less well-resourced groups offer less information value to policy makers, including those in the administrative process. That administrative structure or process reforms, such as new forms of citizen advisory committees for federal agencies, are needed to boost the information value of citizen group influence in the administrative process (Bull 2013) further underscores the influence and incentives that favor well-resourced interests, especially those of business.

The neoliberal-oriented changes imposed on the administrative state over the past several decades have spurred elected public officials to shift away from almost exclusive reliance on hierarchical organizational and institutional arrangements and toward the use of interconnected networks of organized entities, governmental and non-governmental, to achieve policy goals. Much of this was engendered by the "privatization revolution" (Michaels 2017, chap. 4–5) intended to tip the scales further toward business in the ongoing interactions of administered market and the administrative state. Because not all of the changes were about privatization, however, the sobriquet "new governance" or "new public governance" (e.g., Sorensen and Torfling 2007; Bevir 2010; Osborne 2010; Morgan and Cook 2014) arose to capture the broader and more complex character of organized collective action that extends beyond formal government entities.

This expanded and more complex landscape of governance comes primarily in the form of networks mixing public, quasi-public, and private entities of varying sorts connected in relations of widely varying formality, density, and extent. Many of the private entities are nonprofits, the tremendous growth of which was spurred by privatization and by tax code changes that advantage business and wealthy investors (Hohle 2015; Lindsey and Teles 2017). Many of them operate much like for-profit businesses, and they essentially provide a back door by which business can exploit privatization and influence networked governance.

The legitimating idea at the heart of networked governance in a neoliberal administrative state is that public and private entities partner to "coproduce" public goods and services (e.g., Bovaird 2007; Pestoff 2012). This process takes place when government entities, primarily administrative agencies at one level or another, and even across levels, interact with citizens in various organized forms—as contractors delivering services, as watchdogs, or as targets or recipients. The interactions constitute coproduction, with the outputs and outcomes being the goods and services produced and consumed, and their impacts, respectively. Values may be shaped or reshaped as well. Thus, like all administrative processes and actions, coproduction is constitutive as well as instrumental. One such constitutive effect is its reshaping of fundamental ideas and practices of democracy and citizen engagement. This arises as members of the broader public engage in the administrative process, where the most concrete action in governance can be found. Such effects may come in multiple ways not necessarily available or contemplated under more hierarchical administrative structures and processes (see, for example, Morgan and Cook 2014, chap. 7–14). Yet this coproduced governance is not just facilitated by but essentially forced by the market-mimicking imperatives of neoliberal reform. Not surprisingly, therefore, it has expanded business influence on and gains from interaction and interdependence with the administrative state.

Business influence on policy implementation through the administrative process thus does not disappear in a coproduction context. Coproduction can "shift the policy emphasis during implementation" (O'Toole and Meier 2004, 684). For policy outcomes really to be coproduced via networks of governmental and nongovernmental entities requires overcoming even greater problems of complexity and coordination in achieving policy aims than under more hierarchical arrangements. But greater complexity also "tilts the balance of power" because "the scope of involvement shapes the definition of issues and goes a long way toward determining who wins and who loses on policy questions." The effect is that "pressure from network actors" on the public agency at the center of a network can be such that "network nodes seek greater benefits for goals that are favored by more entrenched interests and downplay efforts that favor disadvantaged clientele" (684, 685). Hence networked, coproductive administration can reinforce inequalities and undermine the democracy-enhancing effects that are supposedly at least a byproduct of decentralized, networked administration and other neoliberal changes to the administrative state (Steen, Brandsen, and Verschuere 2018).

Administrative agencies can modulate the bias in coproduction emanating from entrenched interests (Ellison and Newmark 2010) when network partners "are limited in role, capacity, and authority relative to their public agency partners" (McGuire and Agranoff 2010, 390). A pattern of "mixed dominance" (391) in the relations between public and private partners in networks prevails, and agencies "can be substantial counterweights to any financial, informational, operational, or other asymmetries that nongovernmental organizations might bring to the table" (393). This also means that strengthening administrative agencies in their relations with private interests can increase the chances that a version of the public interest, at least as defined by agencies and administrators, may be realized in networked governance. The relative strength of agencies in this regard may depend on realizing a particular kind of "bureaucratic autonomy" (Carpenter 2001). This kind of autonomy is not common or frequent, however. It is also difficult to sustain, and it is not simply bestowed. Administrators must construct it (Long 1949; Carpenter 2001, chap. 4–9). Yet agency efforts to create such autonomy have proven to be interest-centered and dependent on coalitions of already advantaged and engaged professional and economic interests. These interests exercise influence on an agency directly and through elected officials motivated to gain greater control over administration in reaction to agency power-expanding efforts (Durant 2015). Absent larger political-structural changes that would favor sustaining agency-constructed autonomy, such autonomy by itself is thus inadequate for addressing the enhancements to business privilege and the inducements that the second administrative state with its neoliberal overlay have facilitated and continue to sustain.

From the development of the corporate-liberal working constitution onward, the administrative state has posed yet one more problem for the commercial republic. Its fragmented structure, intended to reflect and align with the multiple and distinct business interests of corporate capitalism, combined with its "low-visibility nature" (Elkin 2006, 60), intended to insulate risky policy making from citizen scrutiny and irrational reaction, enabled the development of substructures of policy making that favor narrow and discrete interests, especially those of business that multiplied with the rise of corporate capitalism. These substructures—iron triangles, subgovernments, and the like—were curtailed to some extent by the administrative separation of powers and by policy and administrative design reforms in the 1970s that opened up the substructures to greater outside scrutiny and intervention by nonbusiness interests. Nevertheless, these policy networks not only survived but have multiplied under neoliberal policy and administrative changes. They are insular and exhibit a bias toward narrow, already advantaged interests. The combination of the features of the substructures with the fusion of powers in administrative agencies "has erected additional barriers to the Madisonian impediments to majoritarian government," seriously hampering "the political role of civic majorities" (60) as a counterweight to minority factional interests. This combination of features in the administrative state as it has evolved also "hinders the inducement to the broadening of interests that dividing governmental powers would bring" when the controllers of productive assets are given political advantages to engage in government. Instead, the "political energy" gained from encouraging the propertied to engage in governance is misdirected to "the service of narrow interests" (64). These tendencies have only become more pronounced with the neoliberal overlay on the second administrative state. The administrative state across all levels of government thus does not have just a tendency to enable the service of narrow interests, it has features that are overtly pitched toward serving narrow, mostly business interests, including operating programs that are designed by business to extract rent and funnel it to CEOs and major shareholders (Halliday and O'Flynn 2018; Cooper et al. 2016; Hertel-Fernandez 2016).

As a general proposition, the administrative state in its current form is part of a working constitution that fails to serve the liberal justice to which the commercial republic aspires. Not all would agree that the condition of the American republic has gotten this bad, and it is certainly not completely devoid of any capacity to gain a sense of the public interest and strive for it in concrete ways. Formal administrative processes still exhibit notable tendencies in this regard (Scheffler 2020). As a whole, however, the current working constitution, including the administrative state in its current guise, not only falls short of realizing a commercial republic, it has in significant respects slipped backward. It has retreated from maintaining "a certain kind of political regime that has as a defining feature the politics of self-limitation" (Elkin 2006, 275). Its ever increasing "inducements and political access extended to business point to a degree of factional rule by a minority—and factional rule is, by definition, unlimited" (72).

The historical account of part I shows that, under successive working constitutions, an administrative state has at several short periods of time helped the regime serve the public interest and approximate liberal justice, at least for a portion of the citizenry. Perhaps that is why there have been virtually no efforts to explicitly conceive of some form of an administrative state as a constitutive institution having the capabilities to serve as a fortification for the politics of self-limitation and a procedure by which those capabilities might be developed or enhanced. Instead, the administrative state largely stands as a prime target of denunciation and source of great despair in the republic's recent history. This state of affairs offers the perfect opportunity to explore fundamental questions about how extensive alterations to the administrative state can add to the theory of political constitution of the American commercial republic and improve its practices. The way to do so is to mount the most vigorous case possible for an administrative state as a constitutive institution of the regime that deserves status as a coequal constitutional branch.

A CONSTITUTIONAL FOURTH BRANCH

The possibility of a large administrative establishment amounting to a "fourth branch" has been the object of varying attention and concern in American politics and law for most of the last century. In his treatise on government in modern states, W. F. Willoughby conceived of five separate functions, including administration as a separate branch. The distinction he drew between the executive and administrative functions is that between supervision and action as well as between politics and administration. He conceived the executive function "as the function of representing the government as a whole, and of seeing that all of its laws are complied with by its several parts. The administrative function is the function of actually administering the law as declared by the legislative and interpreted by the judicial branches of the government." Willoughby distinguished the executive function as "essentially political in character; that is, one having to do with the determination of general policies, and involving the exercise of judgment in its use." The administrative function was "concerned with the putting into effect of policies as determined by other organs" (Willoughby 1919, 231).

Willoughby was never fully clear about why the distinction he drew necessitated characterizing administration as a separate branch. Most likely, it was part of his effort to keep administration from being wholly subsumed under the executive function. As he argued, "The whole power of direction, supervision and control of administrative affairs legally is vested in Congress. The executive departments and other administrative services are mere agencies of that body for the carrying out of its orders" (Willoughby 1919, 387). Furthermore, there "can be no question regarding the great powers of direction, supervision and control of the President over the administrative work of the government. These powers, however, are primarily exercised by him but as an agent of Congress, which as a matter of expediency has conferred them upon him" (387–388). Willoughby thus accepted the necessity of separating administration from politics by distinguishing policy formation and supervision of execution from the action of putting policy into effect. Yet he was the most strenuous early proponent of the legislative-administrative nexus as the modern core of government, a position that is Congress's own (Rosenbloom 2000) and is at the center of other investigations and theorizing about the regime design problem that administration poses (Bertelli and Lynn 2006a).

Analysts with an executive-centered conception of the administrative function had a very different perspective on the wisdom of an administrative fourth branch. Pronouncements about the hazards of such a possibility included the hue and cry raised by the Brownlow Committee about a headless fourth branch of disparate administrative units lacking coordination and executive oversight and control (President's Committee 1937, 32). Mr. Justice Robert Jackson declared that the growth of administrative entities had brought into being "a veritable fourth branch of the Government which has deranged our three-branch legal theories much as the concept of a fourth dimension unsettles our three-dimensional thinking" (*Federal Trade Commission v. Ruberoid*, 343 U.S. 470 [1952]). The unsettling extent of the political power of this functionally real fourth branch has even prompted students of public administration to give considerable attention to why and how it must be restrained (Smith and Licari 2006). In contrast, the notion of a more benign administrative fourth branch having emerged informally through political adaptation also gained currency. Possessing various combinations of legislative, judicial, and executive functions and the widely varying discretionary authority to exercise them, administrative agencies, according to this view, gained the capacity to respond to public opinion and engage a broad swath of interests, perhaps even in deliberative ways, engendering a working constitution that may compensate for defects in the founding regime design as it has evolved (Long 1952; Rohr 1986; but in contrast, see Bertelli and Lynn 2006a, 137).

This normative case for recognizing an operational but not structurally explicit governing role for administration, in a constitutional design that is rather conflicted about the possibility, includes the contention that requirements for administrative agencies to engage the public, such as through notice and comment requirements, boost the chances that administrators will get a broader reading of the public on important day-to-day governing matters than the denizens of the constitutional branches can manage. However, the evidence reviewed above on the interactions between organized interests, especially business, and administrative agencies demonstrates that at least on this count the current reality falls short of the normative vision.

Because its origins are almost entirely statutory (see chapter 5 for elaboration), administration as an informal fourth branch remains in a decidedly subordinate position to the formal branches in the constitutional system. This makes it wide open to manipulation during the bouts of "ambition counteracting ambition" encouraged by the separation of powers. The battles between president and Congress, and the judiciary, over control of administration have been attempts to mold administration in the image of one or the other constitutive institutions rather than recognizing the distinctive nature of administration and administrative power, diluting technical and managerial competence and policymaking contribution along the way (Aberbach and Rockman 1997). This has in turn diminished the ability of administration to function as a distinctive counterweight or restraint on business in the complicated interdependent relations of market and state, furthering the privileged position of business interests and even substituting business interests for the general public interest. Again, therefore, the impact of the administrative separation of powers, with its requirements for an open and broadly responsive administrative process, and other features of administrative design that might insulate agencies from undue business influence, often produce the opposite effect. Likewise, the impacts of the most recent set of neoliberal overlays on the administrative state have further exacerbated the problem.

The central question is whether a structural change to the separation of powers design that would make administration a fourth constitutional branch will alter constitutional politics by creating the incentives and empowering administrators to make lawmaking, including policy implementation, more deliberative and thus more likely to give concrete meaning to the public interest. An administrative state elevated to the status of a fourth branch, making it more robust in its support of deliberative lawmaking, would shore up a critical component of commercial republican regime design that has eroded considerably in the late stages of the current working constitution. Would raising administration to fourth-branch status alter the administrative state's current impact from that of an enhanced conduit for business inducements to one that facilitates the essential broadening of the interests of the capital-holding class toward a concern for the public interest? Raising administration to constitutionally co-equal status would enable new perspectives on broadening the interests of the propertied that a conceptually and doctrinally ossified tripartite scheme cannot produce.

There is irony here, as adherence to rigid notions of the separation of powers stemming from Supreme Court jurisprudence and much political practice, particularly with respect to the president's control of administration, has nevertheless enabled a separation of powers repeatedly modified and breached because of the very forces the separation of powers was intended to stimulate (Huq 2014). Much of this proclaimed adherence to the separation of powers, even as it is twisted and stretched in surreptitious ways under the veneer of strict adherence, stems from the desire of elected officials to deflect responsibility for resolving hard political conflicts. Although the courts have accepted a share of this off-loading of responsibility, the administrative state has offered elected officials the better avenue for dispersing the responsibility for the consequences of hard political choices stemming from the interdependence of market and state and the difficulty of giving concrete meaning to the public interest. Yet the constitutional branches give little credence to what the administrative state learns from bearing this responsibility as it pertains to the meaning of the separation of powers and how it serves to enhance the capability of the commercial republic's design to give concrete meaning to the public interest.

In an important sense, across successive versions of the working constitution, elected officials have understood administration as a distinct governing institution that is unavoidably central to liberal-democratic governance in the form of the American commercial republic. Despite fanciful Jeffersonian and Jacksonian rhetoric about plain, simple, and cheap government—and a "*mania* for retrenchment" that even Andrew Jackson once decried (quoted in John 2003, 59)—political leaders have pushed for as much as they have resisted the construction of an administrative state. With varying enthusiasm they have supplied it with important legal and fiscal resources, broad discretion, and the frequent lack of resistance to autonomous administrative action.

The dispersion of responsibility for tough choices to institutions more insulated from public scrutiny and pressure may give elected officials the necessary cover for taking the risky actions that society needs to cope with polycentric problems. Such actions frequently distribute costs and benefits very unevenly (Wilson 1990). Yet playing what Woodrow Wilson called "hide-and-seek politics" (Link 1975, 198) with responsibility hardly helps the separation of powers restrain factional influence, protect liberty, or enhance deliberation about the concrete meaning of the public interest. Instead, it further enhances the leverage of business by placing the application of that leverage in the shadows, making it hard for the public at large to know about it, let alone judge its effects. Occasional media exposés about special-interest influence in the administrative state are largely useless. They are haphazard, biased in favor of the salacious, and lacking in careful analysis because so few journalists are even aware that the regime's design is a particular form of a commercial republic. Furthermore, the responsibility-dispersing and cloaking strategy also exposes what makes the separation of powers in its current form most problematic as part of the design of a government intended not just to protect liberty but also to promote the general welfare: the relationship of subordination and obedience in which it places administration. This relationship generates a grinding friction with the constitutive effect of administrative action (Cook 2014), especially the considerable formative effects that follow from the immense responsibilities for hard choices thrust upon public agencies. A working constitution that mostly generates nothing but general repugnance for public bureaucracy and public administrators and portrays independent administrative action as constitutionally illegitimate is a very poor recipe for increasing the chances of reasoned deliberation about the concrete meaning of the public interest. This is especially so with respect to understanding the public interest in an institutional sense—securing and sustaining the institutional forms that enable individuals to pursue a variety of purposes and support a healthy politics of self-limitation. Regarding an administrative state as primarily a threat rather than a contributor to such a constitutional politics undermines essential pillars of the regime.

Those most fearful for their liberty and thus constantly on their guard for signs of tyranny probably see the subordination of unelected officials and the unintended consequences that follow as a price worth paying for whatever reminders of popular sovereignty it provides. Strange it is that there are rarely objections on similar grounds to unelected judges, some of whom enjoy life tenure. More important, the purchase of some perceived popular sovereignty through the continued abject subordination of administration may simply be replacing one form of tyranny with another, for the relationship of subordination and obedience to the constitutional branches also places administration, and thus day-to-day governance, in a relationship of subordination to business political privilege and the unquenchable business thirst for inducements that it claims are essential for directing its productive assets toward sustaining reasonably broad economic performance.

To empower the administrative state to contribute to rather than undermine the institutional dynamics that generate a politics of self-limitation and the progress toward liberal justice to which Americans presumably still aspire, one critical step is to provide administration with a resource distinct from business influence, organized interest support, and technical expertise. Moreover, that resource must be more widely distributed and more reliable than the very context-dependent instances of agencies as autonomous interest brokers. In short, the resource must be structural. Although public administrators already take an oath to uphold the

Constitution, and they have received counsel to use that oath as their lodestar (Rohr 1986, 186–194), a structural change will give them the political security to engage more frequently with the other authoritative actors in the system in the quest to give concrete meaning to the public interest and what it requires in particular circumstances. Incorporating that structure into the central legal edifice of the regime will undergird the participation of administration in regime politics, bringing administration's special qualities and an administrative power perspective to bear on deliberation about the public interest.

Within the last two decades, powerful critiques have appeared contending that the separation of powers is at best an archaic relic when so much of modern governance is administration (e.g., Magill 2001; Carolan 2009). Why not, then, do away with the separation of powers all together? Because "we have inherited it and almost certainly must live with it," but we can "improve its workings." Moreover, "there are advantages to formal separation, not the least of which is that public officials must carry out in public some of their negotiations on important public matters" (Elkin 2006, 356n16). Although there seems to be something comforting in the number three, at least in western culture (Rubin 2005b, chap. 2), why must we necessarily limit to three the institutions formally separated so as to control factions, restrain the popular sovereign, and energize the state to serve the public interest? If the project of accommodating administration to the tripartite separation of powers has so far failed to protect the regime from the grip of minority faction even as citizens and political leaders alike remain committed to a design anchored in separate institutions sharing powers, then elevating administration as an institution to the status of a constitutionally recognized fourth branch is hardly an absurd proposition. Since it is already in the lexicon of both scholarship and practice to refer to administration as functionally a fourth branch, what would formalizing that function through constitutional redesign entail? How can such a change be consonant with American constitutional and governing traditions? And, how can it address the disturbing developments, especially with respect to business-state relations, evident in the most recent developments of the commercial republic's current working constitution?

Authority for the Steady Administration of Law

The primary Madisonian aims of the separation of powers—checking the threat of majority faction as an auxiliary to an extended republic of varied and conflicting interests and enabling effective governance even in the event that factional interests gain a toehold in government—necessitate making distinctions among the branches in accord with the governmental purposes that they embody and the special qualities and functions they possess (Tulis 1987). Hence, Congress concerns itself principally, but not exclusively, with constituting popular will and giving it concrete meaning in public policy. Its special quality and function is deliberation. One of the most serious threats to republican government to emerge in the working constitution, stretching all the way back to the Decision of 1789, was the significant shift of the locus for constituting popular will from Congress to the presidency. In contrast, in the regime's design the presidency is to concern itself principally, but not exclusively, with constituting and giving concrete meaning to "national security" or "self-preservation." The presidency's special qualities are "energy and despatch" directed toward both national security and setting the government's agenda to sustain the republic's existence. Yet the Constitution also tasks it with "steady administration of law." Finally, the Supreme Court principally embodies the protection of individual rights and giving concrete meaning to enumerated rights. The court's special quality and function is "judgment, not will" (Tulis 1987, 43). In this linkage within each branch between a principal constitutive role and a special quality and function, the presidency is an outlier. It has an additional function that does not match its special quality or its principal role. Or, to state it differently, there are both specific "presidential" and more general "executive"—or better, administrative—powers that the Constitution confers on the same institution (Froomkin 1987).

To bring the presidency into symmetry with the other two branches, its special quality and function can best be thought of as energizing government to achieve and maintain self-preservation and national security. This has been the presidency's primary role in practice, consistent with the clearest and most specific presidential powers delineated in Article II. Presidents have largely relegated "steady administration of law," the faithful execution of the laws, to a secondary, strictly supervisory concern. The nation has suffered whenever presidents have been careless about the capability of subordinates to whom they delegate the administration of the law. Indeed, to add to the points made in chapter 3 regarding the weakness of claims that presidents bring a national perspective to governance as the only constitutional officer elected by the nation as a whole, presidents have rarely, since the rise of political parties, formed cabinets fully composed of individuals with broad, national perspectives on policy and its implementation, as well as the competence and experience to administer the law, make adjustments in the face of shifting conditions, and learn from those episodes. Presidents have also rarely used the cabinet as a vehicle for forming such perspectives (Fenno 1959), instead using it as a representation of major contending interests (Cohen 1988). At present, therefore, none of the core governmental institutions of the regime give steady administration of law the priority it deserves. Steady administration of law requires an institution of its own that is part of the Constitution's basic structure. That institution is clearly administration, or an administrative state, one in the hands of a dedicated, competent, ethical career service enjoying secure tenure that inculcates it with a number of special qualities, including stability, respect for and effective use of "the accumulated wisdom of the past" (Storing 1995, 323; see also Terry 2003), the capacity to balance the instrumental and the constitutive inherent in every public policy (Cook 2014), and the ability and sustained commitment to work across the fuzzy boundaries between the state, civil society, and the market.

Holding in abeyance for now consideration of the particular structural features that might flow from this central design principle of constitutional autonomy for a fourth, administrative branch, how would such a change redress the troubling developments in the working constitution, especially with respect to the scope and pathways of business influence, the character of separation-of-powers politics, and the constitutional politics of the regime more generally? The answer turns first on understanding and accepting administration as a constitutive institution of the regime that functions in ways distinct from legislative, executive, and judicial institutions.

Constitutive Administration: Deliberation, Institutional Politics, and the Public Interest

Administration is a distinctively constitutive institution because it is the setting where, on a daily basis, the instrumental and the constitutive characteristics and impacts of public law become evident at the interface between state and society—the line between interference and laissez-faire. Although it is principally concerned with putting law into action, its engagement in that primary role gives administration a unique "experiencing" function (Cook 2010), a combination of monitoring, learning, and informing responsibilities, particularly about the formative effects of law in action on individuals, groups, and social interactions, including in the market. Indeed, the other constitutive institutions of the regime rely heavily upon administration's experiencing function in the exercise of their authority. The evidence of administration as the "most knowledgeable branch" (Sunstein 2015) can be seen in the rise of a "new separation of powers" in many liberal democracies (Vibert 2007), and particularly in policy agenda settings (Workman 2015). Because in the United States administration as an institution already exhibits these characteristics in its currently subordinate constitutional role, how would elevating it to a constitutional branch make any difference? At least at the national level, the creation of a fourth administrative branch would reinforce and elevate these knowledge and experience effects and thereby refashion constitutional politics and redirect the working constitution in ways more in line with the founding aspirations for the commercial republic.

Three key effects of a constitutionally distinct fourth administrative branch form the foundation of its contributions for reconstructing and enhancing the political constitution of the commercial republic in theory and practice: 1) enhancing deliberative lawmaking, further increasing the possibility that lawmakers will concern themselves with the public interest and its concrete meaning; 2) recalibrating the functions of the separation of powers, particularly by providing a distinctive check on the presidency and focusing the presidential role on regime self-preservation, as well as inserting administration's distinctive perspective into the counteracting and collaborating actions that the separation of powers is meant to engender; 3) broadening the interests of the propertied by forcing them to confront the public-interest perspective that public administrators offer. These effects would flow from the enhanced constitutional status of the administrative state, reducing the risk that administration will remain a subordinate instrument manipulated into serving as a vehicle for rent seeking and the satisfaction of narrow business interests. In addition to these key contributions that a constitutional fourth administrative branch offers, there are also important follow-on effects. Changing the status and repositioning administration's place in the regime can help strengthen the citizenry by developing citizen capacity to scrutinize administrative action and engage in the governance process, and it can help restore the middle class to health as the ruling stratum of the commercial republic. An explanation and defense of each of these effects follows.

Supporting Deliberative Lawmaking

Promoting deliberative lawmaking is part of the public interest of a republican regime. A regime designed with the public interest centrally in mind will have institutional structures and processes that promote deliberation. In turn, deliberation enhances the chances that lawmakers will experience a broadening of their own interests, and those of their constituents, toward finding the concrete meaning of the public interest on particular public questions (Elkin 2006, 33–36). The American commercial republic in its current condition is not entirely bereft of deliberative lawmaking, but the capacity of the constitutive institutions of the regime to deliberate, individually and in their interactions with one another, has been seriously degraded by a working constitution that in far too many instances treats not just administration but all the constitutive institutions as instruments to satisfy business interests.

The most critical resource in lawmaking of whatever form is information. This is so for lawmaking entirely concerned with aggregation and distribution, of which there is likely to be a great deal, especially in a commercial republic. In a commercial republic, as in any liberal democracy, citizens are highly attuned to pursuing their particular interests. Thus politics will frequently be about "who gets what, when, and how" (Lasswell 1936). As a result, lawmakers, and their well-organized constituents, are adept at the pulling and hauling necessary to reach something approaching a social optimum that satisfies competing interests and distributive demands. They are thus also motivated by and proficient in providing the critical information in support of their interests that feeds into the transactional politics of aggregative and distributive policy making.

There are, however, many public questions that require answers beyond the toting up of demands and the distribution of benefits to satisfy them. Such questions centrally implicate the public interest because they concern "the purposes of the regime and its ability to serve them" (Elkin 2006, 238). Indeed, one such question pertaining to aggregative lawmaking is whether the structures and processes of such lawmaking respect the "political equality" toward which liberal democracies strive by "keeping open the channels of political influence for interests that are resource poor or 'insular'" (238). On such questions deliberation in pursuit of the public interest is necessary.

If "the legislature is to do the work of deliberating about the public interest, it must be able to build on a good deal of careful argument and analysis of information" (Elkin 2006, 51). This includes decisions about which problems in society merit legislative attention and action (Workman 2015). When deliberative lawmaking is truly happening, lawmakers will, through their discussions, exchange of information, and articulated rationales, move toward successively better approximations of the concrete meaning of the public interest on such questions as how to help the unorganized promote and defend their interests in the competition for public resources. To do that, lawmakers must know how earlier approximations of the concrete meaning of the public interest have fared, as well as what changes in society have occurred in the interim. This necessity can be fulfilled in many ways, and lawmakers have many sources of information they can and do rely on. The most crucial, substantive, and reliable information on the actual workings of the law with respect to the public interest, however, consists of the observations, experience from action, and consequent learning that public administrators gain from putting the law into effect, whether on their own or in conjunction with other actors.

This information is not perfect. Public administrators are nearly as strongly oriented as other political actors toward seeking out and providing information on the effects of distributive policy because they are so frequently tasked with implementing such policy. The demand is high, and the bias toward technical expertise in bureaucracy makes meeting the demand for information on the performance of distributive policy relatively easy for public agencies. Such information is just not very distinctive because of the incentive that well-organized interests have to independently generate and analyze information on distributive policy effects, unless a public agency has achieved the status of the most trusted source of such information. An example of such an agency is the US Bureau of Labor Statistics (BLS) in the US Department of Labor, briefly in the spotlight in chapter 3 for its role in the rise of the corporate-liberal working constitution. Although frequently embroiled in political-economic controversies, especially regarding industrial labor-management relations across the 1920s to 1950s, the bureau has since the 1970s "generally sustained a reputation for non-partisan data production even while its statistics have served many high-stakes political functions" (Stapleford 2010, 188). Even absent the trusted status of the likes of the BLS and a predominant focus on purely distributive policy, lawmakers may treat as authoritative the information and analyses of policy effects that many public agencies produce in ways that make such information distinctly valid for lawmaking purposes.

The information that administration may provide in support of lawmaking with respect to policy impacts and outcomes can also be biased by the narrowness of professional expertise, the limits of organizational frames for policy learning, bureaucratic pathologies that enhance risk aversion and inhibit internal transparency and candor, and system incentives that favor reporting policy success. This last shortcoming emanates from the highly developed aptitude that elected officials, and legislators particularly, have for deflecting responsibility for policy design and placing the blame on civil servants when law and policy fail to have the intended effects, or worse, have unintended consequences, many of which stem from a failure to take administrative design into account in policy design (Cook 2014, 221–230).

The information that the administrative state has to offer in support of lawmaking generally, and in support of careful deliberation on questions that implicate the public interest especially, is nevertheless highly distinctive because most public administrators understand, even if only implicitly, that they and their agencies comprise the regime's principal organ of experience. In fulfilling this experiencing function they are most attuned to the consequences, intended or otherwise, of the administrative design features, or lack thereof, in law. More generally and importantly, they are attuned to the complex dynamics that arise at the fuzzy boundaries where state, market, and society meet, particularly the stresses and strains that arise where the formality and stability of the law clash with the agitation for change constantly welling up in society. Stated differently, more than any other kind of public official, public administrators are most attuned to alterations in social relations and institutional norms stemming from the law in action. They simply have to be, because they hold the authority to make adjustments as conditions change or peculiar cases arise, up to the point at which the accumulation of such adjustments warrants legislative action. Judges are highly attuned to this, too, but the breadth and depth of their view of this dynamic is limited by the cases-and-controversies requirement and the adversarial formality of judicial proceedings. Not all of the constitutive effects of law and policy involve one party pitted against another.

It is where state, market, and society meet that the public interest is most concretely actuated—or undermined. Public administrators are leading actors in and principal witnesses to this dynamic. They thus have unique information to impart in support of lawmaking generally, but more importantly information that can not only support but further encourage the deliberative lawmaking needed on questions that implicate the public interest and thus the purposes of the regime. Given the primarily instrumental demands on them, however, administrators need incentives that are currently lacking in order to fully attend to, reflect on, and bring to lawmakers information that can inform deliberation on the public interest. Raising the constitutional status of administration and the administrative state to more fully validate the information and insights that administration has to contribute to the lawmaking process, especially with respect to the law's effects and the implications of those effects for the public interest, can go a long way toward creating such incentives.

To make the most of administration's experiencing function as a spur for and input into deliberative lawmaking, lawmakers must regard the administrative state and the civil service that fills its tenured positions as a constitutional coequal—not just a clerical lackey, slave to the personal policy predilections of presidents, an extension of legislators' constituency service staff, or factory for the production and distribution of public goods. Elected officials do listen to what administrators have to say about law and policy in action and its effects. Sometimes they even make adjustments to law and policy in response to what administrative agencies report and advise. Too often, however, the focus is on administrative performance and fixing blame with little consideration of underlying problems in administrative design or lack thereof in the statutes themselves, or on questionable statutory interpretation or excessive exercise of administrative discretion. All these problems associated with the administrative state—administrative dysfunction, dubious statutory interpretation, too much discretion, and the piling up of rules upon rules, pushing the action of the law farther and farther away from the language of the law and whatever may have been its intent—are partly functions of an incredibly complex political economy where expectations for precision and absence of error are wildly unrealistic. More important, however, they are also a function of administration and an administrative state so subordinated to elected officials that the insulation from popular scrutiny that administrators provide incentivizes those same officials to comfortably ignore what administrators have to tell them about the law in action and its effects. A fourth branch thus offers a constitutionally robust way for administration to resist the imposition on administrative entities of discretion too expansive or too vague in its legal implications by elected branches seeking to escape the hazards of democratic politics. Such efforts undermine not only the legitimacy of administration but the legitimacy of law as well.

Many of these tendencies, and their effects, are evident in the prominent example of the Federal Reserve (Binder and Spindel 2017). Over the decades since its inception, the Federal Reserve has been subject to political attacks for its policy failures, real and imagined, during times of severe economic distress. The reforms of the "Fed" that have followed in response to these attacks have generated a pattern of tension between increases in the Fed's centralization, autonomy, and policy remit on the one hand, and on the other hand demands for greater transparency, including through audits and reporting requirements, and occasional trimming of the institution's policy scope.

A key pivot in this saga was the "Treasury-Fed Accord of 1951" sparked by presidential-congressional conflict over monetary policy. The effect of the accord was to free the Federal Reserve from most treasury oversight and influence, but in exchange it "cemented the subordination of the Federal Reserve and monetary policy to Congress" (Binder and Spindel 2017, 12). Since that time Congress has mostly enhanced the Fed's centralization, autonomy, and power over the economy. This has been done less to improve management of the economy and more to enable Congress to insulate itself from much of the popular ire that arises in response to economic downturns, allowing the Fed to be the lightning rod for such popular discontent. The Fed can also manage the economy with an expanded set of tools when polarized politics leaves the branches immobilized in the face of severe disruptions in the economy. When political conditions improve, Congress can swoop in with reforms in response to specific criticisms of the Fed, gaining credit for acting while avoiding much accountability for previous legislative designs that may have contributed to the problems the economy experienced.

The consequence of this pattern, in which the Fed "largely escapes scrutiny when the economy is sound" but "a souring economy encourages Fed-blaming lawmakers to revisit the [Federal Reserve] act, and reconsider the powers and governance of the Federal Reserve," is that it allows few opportunities for the Federal Reserve and the constitutional branches to engage in extended dialogue or deliberation about the administrative consequences of proposed reforms. More important, the ignore-attack-reform pattern diminishes even more the chances for deliberation on the public interest with respect to the design of a money and banking system. It is unclear whether the current pattern allows any opportunity for the Fed in its current "interdependent" (Binder and Spindel 2017, 2) yet subordinate status to push Congress and the president to deliberate about institutional forms that a money and banking system might take that would more likely support the larger, political view of the value of a commercial society. A Federal Reserve that is part of a constitutional fourth branch would gain some strategic advantage, enabling it to push the other constitutional branches to confront those broader questions about the designs of a political economy that better serve the political aims of commercial republican regime design.

Elevating administration to a fourth constitutional branch would thus give agencies the leverage to pressure legislators and elected executives to pay more careful attention to administrative design in law and policy, particularly the formative effects of law and the possibility of unintended consequences. At the national level, it would push Congress to write laws with clearer guidance on the administrative use of statutory authority and less ambiguity that leaves the impression that agencies are exercising unrestrained legislative power. This would force Congress "regularly and routinely into the business of serious revision of laws in light of administrative experience," a distinct contrast to the current Fed-Congress pattern of interaction, for instance, and enable Congress to write statutes with real legal integrity—clarity about the legal rules being imposed and the consequences of violating them—"and yet delegate broad powers to administrators." In turn it would improve the administrative process, as "every administrator would be making decisions with an eye toward review for consistency, and every agency would have incentive to influence this process by [earlier] promulgation" of formal rules. Clarity in statutory design can only go so far, of course. Yet it will enhance the participation of administrators "in the legislative process in a way that is consonant with the Constitution." The effect of "a commitment to serious legislative revision which attempted to fuse administrative experience" (Lowi 1979, 307) would also be a firmer, more reliable way of ensuring general responsibility and public accountability in the administrative state and would decrease the tendency for legislative oversight to focus on administrative failure and casting blame. Elevating administration to the status of a fourth constitutional branch thus has real potential to improve the chances that deliberative lawmaking—lawmaking that at least occasionally transcends bargaining and interest exchange—will occur, resulting in laws that over time are based on successively better approximations of the public interest. In the case of the Federal Reserve, this would be a more satisfying outcome for proposals, such as those that surfaced at the time of this writing to expand the remit of the Fed to address income inequality, especially with respect to racial disparities in employment, wages, wealth, and credit (Long 2020), than the current pattern of congressional-Fed relations tends to produce. More generally, instead of patterns of blame shifting and blame avoidance, administration as a fourth branch can discipline the legislative-administrative process to value longer-term outcomes and sustained reflection on the concrete meaning of the public interest. Elevating administration's experiencing function to promote the greater possibility and quality of deliberative lawmaking is thus an especially crucial contribution that a fourth branch can make to the preservation and enhancement of institutional capabilities. Such a contribution lies at the heart of the public interest in the theory of political constitution of the commercial republic (Elkin 2006, 130–132).

Recalibrating the Separation of Powers

A second significant contribution that an administrative fourth branch can make to the commercial republic is to rebalance the counteracting and collaborating functions of the separation of powers, with respect to both its original design intentions and current conditions. The republic's separation-of-powers dynamics have gotten seriously out of equilibrium. In one respect, separation of powers has become a positive sum game among the existing constitutional branches in which they all gain by piling procedural requirements, directives, and restrictions on administrative action (Rosenbloom, Newbold, and Doughty 2018). Such requirements and restrictions are a poor substitute for the hard task, which the constitutional branches have for some time now actively tried to disown, of designing good legal and policy principles that capture the concrete meaning of the public interest. Beyond this general dynamic, however, the disequilibrium in the separation of powers currently reflects the dramatic shift in power to the presidency since the middle of the twentieth century (Moe and Howell 1999; Howell 2003; Devins 2009; Shane 2009; Bradley and Morrison 2012, 441–448). Giving administration coequal constitutional status can curtail the "one-way ratchet" (Shane 2009, 4) of expansion and monopolization of policy authority and administrative power within the presidency. This shift has not consistently increased presidential ownership of policy consequences, but it has created a second, far more unaccountable bureaucracy within the presidential sphere. This presidential bureaucracy has, as already noted, enabled the president to intervene in and short-circuit the administrative separation of powers. It has also diminished the effectiveness of other subconstitutional mechanisms—advise and consent, legislative oversight, and judicial review, for example—devised to help the separation of powers serve its design intentions.

Alexander Hamilton's case for an administrative service that would help restrain the potential for excess in an elected executive was part of his argument for unity in the executive as the source of energy in a constitutional system. Hamilton offered a complex vision of the executive and of a republican public administration that contrasts with the strict subordination of administration in the current working constitution of the commercial republic. "Hamilton conceived 'the executive' as more than a single personality. The executive was a composite individual, and . . . functioned through diverse ministers acting in its name and under its authority" (Caldwell 1988, 44). More important, Hamilton stressed that these ministers were "holden not of the President, but of the Nation," and he "observed that 'the Constitution has everywhere used the language, "Officers of the United States," as if to exclude the dangerous pretension that [they are] the mere creature of the Executive." Furthermore, they take "no oath of any kind to the President" (90; also, see again Green 2019, chap. 2 and 4).

Hamilton advanced these arguments about the status of executive officers under the Constitution because he was concerned about the possibility that the republican principle of short duration in office might combine with the Constitution's more energetic executive to generate a permanent state of revolution in the public administration, undermining the stability of government and the regime. Despite the Constitutional Convention's rejection of an executive council and related forms of multiheaded executive, Hamilton envisioned what essentially amounted to a semiautonomous administrative service "staffed by qualified men who would be attracted by the permanence of the office as well as its insulation from public opinion" (Bailey 2008, 464). Their efforts would help temper the democratic responsiveness of the elected executive and bring the stability so essential for undertaking the "arduous enterprises" (*The Federalist Papers*, no. 72) of building a regime and sustaining a great nation. Hamilton's strategy to ensure this balance in the energetic executive included a check on the president's removal power. Despite conclusions to the contrary (e.g., Caldwell 1988, 88), Hamilton "never fully repudiated" his interpretation of the Constitution giving the Senate "a veto over presidential removals," and this position was "central" to Hamilton's analysis of duration and energy in the executive (Bailey 2008, 463–464; see also Wise 1993, 259).

Hamilton did not propose a wholly independent constitutional authority for these more permanent officials (Caldwell 1988, 29), although his interpretation of removal provisions implies something just short of such an arrangement. Others certainly did interpret Hamilton's argument and other constitutional provisions to that effect in the debates leading to the Decision of 1789. This interpretation was a distinctly minority position in a debate that resulted in what would retrospectively (*Myers v. U.S.*, 272 U.S. 52 [1926]) be treated as expanded, constitutionally authorized presidential removal powers (but see Shugerman 2020). Nevertheless the advocates of the independent-administrator position insisted that to be internally consistent, the Constitution had to be seen as granting top administrators independence from complete subordination to the president in order to provide a check on executive power. This argument has resurfaced in party conflicts, interbranch struggles, and constitutional jurisprudence across the nation's development, but with notable weakening over time (Cook 2014).

One prominent component of this recurring argument centers on the question of what constitutional authority, if any, Congress has to create administrative agencies independent of direct presidential superintendence and at-will removal power (Froomkin 1987). The possibility of administration exercising a check on the executive remains constitutionally and politically contentious. A unitary executive approach to the presidency currently prevails (Kovacs 2018), yet there remain significant arguments for the constitutional validity of at least some administrative independence from strict presidential direction for even the "principal officers" and the executive departments (Emerson 2021). There is also evidence that some mid-level administrators are able to achieve a form of autonomy for their agencies that enables them to pursue their own policy preferences and get elected executives and legislators to go along, providing an alternative source of energy and direction for policy and law (Carpenter 2001).

This nonstructural, political form of "bureaucratic autonomy," interesting for students of politics and indicative of how administration can shape policy fundamentally, may have salutary practical effects on the function of the regime by helping to "orchestrat[e] the participatory energies of American politics" (Carpenter 2001, 367). Even if it were not constitutionally suspect under current conceptions of the relationship between the administrative state and other governing institutions, however, such ad hoc autonomy is too infrequent and fragmented to serve as a consistent force in shaping separation-of-powers politics by constraining presidential overreach in a way that enhances the capabilities of the administrative state or the presidency. It is also unclear whether this sort of autonomy has any beneficial effect on diminishing the dominance of narrow business interests in the administrative state. It may even exacerbate it. Business privilege is, after all, a dominant form of "participatory energy" in the regime. To realize more of the institutional counteraction and collaboration that a design for separate institutions sharing powers is supposed to produce, creating a fourth branch has much greater potential for resetting and enhancing the strategic interactions associated with the separation of powers.

The general normative effect of a fourth administrative branch on the separation of powers is that through the institutional politics it would engender it can reinvigorate the existing institutions in the separation-of-powers scheme and the public-interest purposes that their interactions are supposed to engender. A fourth branch would have this effect by setting the public interest perspectives and arguments of public administrators on an equal plane, forcing all the institutions to engage one another more openly about public-interest questions. If administration as a fourth branch accomplished this feat by spurring the other institutions to engage on a coequal basis, it would increase the chances of shifting separation-of-powers politics back toward serving the public interest in the most fundamental way: preserving a liberal way of life and serving justice by preventing some groups from seizing control of government to serve their own narrow yet unlimited ends (Elkin 2006, 136–137). This is consistent with a Hamiltonian conception of the function of separation of powers as a key part of a coordinated, unifying representation of the nation's permanent interests, as well as a bulwark against faction. It is attractive especially to the extent that the Madisonian scheme for representation and regulation of faction has proven deficient in restraining the unceasing efforts of particular interests to control the state for their own benefit and at great cost to their fellow citizens.

More specifically, a fourth administrative branch would alter separation-of-powers politics in two critical ways. First, again with respect to the presidency, a constitutional fourth administrative branch would push the presidency toward enhancement of its primary institutional capability—energy and dispatch in protecting the nation's security. It would do so by relieving the presidency of the excess burden of a second primary responsibility for the "steady administration of law," but it would also do so by providing an added constraint on the tendency of the presidency to push toward extremes of action for national self-preservation by having the higher law standing to challenge such presidential tendencies. It would thus leaven the action orientation of the presidency that tends to undermine deliberation across the separation of powers. Such cross-institutional deliberation is sometimes necessary in order to give careful consideration to whether precipitate action serves the public interest. This is precisely why war making powers in the Constitution are institutionally separated but overlapping. National self-preservation is certainly in the public interest, but that does not always require shooting first and asking questions later.

There are many instances of ad hoc administrative restraints on presidential energy and action in foreign affairs, perhaps most famously the deliberations of the so-called ExComm, a subset of the National Security Council membership assembled by President Kennedy during the Cuban Missile Crisis (Allison and Zelikow 1999, 346–347). Although it was not an interbranch group, it represented at least some viewpoint diversity on the crisis and the options for response that circulated within the group. More important, it deliberated even in the midst of what all regarded rightly as an existential threat. Yet the limitation of all examples like ExComm is not so much that they are ad hoc but that they remain subordinate to the president and subject to presidential whim. This is so even for the president's cabinet, which, despite its status as a traditional mechanism of advice and restraint on the presidency, has no formal authority and no political power (see the further discussion of the cabinet in chapter 6). A constitutionally distinct administration would reshuffle the deck with respect to the possibility of executive-administrative, or broader interbranch, deliberation on the concrete meaning of the public interest, whether it is in the core areas of presidential authority or in the vast array of other policy realms where constitutional authority is widely shared.

A fourth administrative branch would alter separation of powers in a second way by forcing the other constitutive institutions of the regime to engage administration on the plane of constitutional argument rather than through the dictates of superiors to subordinates. It would force presidents and Congresses in particular to give more explicit attention to relations with administration because they would have to confront its systemic authority. This coequal engagement would in turn enable administrators as independent constitutional actors to make constitutionally principled claims in support of or in opposition to the enterprises of the other branches. They might invoke such claims only rarely, partly because they are obligated to carry out the law and are busy doing so, but also for the strategic advantage of holding back on the invocation of such claims for the times when they will be most consequential. Moreover, they might still lose the argument despite invoking those claims. This does not negate the strategic value of this constitutionally structured administrative independence, however.

Currently, the permanent bureaucracy has a number of weapons at its disposal in disputes with the constitutional branches. Besides the power of rational-legal bureaucracy itself, and the expertise, and collection and analysis of information, which are among its most distinctive features, bureaucrats can deploy information tactically through leaks and whistleblowing, and other forms of release and dissemination, to blunt attempts at command and control from their constitutional masters. They can also mobilize agency constituencies, whether or not they have achieved that special kind of bureaucratic autonomy. They may even have standing to sue with claims that their political superiors have instructed them to act in contradiction to their legal obligations. The problem with all these tools and tactics is that they are tainted with the air of insubordination, even when they may be legally sanctioned as in the case of whistleblower protection statues.

Without a reconstruction of the separation of powers, a "subordinate autonomy" (Barth 1993, 1995; Green 2019, 107–112; see chapter 5 for further discussion), in which administrators play one constitutional master off against another, may be the best that can be done, given the Constitution's tripartite design and administration's subordinate status within that structure. The legitimacy of such behavior as well as its practical effects is at best suspect. With clear constitutional sanction to check power or facilitate action, however, agencies would be empowered to engage the other actors in the system at a level of political argument that their current subordinate status does not allow. With constitutionally anchored autonomy, administration can bring to the open court of public opinion plans of action enriched with constitutional argument and the higher-law foundation to make those arguments, which together will allow them to engage the other branches in ways that shed light on quandaries regarding the public interest. This stands in stark contrast to the current strategies and tactics, which tend to obfuscate such questions by mixing them with doubts about the legitimacy of administration engaging in challenges to the constitutional branches.

There is certainly legitimate concern that elevating administration to the status of a constitutional fourth branch will shift power too far and make unelected bureaucrats the new imperium. Even under current arrangements, some agencies are able to act beyond a reasonable interpretation of their statutory authority. The so-called "family separation policy" of the US Department of Homeland Security, while of questionable legality under international law (Cordero, Feldman, and Keitner 2020), enabled US Customs and Border Patrol and its contractors to impose extreme deprivation in the detention of the children of cross-border migrants and asylum seekers that clearly violated law and policy (Costello 2019). The existing constitutional branches, acting as overseers, can slap down such instances and readjust power so as to restrain bad bureaucratic actors, but they do not always do so when that behavior serves their purposes. What lies beneath all this, however, is that in most instances such horrid bureaucratic behavior is the result not of bureaucracy gone rogue but of public bureaucracy, and the administrative state and civil service more generally, that is too weak and subjugated to resist the unethical or even illegal commands of political overseers. A conception of constitutional authority and the separation of powers like the unitary executive—in which presidential interpretation of the law is the law for all intents and purposes—requires a far harder corrective than marginal institutional tinkering or constitutional reinterpretation will provide.

How political principals attempt to control administrators and how administrators respond under the current form of the administrative state reveals something about separation-of-powers politics after the creation of a true fourth branch. Even under ideal conditions of political control, for example, the particular values of bureaucrats and administrative agencies will shape policy effects in ways that deviate from the intentions of political principals. Such deviance reflects the behavior of bureaucrats as strategic actors, responsive to many external pressures (Meier and O'Toole 2006, 115–119). Giving them greater, constitutionally anchored autonomy will expand the influence of distinctive bureaucratic values, complicating constitutional politics. This need not mean out-of-control bureaucrats and the destruction of democratic constitutionalism, however. It might mean that administrative values bolster or leaven the values that other political institutions bring to separation-of-powers politics, including restraining their excesses. Bureaucrats show greater inclinations toward values and interests that are "under- or unrepresented in the short-term electoral cycles," including "members of future generations" (135). They are also generally "more public-regarding . . . than the general population," as well as "more civic minded, more efficacious, and more willing to use the instruments of the positive state" (137). The point is not that these values should be dominant, only that a fourth administrative branch increases the chance that they will gain a purchase in constitutional politics that they do not enjoy now. In its interactions with the constitutive institutions, a coequal administrative branch can raise the public visibility of those values, helping to enrich the educative effect of politics.

Dynamics of this sort may already exist because of a "subconstitutional regime of institutional counterweights" (Michaels 2015, 540). Yet this has not stopped the threat to the regime from privatization (again, see Michaels 2017, especially chap. 6), so the critical problem of excess political privilege for business is largely untouched by such *sub*constitutional politics. Elevating administration constitutionally must, therefore, speak to the central liberal-democratic concern for market-state relations, the commercial republic's experience with the influence of business in the administrative state, and most importantly, the preservation and improvement of a regime design relying on a distinct class as the social basis of the regime.

Broadening the Interests of the Propertied

Apart from the foundational elements of society that would tend to make the owners of productive assets susceptible to a broadening of their perspective on the public interest in a commercial republic, Madison and Hamilton sought institutional designs to reinforce that tendency toward gaining a broader public-interest perspective. Madison "assumed that the various components that go into making up the propertied class would be spread among the branches of government" (Elkin 2006, 223). With the presence of "an attentive citizenry, property holders of various kinds would find themselves arguing in public about what they have in common—and they would look to a version of their common interests broad enough to attract" significant citizen support (224). Hamilton recognized that the propertied, especially the holders of capital, would be ambitious, not just for wealth but for the public recognition that would come through public service, whether by serving in government or supporting its functions. The energy of that ambition could be harnessed to serve the common interest in prosperity, growth, and national strength. That ambition carried risks, however, and thus had to be restrained by an institutionally multifaceted representation, including an expert administration.

The rise of corporate capitalism changed the equation for broadening the interests of the propertied. The fragmentation and narrowing of the interests of the propertied class through corporate consolidation and control of the economy diminished the foundational tendency of the propertied to have a sense of the larger public interest, except, perhaps, for the sense that the satisfaction of their interests overlapped with the permanent interests of the regime. The concomitant reconstruction of the administrative state in the corporate-liberal consensus provided a form of legally and politically robust and technically expert administration to counterbalance the more narrow, multiplied interests and ambitions of a corporate capital class. Key design elements of the second administrative state nevertheless greatly expanded the opportunity for the propertied to seek satisfaction of their interests, not in open public debate attracting the attention of the citizenry but through interaction with and influence on administrative agencies that operate with at least partial legislative, executive, and judicial authority applied to narrow missions that often parallel specific lines of corporate interests.

The holders of capital forming the new propertied and the social basis of the regime now have political privileges and avenues of influence that go well beyond what is necessary or wise in a commercial republic. Such a regime depends on those "who control large-scale productive property . . . by which economic prosperity is generated" and thus forces public officials to negotiate with them a role that is "attractive enough to make them staunch adherents of the regime" (Elkin 2006, 220). Yet the current working constitution too often rewards them for pursuing their narrow interests and acting factionally, including by "the shaping of citizen volitions" and other efforts that "weaken elections as a control on minority faction" (220; see also Angresano 2016, chap. 4). One way to counteract these conditions directly is to expand the size of the capital-holding class, one that, if defined as the richest 1 percent of the population, owned 53 percent of stock and mutual fund assets as of 2016 (Inequality.org N.d.). Extending the breadth of capital ownership or diversifying its organizational character are intriguing possibilities for broadening the interests of capital, although it is not entirely clear that either strategy would actually result in this broader group of capitalists thinking much differently than the current ones (Elkin 2006, 220–223). An indirect strategy for broadening the interests of the capitalist class is that used by the regime design itself—the separation of powers and other institutional arrangements. If the nature of the administrative state in its current iteration is a significant part of the problem, then it deserves particular attention in this regard. This suggests directing consideration back to efforts to make the administrative process, with its fusion of legislative, executive, and judicial powers, more public and open as through the Administrative Procedure Act and the administrative separation of powers.

Several prominent reform approaches that focus on the existing constitutional branches, as well as several new attempts to reconceive the role of administration within the separation of powers, are the focus of the analysis and critiques of chapter 5. For now, however, the evidence considered in chapter 3 and this chapter shows that restructuring the administrative state along such lines has not so far solved the problem of a working constitution that far too often fails to broaden the interests of the propertied toward a sincere consideration of the larger commercial public interest. The propertied have "too much power" to get government to serve their interests, only exacerbating the "dangers of faction" (Elkin 2006, 221).

Given the tight interweaving of business privilege and influence through the structure and function of the administrative state itself, how would the creation of a constitutionally legitimated fourth administrative branch help broaden the interests of the propertied? There is some evidence that despite narrowly interested business dominance in the administrative state, administrators already can and do encourage some interest broadening among the propertied. Actions of National Labor Relations Board regional offices, for instance, indicate that "case processing is a dynamic system of clientele and staff interaction and reaction" (Schmidt 2002, 208). Regional staff "balance or structure decision outputs so that they protect the weaker interests against the strong but accommodate politically or economically important interests whenever prudent to do so" (209). If administrators in other agencies act similarly, they can be said to model for the stronger interests various ways to accommodate multiple, competing, and legitimate claims on public action. Through frequent business-agency interactions, business interests might be broadened.

One other example of an avenue by which administration may already help broaden the interests of the propertied is the federal advisory committee process. The Federal Advisory Committee Act of 1972 (FACA) was one of many efforts in the early to mid-1970s to open public-policy decision making to a broader array of citizen interests. The FACA's aim was "to help control the undue influence of special interests on advisory committees by balancing committee membership, opening committee meetings and minutes to the public, and controlling the number of committees formed" (Bierele and Long 1999, 10400). It may be numbered among those reforms in which Congress sought to modify an administrative process dominated by executive values so that it more closely reflected the value of representation that is central to a legislative perspective (Rosenbloom 2000).

Most FACA committees are oriented toward obtaining advice from subject-matter experts or guidance on policy development from a cross-section of agency stakeholders. Representation on the average FACA committee is dominated by universities and researchers, and business and industry representatives, because of the scientific and technical expertise sought (Karty 2002, 217, fig. 2b). The FACA process and its effects have been the target of considerable criticism since its inception. Two key criticisms are that it has restricted broader public participation in administrative processes, and it has served as a pathway for regulatory capture, leading the OMB to restrict lobbyists from serving on advisory committees (Straus et al. 2015). Despite these flaws, with over 1,000 FACA committees across the federal government, the FACA process provides a forum for regular, and most importantly public, contact between business and public agencies in the governance process. Although FACA committee meetings are almost always dominated by very specific, often highly technical policy questions and debates, the cross-sectional nature of their stakeholder representation is such that there is incentive to lift the discussion on occasion to general questions of what constitutes good public policy. There is thus the potential that the meetings might broach real public interest questions and force business representatives to think about them. The existing FACA process may suffer from path-dependent faults that cannot be rectified. The point, however, is that something like the FACA process, instituted by and for a constitutionally sanctioned fourth branch, might enable a public, deliberative process where business representatives must directly state their views about what constitutes the public interest in the context of a specific policy question. They must also then listen to alternative and possibly contending views in circumstances where the determination of concrete policy actions, and possibly larger questions of institutional design, are at stake (see, for example, Lavertu, Walters, and Weimer 2011).

It is also worth considering, in what is now a networked, coproduction-oriented administrative process, that at least at the state and local level and in the delivery of public services, business might be forced to acknowledge the multiplicity of interests. The collaboration necessary to achieve shared aims might thus broaden their perspective on what constitutes the public interest. As already noted, however, networked administration and coproduction has a "dark side" (O'Toole and Meier 2004), where "co-contamination" rather than coproduction for achievement of broad public goals occurs (Williams, Kang, and Johnson 2016). The result, again, is bias toward "goals that are favored by more entrenched interests" and the discounting of "efforts that favor disadvantaged clientele" (O'Toole and Meier 2004, 685). Still, administrative agencies "can be substantial counterweights to any financial, informational, operational, or other asymmetries that nongovernmental organizations might bring to the table" (McGuire and Agranoff 2010, 393). Whether this has a broadening effect on the perspectives of business and the property-holding class with respect to the public interest, which they likely think of in strictly aggregative terms and equate with their own specific interests, is an open question. There are at least some hints that in their interactions with public administrators and public agencies, narrow business interests might be exposed to other interests and other perspectives on what constitutes the public interest. How would elevating administration and the permanent civil service to the status of a constitutionally recognized fourth branch build on existing tendencies and perhaps even alter the fundamental dynamics of an administrative state pervaded by narrow business interests?

Most administrative agencies are mission oriented, whether their missions entail broad public aims like predicting the weather accurately or protecting air, water, and land from pollution or serving more specific clientele, such as veterans, farmers, or broadcasters. Although they may be vested with considerable statutory authority, their power to succeed in their missions relies on a "structure of interests friendly or hostile, vague and general or compact and well-defined" that "encloses each significant center of administrative discretion. This structure is an important determinant of the scope of possible action" (Long 1949, 258). While the second administrative state was still fairly robust, agencies, and administration more generally, were not stuck in a subordinate and completely dependent status with respect to that structure of interests. Public administrators could, and did, exercise agency in assembling the resources at hand into the power necessary not just to fulfill their missions but to counterbalance "the massive feudal power of organized business, organized agriculture, and organized labor" (263).

This particular perspective on "power in administration" generally discounted the power value of formal, statutory authority but did not dismiss it entirely. Although the regime may now be a "republic of statutes" (Eskridge and Ferejohn 2010), bedrock constitutional authority is bound to carry considerable authoritative force and thus practical political power. Hence, giving administration elevated constitutional status can provide agencies with the foundation to leverage the interest-based power resources on which they currently rely toward giving due regard to broader conceptions of the public interest. The platform of higher constitutional status at least increases the chances that administrators will confront their more narrowly interested clientele with arguments grounded in constitutional values and admonitions to aspire to being part of broader coalitions tied to the "enlarged and permanent interest" (*The Federalist Papers*, no. 42). The critical point is to expand the power base of administration beyond an exclusive reliance on interest-based power. As a constitutional fourth branch, the administrative state might then help to lower barriers to the formation of civic majorities on important public questions, or at least reinforce in policy implementation and in later policy creation and refinement the effect of civic majorities that do form despite the barriers in the regime's design.

At a minimum, coaxing narrowly interested clientele into defending their policy stances publicly, making them explain and defend openly that what they do is an essential component of the common good, would be an improvement over current arguments that amount to no more than that government must be concerned principally with serving "vital" interests, or even more narrowly, with reducing business costs and increasing shareholder value to induce business to create jobs. With elevated constitutional status, administration might have the independence to redefine agency missions toward serving the "objective interests" of the community (Cook 1992, 424), rather than narrower clientele interests, and drag their stakeholder coalitions along in the quest to define and serve those broader community interests. Any modern nation is likely to have, for example, a general interest in agriculture, or forestry, or manufacturing. Even in a commercial republic, such interests are not, or at least need not be, coterminous with the interests of the businesses engaged in those endeavors. Seeing national or common interests in this way is also consistent with Hamilton's conception of representation as realized through multiple government institutions, including administration, in contrast to representation manifested only as particularistic interests selecting legislative representatives. Administration's contribution to institutionally based representation is also partly that it buffers factional interests through its professional temperament and commitment to rule by law.

A constitutionally grounded administrative state can also increase the chances that the interests of the corporate capitalist class can be broadened by short-circuiting the extreme dependency relationship between business and the state that has emerged in the most recent developments in the political economy and the neoliberal overlay on the administrative state. Critics of social-welfare programs have long contended that they create in welfare recipients a dependency that is socially and morally degrading for the individual and politically and morally damaging for a liberal-democratic regime. This contention is rooted in a highly gendered, racialized, and ahistoric social construction (Fraser and Gordon 1994), however, that is largely intended to keep a particular segment of the population in its place (Soss, Fording, and Schram 2011). Moreover, claims of social and moral deviance across generations caused by reliance on public-assistance programs lack supporting evidence (Schneider and Jacoby 2003). To the extent that social welfare recipients are too reliant for too long a time on public assistance because of the perverse design of public policy and a lack of reasonable political-economic alternatives, however, they are truly bit players compared to business. Large swaths of the corporate class have become so dependent on ever greater inducements to performance, and opportunities for rent seeking, that "corporations can no longer be expected to provide jobs, to invest, or to produce without government assistance." This has grown to the point that it has created "an 'endless cycle of dependency'—a 'way of life' for a whole group of people" (Olson and Champlin 1998, 769), namely corporate CEOs and shareholders, investment banks, and hedge funds.

Through its greater autonomy and constitutional authority in a separate fourth branch, the administrative state would break the cycle of dependency by returning the interdependence of market and state to a level that is more in keeping with the commercial public interest. A civil service that is more robust because of the greater political leverage gained with constitutional status would be more capable of and confident in pushing back against corporate dependence with evidence gathered through its experiencing function. It would gain a proper sense of the place of the corporation in a commercial republican political economy and fight against policy designs that sustain rent-seeking advantages and perpetuate the cycle of dependency. Its authoritative political leverage would enable it to push for statutory authority to prohibit privatizing schemes that entail below-market rents, sole-source contracts, below-market contract payments, and other forms of hidden subsidies and rent extraction. Constitutionally grounded authority and political power would also enable agencies of the administrative state to better resist efforts by business to gain special favors in the form of favorable interpretations of statutory provisions and other ways in which business can manipulate an administrative process that already has features favorable to its interests. Indeed, in its most expansive potential effects, constitutionalizing the fourth branch might give it the political energy to push for fundamental changes in the administrative process that force business to confront contending interests and articulate in detail and on the record a public-interest rationale for the outcomes it seeks, harnessing rather than merely submitting to business political energy in service of giving concrete meaning to the public interest.

Strengthening Civic Capacity

Ultimately, in a "fully realized commercial republic" (Elkin 2006, 218), it is scrutiny from a public-spirited citizenry that is key to broadening the interests of the propertied. It is such a citizenry "that will encourage the various components of the business class to search for a broad and appealing account of their common interests" (224). It may be difficult to imagine that the now-fabled "one percent," who currently hold such a disproportionate share of the nation's productive assets, would even acknowledge let alone respond to such citizen scrutiny. This is where a real civil service formed in a constitutional fourth branch might tip the balance, however. Because the second administrative state was in part created to be and has thus been seen as a barrier to broader public scrutiny of law and policy making, a substantial body of theory, analysis, and practices has developed in a countereffort to make the administrative state less of a barrier to real citizen engagement in governance. This is in part what the new public governance has sought to encapsulate and advance. It is also consistent with a "democracy against domination" approach, contending that "regulatory agencies actually possess unique attributes that can be tapped to deepen democratic agency, engaging and empowering a wider range of stakeholders in the actual day-to-day work of making public policy" (Rahman 2017, 29), illuminating "the potential of regulatory agencies as sites of democratic action; and the scope to innovate new institutional forms for democratic agency" (30). The more general intellectual and programmatic effort to expand citizen engagement in the administrative process continues apace, with some modest successes as well as much frustration continuing to arise (Dudley, Webb Farley, and Banford 2018).

Much of this continuing effort has concentrated on getting agencies to respond to and engage with citizens and enable that interchange to shape law in action. It may seem counterintuitive that giving the administrative state constitutionally rooted authority would make public agencies more receptive to citizen engagement and influence in the administrative process. As noted above, however, greater foundational authority might make public agencies less dependent on well-organized, economically and politically advantaged interests for their power and autonomy. Perhaps the incentives would still be weak in this regard. Because administrative agencies already appeal to and even purposely organize public support under conditions of legal and political subjugation, however, constitutionally grounded authority might lower the risk of blowback from elected officials that administrative agencies frequently encounter and increase their motivation to marshal public opinion for positions that are distinctive from the other constitutional branches on questions that implicate the public interest.

There is also the question of whether, through more substantial engagement with citizens, administrative agencies can help forge a more engaged and attentive public. This hints at the possibility that a constitutionalized administrative state might help address a weakness in the Madisonian regime design—how to cultivate the public-spirited populace essential for the republican principle to work as Madison envisioned (Elkin 2006, 65–67, 179–182; see also Banning 1995, chap. 3). There is considerable evidence that administrative action can have constitutive effects on political efficacy and other participatory behavior, for good or ill (Mettler and SoRelle 2014, 116–121). These effects are observable at all levels of government, but much of the normative concern for ways to enhance administrative cultivation of public engagement is focused on the local level. This squares well with the importance, in the theory of political constitution of the commercial republic, of altering the political outlook of the citizenry through reforms of local political life (Elkin 2006, 279–285). As noted, creating a constitutional fourth administrative branch can force the other constitutional branches to engage with administration as a coequal, increasing the chances that the disputes and arguments for accommodation will be out in the open and at a sufficiently high level of political import to draw the concentrated attention of the press, and thus of the attentive public, which otherwise rarely pays much attention to goings-on in the administrative process. A corollary is that greater formal autonomy for administration raises the level of citizen engagement in the administrative process. There is some evidence that greater budgetary autonomy (Neshkova 2014) and autonomy through direct election of administrators (Miller 2013), for example, are each associated with more meaningful citizen participation in governance and policy more responsive to public preferences.

With citizen attention increased when administration has greater structural autonomy, the propertied have less opportunity to hide their arguments and maneuvers for serving their own narrow interests in the darker recesses of the administrative state. The propertied will still prevail more often than not, for that is what having designed-in political advantages means. Yet a dramatic structural change can, again, force the propertied into reformulating their arguments about how their interests are coterminous with the public interest, nudging the commercial republic toward "a politics that would overcome the political advantages that stem from business privilege with its narrowing effects" (Elkin 2006, 224). Certainly rhetorical change is not the same as behavioral change, but the whole point of institutional arrangements that require advocates to publicly defend their interests and hear others do the same is that there is a chance that those engaged in contention and deliberation will come to see things differently and perhaps glimpse where the common interest lies. This is politics in its truest sense, and there are good reasons to contend that raising public administration's engagement in politics, especially public-interest politics, is good for the administrative state and the regime (Spicer 2010).

Finally, a more constitutionally secure administrative state, in its various manifestations across the levels of government in the federal system, has the potential to fortify a positive relationship between public administration and civil society. As constitutive institutions of the regime, civil society and the administrative state exhibit several similar features. The components that constitute them are diverse in their size, goals and purposes, and internal characteristics. In both institutions these components vary considerably in how tightly or loosely coupled they are with one another, and there is considerable interaction among the components within each institution across the formal and informal boundaries of governmental levels in the federal system. There are local and state affiliates of national civic associations, for example, just as there are transportation departments of varying scope at the national, state, and local levels. In a number of ways, moreover, the missions of civic associations overlap with agency missions in the administrative state. One prominent such area is the franchise. There are both public agencies and civic associations focused on organizing, managing, and promoting the exercise of the right to vote. In many ways, therefore, the fuzzy boundary between state and society is primarily the boundary between the administrative state and civil society.

Of course, the administrative state and civil society are separate for a very important reason. Civil society is a distinct and critical constitutive institution of a republican regime precisely because it is not part of the state. "A civil society is composed of groups of people who come together for common purposes and whose activities are facilitated by a system of law that is not itself a product of the central government. These civic associations must not depend on nor be authorized by government lest they become agents of governmental authority" (Elkin 2006, 136). Civil society's system of law is the common law, which highlights a distinct and critical connection between civil society and the courts as the articulators and interpreters of the common law. The more important point, however, is that the strength and vibrancy of civil society is not just a function of a public cooperative spirit. It is also a function of the strengths and weaknesses of the "internal law" of civic associations and the common law that supports, structures, and guides civic life. In turn, although outside the state, the strength of civil society is also a function of its relationship to the state. Again, that implicates the courts, but it also implicates public administration.

Certainly there are notable antagonisms between civil society and the administrative state, on matters such as the exercise of rights and the administrative state's regulation of public health and welfare. There can be direct interactions between civic associations and administrative agencies in this regard, but they often take place through the venue of the courts, where a varying mix of common law and statutory law sets the terms of the interactions on any given matter of dispute. Such tensions between major constitutive institutions of the regime are inevitable and in important respects healthy. They reflect alternative institutional conceptions of the public interest as well as active forms of restraint that those institutions impose on one another, a sign of a healthy regime. They also further highlight that the administrative state has prominent connections to the common law and its restraints—and through it to civil society and the courts—that are distinct from the relationships to civil society of the three constitutional branches that are the administrative state's formal overseers.

As the travelogue of the development of American commercial republic theory and practice in part I showed, there is also a critical cooperative dimension to the relationship between civil society and the administrative state. Not just in the highly networked form of governance that is so prominent today, but across the entire span of American political development, the administrative state has relied on civil society to put the law into action and increase the chances that the law will have its intended effects. The administrative state works with civic associations to deliver services, communicate with the public, and receive reconnaissance on public reactions to policy implementation and outcomes. In turn, the formal and informal support that the state provides to civic associations flows through the administrative state. If not exactly a mutual dependency, then at least there is an extensive form of mutual cooperation and support between civil society and the administrative state. What, then, does creating a constitutionally independent fourth branch have to do with this existing dynamic?

Civil society has a significant connection to the market and business. With the orientation of many civic associations centered on protecting and promoting rights, including property rights, civil society is likely, in general, to support the maintenance of an "enterprise-based market system" and "private ownership of productive assets" that promote "economic prosperity" (Elkin 2006, 168). That does not mean, however, that civic associations in general seek to operate as businesses or to promote a business-interest orientation to public questions. Many components of civil society have the specific aim of exercising a counterweight to business interests. Labor unions are the primary example, but many civic associations promote values and conceptions of the public interest that are distinct from those of business and the market. Unfortunately for the health of the American commercial republic, many of the same dynamics that have made the administrative state more a conduit than a counterweight for business political prerogatives and the domination of business interests in debates about the public interest have infected civil society as well. Part of the breakdown of the corporate-liberal consensus after the middle of the twentieth century involved civil society becoming nearly as great a target of and avenue for the expansion of business influence and political privilege as the administrative state. Nonprofit charitable, educational, scientific, professional, and human-service organizations have grown substantially as a component of the American political economy especially since the 1960s (Hammack 2002). Some of this growth was driven by business efforts to fund nonprofits that would be the intellectual incubators of the antitax and antiregulatory movements. Much more significantly, however, public nonprofits, including educational institutions and philanthropy, have been subject to sweeping marketization (Salamon 1997; Eikenberry and Kluver 2004). This far-reaching marketization of civil society raises serious concerns about corporate cooptation of the nonprofit sector (Bauer and Schmitz 2012), as well as the degrading of civil society as a distinct constitutive institution preserving and promoting particular values and conceptions of the public interest (Nickel and Eikenberry 2009). This latter implication is the most worrisome for the health of a commercial republican regime.

The more general implication is that not only have the administrative state and nonprofits of various sorts been closely linked as twin instruments of the privatization revolution writ large, they have been increasingly subordinated to the service of business interests, and their contributions as distinct constitutive institutions of the regime that help make the commercial republic what it is, or should be, have been devalued. In one respect, the privatization or marketization of both the administrative state and nonprofits that has driven the expansion of networked governance can mean greater intrusion of the state into civil society. The latter is being squeezed by both the market and a marketized state, turning civic organizations into instruments of a neoliberal state apparatus—and by extension instruments of business interests and vehicles for expanded inducements to business performance and even rent-seeking. Creating a constitutionally formal fourth administrative branch is the most effective way for administration to escape the extreme subordination that diminishes its contributions to the regime as a distinct constitutive institution. By gaining significant capacity to counterbalance business interest through constitutionally anchored autonomy, the administrative state might also aid the third sector by lessening the grip of business interest and market logic on civil society, through interaction with civil-society organizations in ways that reinforce the nonpecuniary public interest values that the two institutions share, particularly the value of public service (Park and Word 2012; Ingrams 2020).

The possibility that creating a constitutional fourth administrative branch, and constitutionally legitimating administration more generally, might help reinvigorate civil society as a distinct constitutive institution that promotes the "moral pluralism that characterizes a free society" (Elkin 2006, 135) is admittedly speculative. It also should not be carried too far. The relationship between civil society and the administrative state will remain antagonistic to a considerable extent, which is generally a good thing for the health of the regime, as this reflects both the distinct aims and characteristics of the two realms and the moral pluralism to which they contribute as distinct constitutive institutions. Moreover, both public agencies and nonprofit organizations of various sorts will find it very hard to loosen the hold of a narrow, business management orientation to their operations and relations with one another. The spread of business management techniques and market-based managerial processes, such as performance-based budgeting, has been going on for a very long time. Nevertheless, the benefits for civil society of a constitutionalized administrative state, even if conjectural, are not incomprehensible. Something must change to get the American commercial republic back on the path toward a fuller realization of its essential aspirations, and part of that endeavor entails reinvigorating both civil society and an administrative state as constitutive institutions of the regime.

The Middle Class and the Administrative State

One final contribution the creation of a constitutionally formal fourth administrative branch can make to the theory and practice of political constitution of the American commercial republic deserves consideration. This contribution relates to the classical idea of a ruling stratum in the constitution of good regimes (Elkin 2006, 89–96). Madison's idea that the design of an American commercial republic must be anchored in a particular class that constitutes the social basis of the regime is not the same as the notion of a ruling stratum. A regime striving for popular self-government may require as its social basis a class comprised of those not necessarily "most devoted to this manner of governing and the justice at which it aims" (90). A class composed of those of considerable wealth and control over productive assets does not necessarily need a regime of self-government to sustain its lifestyle and wealth-generating pursuits. The interests of those in such a class cannot be ignored, however, if the regime is to be of the kind to which the regime designers and those who have ratified the design aspire—one that interconnects a large sphere of private, acquisitive activity with popular rule and a robust public sector with constraints. The interests of the class forming the social basis of the regime must therefore be taken into account in such a regime and its energy harnessed by an arrangement of institutions that will broaden its interests so that they do not come to dominate the regime and pervert it with respect to the manner of governing and the idea of justice it seeks.

In contrast, the ruling stratum of any regime is comprised of those who *are* devoted to the form of governance and kind of justice the regime seeks to realize and sustain. "The political influence of the ruling stratum reinforces the logic of rule" to make "what otherwise would be a disparate set of people, rules, and institutions into a political whole." In "a popular regime, the ruling stratum will be large in number, perhaps as much as a majority," but it "need not be politically dominant in the sense of controlling the full substance of law and policy." It "rules, at a minimum, in the sense that its conception of political rule and justice is the one given expression in the institutional design of the regime." It is also the essential source of "political justification" of public action when such is needed (Elkin 2006, 90). In short, even a good political regime cannot transcend some form of class politics. There are only partial interests in any regime, even if one stratum of interest extends across a majority of citizens. In that particular instance, class politics and class rule are likely to be "partly disguised" (244). The possible obscurity of class divisions and class politics does not negate the reality that because of partiality there will be contending interests and therefore mixed rule. This is a good thing, for a mixed regime is a moderate regime, and moderation is "a political virtue" because it enables a regime to better contend with the inevitably unattractive happenings in social, economic, and political life (244).

A mixed regime does not mean there will be no class advantage, however. Class advantage is inevitable, but it also is part of what defines and serves the public interest. This is best illustrated by considering the commercial republic and its public interest. In "a fully realized commercial republic . . . the ruling stratum is the middle class" (Elkin 2006, 90). When the middle class is advantaged, it will help to "reduce the danger of factional rule by the propertied" (244). The middle class cannot rule on its own, however. It needs the "cooperation of those who control large-scale productive assets" (244) to sustain a productive economy and achieve the level of economic well-being and quality of life that defines what it is to be middle class, and by extension the conception of the good life to which a commercial republic aspires. Likewise, without at least the acquiescence of the middle class, large-scale asset controllers cannot gain a politically privileged role with proper limits that draw their energy into government and harness their self-interest and ingenuity to sustain a productive economy.

There is, of course, at least one other economic class in a commercial republic, comprised of those who sell their labor and those who are on the very edges of the economy and society—a working class and the poor. There is obvious incongruity in roughly defining such a class in this way, but it serves to highlight the point that social classes are likely to be heterogenous and have fuzzy, semiporous boundaries (Baritz 1989; Samuel 2014). In recent times a near majority of Americans have defined themselves as middle class (47 percent), a small segment as upper-middle class (11 percent), and a larger segment as lower-middle class (29 percent) (Pew Research Center 2015, 14). Hence nearly nine-tenths of Americans see themselves as middle class in some way. Despite the messiness inherent in trying to define socioeconomic classes, there will be classes and class interests in mixed regimes like a commercial republic, and those class interests will only partially overlap. Members of a middle class will share some interests with, but also regard with some antagonism, both an "upper class" of owners of large-scale capital assets and a class of manual laborers and marginalized poor. More to the point, for the theory and practice of political constitution of the commercial republic, a "secure and confident" middle class is vital (Elkin 2006, 243; also see Birdsall 2016). Under the current working constitution, however, the American middle class is neither, with respect to both self-perception and a variety of external indicators (Pew Research Center 2015; Pressman 2007; Samuel 2014; Styhre 2017; Unger 2019). This is where the creation of a fourth branch comes into play.

In addition to its contributions to supporting deliberative lawmaking, shifting and enhancing separation of powers politics, broadening the interests of the propertied, and strengthening civic capacity, a fourth, administrative branch is further justifiable in the theory of the commercial republic because it is the "natural" home in government for the middle class—the ruling class in the mixed regime of the American commercial republic. There was at least a glint of this notion in Hamilton's regime design theorizing. As the American republic developed, political leaders increasingly recognized the economic and political importance of a "middling sort" of professionals, merchants, and related occupations (Aron 2001; Bledstein and Johnston 2001; Stromquist 2006). As members of this nascent middle class slowly but steadily increased their presence in administrative positions in government, there was a mutually reinforcing relationship between an emerging middle class and the first administrative state. Increasing administrative responsibilities associated with national expansion and development enabled expanding lines of professional work like engineering and management. As the administrative state expanded, it was increasingly attractive to those seeking a career that would lead to a middle-class life.

The rise of a second, larger, more authoritative and powerful administrative state intertwined with managerial capitalism cemented the connection but also revealed that a relatively substantial, competent public sector and the services it provides are a vital source of support for sustaining a secure and confident middle class and lifting more people into it through the protection of labor rights and other programs that provide financial stability to those of modest means. The middle class provides the main societal support for a healthy public sector and its active regulation of the market because most members of the middle class "do not have the resources to insulate themselves from a poorly run public sector" (Elkin 2006, 297). A public sector especially unable or resistant to restraining an "investor capitalism" is a particular problem for the middle class, for it makes not only blue-collar but white-collar work less secure in the constant pursuit of enhanced shareholder value (Styhre 2017). This is a fact well demonstrated by the effects of the "financial liberalization" that eliminated several of the primary statutory and administrative underpinnings of financial-services regulation, a key cause of the so-called great recession of 2009 (Arestis 2016; see also Green 2014, 28–32; Kwak 2013).

The relationship between the public sector and the middle class is mutually reinforcing in an even more critical way. The civic majorities that a republic needs to form for effective rule are animated by a public spiritedness in the citizenry of sufficient breadth and depth. Because it is the ruling class in a commercial republic, the middle class's idea of what it means to be public-spirited will not be the exclusive idea, but it will be the predominant one. Hence, civic majorities, when they arise—often shaped and mobilized by political entrepreneurs (Elkin 2006, 234)—will be composed of class coalitions that will nearly always include a considerable contingent of middle-class citizens. This same public spirit that grounds civic majorities is carried into government, certainly by some of those who are elected as legislative representatives and appointed as judges, but to a far greater extent by those selected by merit to fill the administrative positions that dominate government employment. For some time now a particular manifestation of this public spirit has been evident in public, administrative work. It also shows up in the parts of the nonprofit sector that are in an increasingly networked and cooperative relationship with public agencies. Administrative science has captured elements of this public spiritedness in the "public service motivation" construct, which nevertheless remains somewhat murky in its dimensions as well as its antecedents and effects (see Ritz, Brewer, and Neumann 2016 and works cited therein; also Bozeman and Su 2015). No particular precision in conception, measurement, and testing of precursors and consequences is necessary for present purposes, however. Enough is known to be able to state that this public spirit, whatever it is exactly, energizes public work, and public work properly managed reinforces it. All this is primarily a middle-class phenomenon. Public spiritedness expressed in the work of the administrative state can also be damaged or at least diminished when under stress by privatization and other neoliberal marketized distortions of the administrative state (Moynihan 2008; Steen and Rutgers 2011). For that public spiritedness to fully express itself and help shape and bind the regime, therefore, the civil service and the administrative state must be less subordinated to the self-interested political ambitions of those exerting overhead political control and to business with political prerogatives and influence far in excess of that imagined by the regime's designers or safe for a regime aspiring to sustain a republican character.

The deeply ingrained response to the possibility of greater autonomy for administration is the fear of bureaucracy and the insistence that bureaucrats, with all their powers, must be subordinated and made accountable by politics and those who supposedly represent the public will more directly (see chapter 6 for further exposition). Both formal and informal theories of political control of the bureaucracy rarely take the actual values and goals of bureaucrats into account, however, generally just assuming "goal conflict between politicians and bureaucrats" (Meier and O'Toole 2006, 29). The general normative theory of accountability through political control is largely a myth, moreover. It is actually administrative bureaucracy that possesses both an adequate theory of and the primary practical safeguards for accountability (Rubin 2005b). There is thus no loss of accountability in a systemic sense under a more constitutionally independent administrative state so long as the accountability supposedly achieved through political subordination of the bureaucracy is replaced with accountability generated by very public political engagement and argument among constitutional coequals. This happens now under the current working constitution, but in an excruciatingly twisted way, such as when an administrator confronts accountability demands from one political overseer while trying desperately to maintain subservience to another constitutional master (for an illustrative example, see Flynn 2020).

With greater independence and the accountability that comes with having no layers of politicized bureaucracy behind which to hide, responsible decision making in the use of legal authority will be more likely across the constitutive institutions of the regime—and at least marginally less strained. The educative function of government also will be enhanced. While much of the interbranch exchange that would occur with the addition of an administrative fourth branch might be no less contentious than it is now with three branches, the bureaucratic values that an administrative branch brings to the exchange could just as well enrich the interbranch deliberation that the separation of powers is meant to facilitate. Reinforcing the public spiritedness that is prominent in public administration by increasing its constitutional autonomy in the form of a fourth branch also reinforces the support for deliberative lawmaking that a fourth branch is capable of providing. Because deliberative lawmaking is "unlikely to occur without a public spirited citizenry" (Elkin 2006, 153), reinforcement of citizen public spirit through the mutuality of the middle class and public administration increases the chances that lawmaking in the public interest will occur.

Claims about the normative value of a fourth administrative branch resting on the reinforcing linkages across a secure and confident middle class, the presence of a public-spirited citizenry sufficient for republican aspirations, and the administrative state may be a bridge too far for many skeptics. What may be said, for example, about the apparent rise of an "upper-middle class" of knowledge professionals that may be more inclined to align with the propertied than with the public-spirited values of the middle class? Moreover, is it not clear that public bureaucracy and its pathologies are more likely a spirit-breaking prison than a place where public spirit is strengthened and expanded? The first question articulates a genuine worry, but there is no particular reason to conclude that this new knowledge-based upper-middle class is more likely to align with the propertied elite. It is at least equally possible that it would continue to identify as middle class and retain middle-class values and orientation to rule. Because many of these new knowledge professionals are in administrative government, the effect would be to reinforce the interest-broadening effect on the propertied of a constitutional fourth branch. Whatever personal or relational distortions working in a bureaucracy may have, such as its tendency toward exaggerated concern for turf and aggrandizement of personal position and status, the fact remains that public bureaucrats are more "public-regarding," "civic minded," and "efficacious" than the public generally (Meier and O'Toole 2006, 137). It is difficult to see what additional risk there would be to the health and improvement of the regime in the areas of class politics and the necessity of a public-spirited citizenry from the creation of a constitutionally structured fourth administrative branch. There is certainly the possibility of nudging the regime farther along the path toward a fully realized commercial republic by such a move.

CONCLUSION

The ultimate aim of republican constitutional design is to foster a politics that can sustain a vigorous, but limited, popular sovereign that aspires to liberal justice. The peculiar American form of this design—a commercial republic—has strayed from this aim because elements in its original regime design, combined with crucial design adjustments and political-economic developments, have significantly weakened the capacities of the constitutive institutions to maintain a form of interdependence of market and state that keeps the commercial public interest in sight. The primary normative case offered in this chapter for one dramatic, albeit partial, corrective to the current condition of the regime in the form of a constitutionally formalized fourth administrative branch is undeniably hypothetical. The case for the constitutional redesign presented in 1787 was no less hypothetical, however, even if its underlying theory and evidence was ultimately persuasive and to a considerable extent borne out in practice.

Readers will draw their own conclusions regarding the theoretical and evidentiary plausibility of the normative case for a fourth branch. It is worth pointing out, however, that the more provocative elements of the 1787 redesign—the extended republic, separate institutions with distinct but shared powers, property-based political privileges—met with considerable skepticism and even outright opposition. Support emerged for less radical forms of constitutional reconstruction. The case for a fourth branch deserves a similar reality check. The next chapter considers several alternative ways to address the current troubles of the administrative state and the American regime that fall short of radical constitutional redesign. This exploration details how those alternatives diagnose and respond to the troubles of the administrative state in its current condition. The chapter then offers a rejoinder to these alternatives, explaining why they fall short as viable responses to the serious difficulties that enmesh the commercial republic.

5. Alternative and Competing Solutions

The problem that administration generally, or an administrative state specifically, poses for the American constitutional system has always and almost exclusively been defined as the problem of reconciling it with the tripartite system of separate institutions sharing powers. This requires legitimating the unavoidably extensive exercise of governing power by administrative entities staffed by unelected public servants, most of whom are not beholden for their jobs to the latest political winners. Administration must be powerful to be effective, but that power must be restrained to be legitimate, which in turn enhances its effectiveness. Because the regime's design relies on the tripartite separation of powers as a crucial device to both effectuate and restrain power, the question has always been where, and how, does administration fit in that three-branch scheme?

Considerable debate continues to simmer regarding whether the framers failed to address the question adequately, leaving "a hole" in the Constitution "where administration might have been" (Mashaw 2012, 30), or whether "principles of administrative law that emerged from the debates surrounding administration during the framing and ratification of the Constitution can be discerned" (Postell 2017, 30). In an important sense the debate is superfluous because whether the efforts of successive generations of political leaders and prominent thinkers to address the constitutional problem of administration in practice have proceeded with or without the guidance of the framers, the result has been the same. Administration is an unresolved, or at least ill-resolved, constitutional design problem that is "still evident to constitutional lawyers as well as the general public. The crisis of legitimacy has not subsided" (5). One not entirely unreasonable reaction to such claims and the state of affairs they represent, is cynicism. Perpetuating a state of crisis regarding the constitutional legitimacy of an administrative state serves particular interests, both the interests of the powerful whose pecuniary or ideological positions chafe under any significant exercise of administrative power, as well as those who write law journal articles in service to or in affinity with the powerful and their pecuniary or ideological interests. Such cynicism is generally unfair, however, at least with respect to thoughtful members of the public in any walks of life who are genuinely concerned that the design of the American commercial republic in theory and practice is flawed, in trouble, and could be made better.

Hence, it is not only appropriate but imperative to consider other schemes for addressing the problem of administration and an administrative state in the theory and practice of the American republic, whether or not they are explicitly concerned with the republic's commercial character and the nature of the public interest. Far too many such contrivances have emerged over the course of the republic's history, however, and even over just the past century of "self-aware" (Waldo 1984, xi) study about the problem of an administrative state, to be given adequate attention here. Instead, a limited representation of ideas for design and action drawn from public administration and public management studies, and constitutional and administrative law studies, will have to suffice. The schemes considered in this chapter capture some diversity in the definition of the problem as well as in the normative underpinnings for the designs and actions proposed. They represent three roughly distinct categories of theorizing about how to reconcile the administrative state and the Constitution: 1) a rights-oriented, moral and attitudinal approach, 2) a public choice and institutional design approach, 3) and an approach steeped in law. They nevertheless all reflect the dominant thrust of twentieth and twenty-first-century thinking about the Constitution and an administrative state: that constitutional principles or values, and structural arrangements, are largely fixed, and that they boil down to the separation of powers, checks and balances, and similar notions. The conclusion follows that an administrative state has already been successfully adapted to existing constitutional arrangements, or can be (further) adapted theoretically and in practice, to reduce the tensions and lower the dissatisfactions with the reality of modern governance dominated by administration.

SUBORDINATE AUTONOMY AND SEPARATION OF POWERS BALANCE

Several prominent normative theories arising within the public-administration and public-management fields have attempted to reconcile the administrative state with, or adapt it more explicitly to, the separation of powers with the aim of enhancing the effectiveness of both. Two such theories deserve further consideration because they stand as counterpoints to one another and to the case for the necessity and possibility of creating a fourth administrative branch. The first portrays administration as possessing a "subordinate autonomy" within the constitutional system enabling it to act as a "balance wheel" for the institutional rivalries engendered by the separation of powers (Rohr 1986, 181–186; Barth 1993). The second theory envisions incorporating a separation-of-powers dynamic into the administrative state, not so much in legal and structural form but as a managerial and organizational "precept" (Bertelli and Lynn 2006a).

The theory of subordinate autonomy for "the Public Administration" is predicated on the claim that the principal aim of the separation of powers is to "maintain the constitutional balance of powers in support of individual rights." This is the "unity of purpose" for all the major institutions of government (Rohr 1986, 181). Administration is one such institution. Administration, however, "neither constitutes nor heads any branch of government, but is subordinate to all three" (182). Administration must accept this subordination, but that status, along with "exercis[ing] all three powers in a subordinate capacity" enables administration to play a crucial role in promoting and modulating the separation-of-powers dynamic. This role amounts to a judicious balancing, a matter of "choosing which of its constitutional masters" administration will "favor at a given time on a given issue" (182). Again, the idea is that its subordinate place in the constitutional system is exactly what affords administration the capacity and opportunity to tend to the balance-of-power politics that the separation of powers is meant to engender to protect rights. This includes property rights, one of several "regime values" (Rohr 1998, 23–28) that can serve as worthy guides for the balancing effort.

Subordinate autonomy and the balance-wheel metaphor should be regarded as attitudinal positioning far more than as actual strategy prescriptions. They are meant "to encourage administrators and the public to think about administrative behavior in constitutional terms" (Rohr 1986, 182–183) in order to make possible a vision of bureaucrats, however they operate, as "administrative statesmen" (183). Certainly administrators will have substantive policy views and will "use their discretion to favor those policies that they think are most likely in the public interest." But doing so with reference to "constitutional principles" is crucial. The reality and necessity of administration's constitutional subordination "preserves both the instrumental character" of administration and "the autonomy necessary for professionalism." This should reassure the public that administration is "subordinate to the political leadership of the day," as well as "professionally exempt from political interference" (183–184). Among possible "normative models that recognize the realities of life in public bureaucracies" (Barth 1993, 178) that might guide the use of administrative discretion, subordinate autonomy is particularly attractive because it accepts constitutional arrangements as they are and does not seek to impose complicated structures or processes to ensure that administration acts constitutionally.

Nevertheless, "exercising discretion to maintain the balance of powers is a vague concept at best for top-level public administrators who deal with the three branches of government on a regular basis, let alone mid-level careerists who rarely see the head of their own agency" (Barth 1993, 163). This makes professionalism of central importance to any effort to translate the theory into governing practice. Professionalism is "inherent in subordinate autonomy" (177), for it is the source of the prudence and judgment, further refined through practice and experience in exercising multiple powers, that enables administrators to see the sometime clashing, sometime aligning powers in a way that might lead them toward finding a balance. This especially distinguishes administration's constitutional role "in a regime that valorizes ambition" (Newswander 2015, 22). However, professionalism external to administrative agencies and rooted in the learned professions with their distinct forms of knowledge and norms, as well as professionalism that develops within agencies with respect to agency missions, also poses challenges to the attitudinal realization and context-specific actualization of subordinate autonomy and the balance-wheel effect.

The administrative state operates across "an enormous variety of institutional settings" (Barth 1995, 232). The "host of interrelated concepts that define" and distinguish the agencies as institutions within which administrators operate, are "not a neutral factor" in the attitudes and judgments of civil servants. What, then, "does the concept of serving multiple masters through subordinate autonomy mean in different institutional contexts" (233)? To understand how the theory of subordinate autonomy might operate in practice, it is necessary to take account of the particular "institutional values" that weigh on administrator attitudes and judgment. Such institutional values are primarily defined by "agency mission, organizational culture and professionalism" (233), and they create complexities for practicing, or at least orienting attitudes to, subordinate autonomy. For example, although "grounded in statute," (233) agency missions are loose enough to be open to interpretation. How does an administrator, or an agency, determine when serving its mission is compatible with choosing which political master to serve in a particular instance of clashing institutions spurred by the separation of powers? Agency culture is closely related to professional standards, moreover, and there tend to be tensions "between norms and standards . . . of traditional professions and the demands of the governance process" (234). Hence, the "tensions created by membership in a separate profession while serving as a public administrator" can generate "conflict between actions . . . based on adherence to strict professional standards and actions" seemingly compelled by "the political process" (243).

In sum, "the question of where to draw the line and exercise autonomy versus subordination in the midst of competing institutional pressures is an ongoing dilemma for the public administrator. However, this tension also reflects the reality of governance." At best, "autonomy grounded in subordination fosters an attitude that embraces the ambiguity of governance, and will heighten awareness of what it means to practice administrative statesmanship in a government of shared powers" (244). It may provide a constitutional sense of place for those toiling in the nether regions of the administrative state, a comforting ennobling of the administrative state's current plight. Because the "grand prize of contemporary politics" is "the control of the Public Administration" (Rohr 1986, 184), however, it is difficult to see how administrators more consciously embracing subordinate autonomy would do much to alter the reality that administrative agencies are as much pawns in interbranch battles as active agents in those battles. The outcomes, moreover, often enough are that agencies become the receptacles of the blame avoidance moves of self-interested elected officials. Agencies are also the means by which elected officials can feed inducements to business while looking like they didn't, or at least didn't do so to such an excess as to spark the public's ire. Perhaps even more distressing, if the administrative state in its current form is the primary pathway for business influence and the enhancement of business political privilege, administrative agencies actually making choices to favor one political master over another in particular circumstances will do little to introduce balance in separation-of-powers politics in ways that protect rights other than the property rights and political advantages of corporate capitalists. That is not an effect that the progenitors of subordinate autonomy theory seem to have considered—and presumably not one they would find reassuring.

PUBLIC MANAGEMENT INFUSED WITH THE SEPARATION OF POWERS

Rather than an institutional perspective that places the separation of powers external to administration and seeks, by promoting a high-minded attitudinal orientation among administrators, to justify administration engaging with and even harnessing on its own accord the separation of powers to satisfy constitutional values and principles, perhaps it is better to determine how to enhance the institutional capabilities of the administrative state internally by defining professionalism in terms of the separation of powers and building a cadre of administrators on that basis. This is the essence of the proposed enterprise for creating a constitutional public management (Bertelli and Lynn 2006a).

Like the concept of subordinate autonomy, the "concept of managerial responsibility under the separation of powers" (Bertelli and Lynn 2006a, 6), portrays public management "as a *distinctive institution*, with the president, Congress, and judiciary," which is vital to making the separation of powers work to ensure responsible governance under the "Constitution as written" (164, emphasis in original). In contrast to subordinate autonomy, however, this institutionally distinct public management, and the public managers who fill its ranks, do not aim to function as a balance wheel for the constitutional branches. The aim is to fashion public management as a "repository of responsible *legislative* agents" (emphasis added) and "not an unreliable corps of 'administrative statesmen'" (164). The administrative-statesmanship vision of subordinate autonomy requires substantive representation, which creates "in the bureaucracy a secondary legislature, congealing preferences and gaming the other branches." This would ultimately lead to "a doctrine of bureaucratic nullification of acts of Congress," a prospect that is "both dangerous and unnecessary" (137). Instead, under the separation of powers, "representation passes through the political branches and restrains factions." Bureaucrats need only be reliable and responsible agents for carrying out the results of the political contestation and cooperation that emerge from the separation of powers. In so doing, they will link law and policy design, and implementation, to popular will (137).

Public management's contribution "in a republican sense" to responsible government "turns on the character of public servants" and therefore the proper design of "the personnel function" is the core challenge (164). This necessitates the development of a "precept of managerial responsibility" that addresses "the principal challenge of an administrative state that Madison and the framers did not fully anticipate: how to get administrators" to "credibly commit to gathering and using information and making policy" so that "legislators could trust them with policy choice because they would know that though circumstances might change, administrators will act in a reliable way when adjusting to new or novel circumstances" (Bertelli and Lynn 2006b, 42). This approach requires the design of a "mechanism" (Bertelli and Lynn 2006a, 125) that can solve "the central problems of administration by unelected bureaucrats in our constitutional system: the delegation of authority and the political control of the bureaucracy" (103–104). The approach draws on the original constitutional debates, traditional public-administration treatments of the separation of powers challenges, administrative law, and social-choice theory to derive the mechanism, centered on the personnel function, which is designed in accordance with a precept of managerial responsibility.

A set of four "axioms of responsibility" derived from the Constitution comprise the precept. The four elements—judgment, balance, rationality, and accountability—"are the most basic that can be incontestably related to the constitutional scheme" (Bertelli and Lynn 2006a, 141). Judgment is the overarching element, and is "synonymous with autonomy or discretion" (142). The constitutional system has no choice but to entrust unelected public servants with discretion, so the system must ensure that such discretion is used judiciously. Good judgment in the use of discretion will consist of balance, which may take many forms, including balancing "collective justice," which reflects groups interests, and "individual justice" (143). However, the "public manager is not obliged to weigh in the balance interests that are neither represented in nor of concern to the face-to-face community. Their purview is circumscribed by legislative and judicial mandate" (144). In other words, the introduction by administrators of their own interests or sense of values is out of bounds, but so are interests not already represented by organized actors. The public interest defined as maintaining the constitutive institutions of the regime that provide for a politics of self-limitation is not within the ambit of administrator concern. Judgment must also be guided by rationality, which means taking "due regard for means-ends relationships" (145). It is reasoned decision making, which includes careful gathering of relevant facts and deliberation on them.

Finally, accountability "is the entire purpose of public management as an institution among the separate powers." By realizing "high levels of accountability over time . . . , the administrative state becomes a reliable pool of agents for congressional delegation and judicial deference," both of which lessen the encroachments of the legislature and the judiciary on the executive branch (Bertelli and Lynn 2006a, 146). Hence, somewhat paradoxically, while primarily a body of *legislative* agents, public management's principal role in the separation-of-powers dynamic helps the executive branch resist the encroachments of the other two branches. Such limitation of encroachment will come about because those other branches trust public managers to be faithful agents. What happens when presidential interpretations of law and judicial decisions, and instructions to administrators, contradict those of the other branches is left unaddressed in the theory, but presumably such conflicts will be tackled in the high-level clash of separate institutions sharing powers.

The precept defines "normative standards of action" that "should be invoked as a matter of course at every level of executive government in which office holders perform managerial roles" (Bertelli and Lynn 2006a, 147). As the description of the theory just sketched out suggests, the concern is with avoiding any external normative guides for or controls on public managers not grounded in separation-of-powers principles. The theory relies on a personnel function that selects on those principles to create that pool of responsible and reliable agents of the law as enacted by the legislature. Execution of the personnel mechanism will select in, and select out, in ways that ensure that public managers do not presume that they know best how to rule, are not selfish or factionally biased, or behave in ways not responsive to political superiors and hence not dependent ultimately on popular will.

This "positive theory of public management in the separation of powers" (Bertelli and Lynn 2006a, 165) does not offer any insight into the strategies that would be necessary to design the personnel mechanism and implement it through concrete reforms of the administrative state. That is because it is offered as "a normative ideal. As such, its fulfillment will not result from the usual tâtonnement processes and interest-group influence characteristic of our constitutional scheme. Its use as a means for resolving the constitutional dilemma of public management will require affirmative action by all those involved in promoting the success of democratic public management" (Bertelli and Lynn 2006b, 49). It is principally concerned with combatting notions that public administration might still function as a headless fourth branch "pretending to an autonomy that is above the law." Its underlying concern is with the legitimacy of the unelected public service, which can only be realized within the confines of "the Constitution's separation of powers" (Bertelli and Lynn 2006a, 166).

This theory, turning on a precept of managerial responsibility derived from a careful reading of the Madisonian design for a separation of powers, is rooted in impressively rich analysis and insight into the critical role of the personnel function, and it is inspiring in the normative ideal it articulates. That ideal is to create "a trusted cadre of administrators" who will be "the linchpin of constitutional public administration." They will fulfill that institutional function because they are trusted by their constitutional superiors to carry out "those laws enacted through the pulling and hauling among political elites," and will do so in a way that is neither servile to any particular interest nor wholly independent of all of them (Bertelli and Lynn 2006a, 109).

From the perspective of a concern with the distorting effects of business privilege, and market-state relations generally, which lie at the heart of a commercial republic, this scheme for responsible public management makes sense to the extent that administrative decisions and actions that prove to be biased in favor of business are the result of faithless or irresponsible agents. However, what if the administrative agents are faithful to the laws enacted, or are made responsible through deployment of the precept, but factional bias lies in the design of the laws themselves, or even in the design and function of the working constitution more generally? Would it be responsible for the agents to refuse to implement those laws or use their discretion to somehow reduce the bias? It is difficult to see how agents following the axioms of the precept in this situation would do anything other than perpetuate such factional bias in the execution of the laws or, resisting that bias, act in ways that uncomfortably approach "nullification of acts of Congress" (Bertelli and Lynn 2006a, 137).

Would the responsible agents be able to bring to bear on the lawmaking process the information they gather and use for their own purposes in implementation? The theory does not speak directly to the role of these responsible agents in the lawmaking process, although its principal-agent foundation implies that such activity would be out of bounds. In a regime in which business political privileges and limits on them are of central concern, a constitutional theory of public administration that hardly acknowledges that public administrators may have something to say on those matters, derived from their experience in carrying out the law, seems seriously deficient. This seems particularly so if the extent of and limits on business political influence are left to the "pulling and hauling among political elites." That is precisely the problem with the separation of powers in the current incarnation of the commercial republic.

More generally, the vision for bringing the precept and thus a constitutional public administration into operation requires a politics—call it a constitutional politics—that goes beyond the "processes and interest group influence characteristic of our constitutional scheme" (Bertelli and Lynn 2006b, 49). The theory ascribes no role for public administration in this constitutional politics. It is relegated to an instrumental role within the confines of the pluralist politics of the separation of powers. While masterly in its synthesis of several lines of inquiry and ambitious in its theorizing, therefore, this design for constitutional public administration falls short in a very critical way. As a species of pluralist constitutional theory, it mistakes a part of the regime design for the whole—and mistakes Madison for a pluralist as well. There is widespread focus in pluralist theory on the separation of powers as the essence of Madison's design, one that, if the institutions function in accord with their allocated powers, creates a kind of "self-regulating system" (Elkin 2006, 270). Madison's design, including not just the separation of powers but the extended republic and other elements, was not just a design to bring competing interests into government and enable them to self-regulate. Madison understood that no regime design could eliminate self-interest or dispense with factional spirit, so the aim was to restrain, filter, control, and harness these forces, not simply to design an arena for factional contestation. Government "is to control interests, not be controlled by them," meaning that the inevitable clash of interests "should be the subject of lawmaking, not a description of how it should work." Controlling the effects of faction has in particular "the purpose of freeing lawmaking to serve the public interest" (Elkin 2006, 30).

The only significant difference between the theory of subordinate autonomy and the precept of public management is that the former permits, even encourages, administrators to bring their own perspectives on constitutional values and principles to bear on conflicts engendered by the separation of powers, while the latter regards such perspectives as extra-constitutional, therefore dangerous, and deploys institutional design to expunge the possibility. Designs for a constitutional public administration that consider only how an administrative state fits into and might possibly enhance the separation of powers fails to follow the example of Madison and other founders, that thinking constitutionally means thinking about the whole regime, what its complex parts should and can be, and how they can best be fit together. Administration is such a part of the regime—and a major one. To consider it only in relation to one other part of the design is to forego the opportunity to consider how a civil service and an administrative state fit into and contribute to the functioning of the commercial republic as a whole and how to nudge that regime design closer to the realization of its aspiration to liberal justice.

Perhaps new and grand theorizing about the role of administration in the whole regime is not necessary, however. That might be so because the administrative state has already been well fit into the regime, and it is only a matter of keeping that arrangement in good repair. Such is a reasonable inference that may be drawn from constitutional-law and administrative-law theory and practice aimed at the problem of the administrative state.

THE ADMINISTRATIVE CONSTITUTION

A prominent position in modern administrative law is that a securely constitutionalized fourth branch already exists. The statutes, judicial rulings, and executive decisions that established the second administrative state and over time fleshed out its structure and operating processes created a distinct governmental institution and imbued it with constitutional values, norms, and internal devices that guide and restrain the exercise of administrative power in the same way that the Constitution guides and restrains the exercise of public power more generally. This "administrative constitution" (Mashaw 2012) or "administrative constitutionalism" (Eskridge and Ferejohn 2010, chap. 1–3; Metzger 2013) is not the higher law of the Constitution itself, but akin to an "unwritten constitution," much like the British constitution (Bremer 2015). It has evolved "to accommodate the administrative state, filling the Constitution's silence" about administration with "a body of seemingly disparate rules that extends a uniform and recognizable set of substantive constitutional values into the modern administrative context" (1272). This "small 'c' constitution" is primarily comprised of "superstatutes" like the Administrative Procedure Act and has not only transcended the "libertarian bias" of the original Constitution's negative-rights orientation, but has "transformed our polity into a governance structure that transcends the original Constitution" (Eskridge and Ferejohn 2010, 5, 7, 10). In its most expansive conception, this administratively centered republic of statutes is even more encouraging from a republican regime design perspective because it is both based on and fosters "republican deliberation." The amendment process in Article V is emblematic of such deliberation in the original Constitution, but in America's republic of statutes, republican deliberation over fundamental commitments has migrated, relatively speaking, away from Constitutionalism and toward legislative and administrative constitutionalism" (16).

The case for an already extant fourth administrative branch fully legitimated and properly harnessed to ensure that administrative power is used in service to liberal justice is impressive. It has roots that go deeper than the rise of the second administrative state (Mashaw 2012), and it was shaped as much by "administrative practice" as by "congressional statute and executive leadership" (313). This "internal law of administration" (313), or accumulation of "agency conventions" (Bremer 2015, 57–59) showcases how administration and an administrative state in its normal operations is a constitutive institution of the regime. Administrative constitutionalism is also dynamic in ways that overcome the rigidities of the higher law Constitution (Eskridge and Ferejohn 2010, 65–68, 270–290). Much of that dynamism is generated within administrative agencies and through agency interactions with legislatures and courts. This characteristic of the administrative constitution suggests that the distinct fourth branch that emerged with administrative constitutionalism is consistent with key points in the normative case for a structurally constitutionalized fourth branch. First, the administrative interpretation of statutes and related constitutional principles is legitimate and on a relatively equal plane with at least two of the constitutional branches. Second, such interpretation and the institutional interaction it generates is grounded in administration's experiencing and informing function and expertise. Third, this relatively coequal interpretive standing for administration generates a robust separation-of-powers politics of contestation, deliberation, and cooperation.

There are, however, worries about the nature and performance of the administrative state under administrative constitutionalism, specifically with respect to what should be the central concern of commercial republican regime design in theory and practice. That central concern, again, encompasses the market-state relationship, the privileged position of business, and the evolution of the second administrative state into a conduit for further enhancing business political advantages to an extent that weakens institutional arrangements intended to promote sustained concern for the public interest. Attention to market-state relations and the political advantages that business enjoys is limited in the theory of administrative constitutionalism. The case of administrative constitutionalism's transformation of the public-interest meaning of the Sherman Anti-Trust Act of 1890 illustrates the positives and negatives of an "unwritten" fourth branch.

"As amended and expanded, the Sherman Act is an important foundation of America's constitution of the market" (Eskridge and Ferejohn 2010, 120). The act came into force relatively early in the nation's struggle to reconstruct the political economy and the administrative state in response to the destructive competition of unrestrained industrial capitalism. It helped establish the "enduring principle" of the corporate-liberal reconstruction of the regime, "that the government is responsible for the operation of a 'competitive market'" (121). The sponsors of the Sherman Act understood government responsibility for the operation of a competitive market to mean the "protection of diffused industry structures and of small competitors" (121). Within twenty years of the Sherman Act's appearance, however, the emerging corporate-liberal consensus was well on its way to pushing the concrete meaning of the public interest regarding government assurance of a competitive market toward corporate consolidation. Much of the continued evolution of the political economy along these lines took place within the administrative state, evident in the transformation of the Sherman Act's "civic republican" norm promoting a "republic of small producers" into a "republic free of market bottlenecks" through administrative and legislative small "c" constitutionalism (123–145). The key and most dramatic transformation of the public-interest meaning of market competition was, however, the emergence and legitimation of "maximization of consumer welfare" as the central norm guiding the government's exercise of its responsibilities with respect to the market. This transformation brought with it "tolerance for a great deal of market concentration, to the extent that concentration is consistent with welfare maximization" (121). The problem has become, through this administrative and legislative constitutionalism since 1970, that market concentration is now by definition consumer welfare maximizing.

The story of the transformation in Sherman Act interpretation into a "republic of consumers" (Eskridge and Ferejohn 2010, 145) through administrative constitutionalism is the story of the emergence of new economic theories in the academy regarding the nature of competition and market efficiency, and the migration, or importation, of those ideas into key federal administrative agencies, particularly the Department of Justice (see also Eisner 1991; Wu 2018, chap. 4 and 6). That emergent "administrative constitutionalism viewed government policy as often part of the bottleneck" holding back consumer-welfare maximization defined primarily as price competition and "approached business concentration less skeptically." The new and increasingly well-ensconced norm, "came from academic economists, public intellectuals, and voters' intuitions," the latter presumed to have been expressed through the election of presidents and legislators advocating deregulation, suggesting public-opinion ratification of the new conception of market competition. After taking "root in the Department of Justice" the "ideas spread to the other branches" (Eskridge and Ferejohn 2010, 151). Reinterpretation of the Sherman Act's "public-regarding purpose" is consistent with other cases demonstrating that "*few* of the fundamental institutions, principles, and policies of our republic should be hard-wired into the impossible-to-change Constitution" (122, emphasis in original). The public-regarding purpose evolved under administrative constitutionalism "to the notion that democracy requires maximizing consumer satisfaction." It reflects a shift in "emphasis as to what constitutes economic justice" from "justice to competitors, who invest their money and sweat to build their businesses, toward a greater focus on justice to consumers, who deserve a fair price and participation in the bounty of America's market economy." It also reflects a shift in "what gives government its legitimacy" toward "government providing citizens security to ensure their flourishing through free choices" (122).

Has the transformation of the public-regarding purpose of the Sherman Act through administrative constitutionalism produced these substantive outcomes of greater consumer participation in the market's bounty and citizen flourishing through greater free choice? The account purposely sidesteps the question, noting only that "many experts . . . dissent" from the dominant economics orientation of antitrust regulation in the Department of Justice as "excessively deregulatory," and "most experts lament" recent instances of the "collapse of antitrust enforcement" (Eskridge and Ferejohn 2010, 158; see the identification of such experts in Wu 2018, chap. 6). Evidence regarding the substantive outcomes is not favorable to the administrative constitutional reinterpretation of the Sherman Act, however. Economic concentration today rivals the Gilded Age (Grullon et al. 2015, cited in Wu 2018, 153). Welfare effects external to price competition and the market as a whole, such as "the 'dynamic' costs of monopoly, like stagnation or stalled innovation" (Wu 2018, 90), and the political effects of the concentration of economic power, have left many citizens distinctly dissatisfied with their supposed economic security from market concentration and what now are frequently phantom consumer choices (chap. 7).

Law and policy changes do not always succeed, of course, even through the most structurally fundamental and legitimate form of Article V constitutional change. Because institutional design and process effects are always central to matters of regime design and possible redesign, it is important to assess the transformation of the public-regarding purpose of the Sherman Act through administrative constitutionalism on the alternative plane of political legitimacy. Based on the deliberation-centered model at the center of the defense of administrative constitutionalism, the sweeping transformation of market-state relations with respect to the organizational structures of the market was only partially legitimate. The administrative efforts were "a thoughtful and well-publicized response to unanticipated statutory problems" and were "subject to judicial review under circumstances where the substantive grounds . . . were thoroughly examined." However, "in light of . . . economic support for an anticoncentration norm, and the fact that Congress has supported the norm in major antitrust statutes, the deliberation [was] insufficient" to legitimate "such a policy shift in a democracy" (Eskridge and Ferejohn 2010, 161).

The antitrust, antimonopoly story thus raises serious questions about the sufficiency of an unwritten administrative constitution as the basis for establishing the legitimacy and safety of a functional fourth branch. It is also raises doubts, however, about the case for a "written" constitutional fourth branch because the characteristics and actions that the administrative entities exhibited in the saga of the antitrust revolution seem to reflect the distinct features and contributions of an administrative state to liberal-democratic governance on which the constitutional fourth-branch case relies. In the antitrust case, the relevant agencies monitored their environment for and learned from advancements in technical and scientific knowledge, which they then incorporated into interpretation and implementation of the law. This learning then "spread to the other branches," although the extent to which that diffusion extended beyond the judiciary, which was also engaged in its own typical monitoring and learning, is unclear. Both the president and Congress adopted, or at least acquiesced in, the new, narrower price-based consumer-welfare antitrust constitutional norm. The critique of the public deliberative dimension of the transformation suggests, however, the inadequacies, or even the absence, of any Department of Justice effort to encourage, and engage in, debate and deliberation that exposed the proposed transformation to sufficient public scrutiny. This is so especially with respect to Congress and the importance of administrative agencies helping Congress deliberate about potential statutory change in light of what administration has learned. Since the start of the effort to transform the public-regarding purpose of the Sherman Act, Congress has put into law only one significant modification of antitrust law. The Hart-Scott-Rodino Antitrust Improvements Act of 1976 (Public Law 94–435) added a fairly modest requirement in the form of premerger public notification. In important respects the Department of Justice tried to discourage Congress from engaging in more searching deliberation about the concrete meaning of public interest regarding market competition.

Even more worrisome in the antitrust saga is the dark side of the agency monitoring, learning, and legal purpose reinterpretation effort. The agencies involved, especially the Department of Justice, seemed all too susceptible to what was essentially ideological capture given that the consumer-welfare transformation of antitrust law was part of the conservative attack on liberal judicial activism (Wu 2018, 91). More to the point, the convergence of new tools from economic science with the ideologically rooted promotion of so-called judicial restraint posed a significant external threat to the established antitrust philosophy and operations of the Justice Department. New appointees, particularly President Reagan's first assistant attorney general for the Antitrust Division, William F. Baxter, Jr., brought the consumer-welfare orientation, economic-analysis tools, and philosophy into the department. These key actors successfully altered "organizational frames"—the constructs through which bureaucratic organizations filter and interpret information. A shift in organizational frames results in changed organizational routines, where the cognition associated with new organizational technologies and ideologies become embedded. Organizational frames and "knowledge-rich organizational routines" become self-reinforcing, making public bureaucracies resistant to change even when new monitoring and experience suggest that reality is deviating from the existing organizational frames and the information embedded in routines (Eden 2004, 51–60). Worse, the now-dominant consumer-welfare "paradigm" in antitrust established through the administrative constitutionalism of antitrust law and policy stands as a significant barrier to the promotion of open public debate within and across the constitutional branches as new information and new learning about the effects of law and policy transformation continue to emerge. Instead, the "righteous and self-restrained" (Wu 2018, 91) paradigm is constantly defended against the "antiquated and economically misguided" proposals of reformers (Delrahim 2019, 3).

It is certainly possible that under the existing administrative constitutionalism, new appointees and new career staff might bring a new paradigm for antitrust, or a return to the more traditional anticoncentration norm, to the Department of Justice and change organizational frames in the same way that the consumer-welfare conception of antitrust won the day. Moreover, under a constitutionally structured fourth branch, a Department of Justice might still lock in a paradigm of antitrust that is most favorable to corporate interests. The key difference is that under a constitutionally structured fourth branch, the other constitutive institutions have an incentive to combat a lack of transparency and openness to public scrutiny in administration, as they contend with it in the same way they wrestle with one another under the separation of powers. In contrast, under the current form of administrative constitutionalism, administration is still subordinate and subject to attempts at control and manipulation to serve the interests of the other branches. Although the battles among them to exert control of administration may neutralize much of their respective control efforts, it is still in the interest of each of them to make administration less transparent and less subject to wider public scrutiny to protect their efforts at control and manipulation of the administrative process. The evidence suggests that this is particularly true of the presidency.

The key strength claimed for the administrative constitution is its combination of "transsubstantive" components. These place "constraints on agency process to ensure reasoned and fair decision making," and include "internal checks and balances, judicial oversight, and transparency." Through this combination of features "the administrative constitution plays a dual role: it constrains administrative action in various ways, and, as a result, it legitimates that action" (Sohoni 2016, 934; see also Michaels 2017, 59–75). A prominent example of an internal structural constraint is the separation of an agency's "rule-making and adjudicative functions" and its "investigation and enforcement functions" (Sohoni 2016, 939). A professionalized career cadre in administration helps restrain "hyperpartisan interests" from breaking through legal boundaries to achieve their policy objectives (940). There is, however, a growing concern about a pronounced weakening of the elements of the administrative constitution that keep the administrative state within bounds. The administrative constitution is in danger of being "exiled," as its "basic constraints" on the administrative state "have become attenuated" (927).

The transsubstantive elements of the administrative constitution are breaking down, or being overridden, as existing "loopholes" and "exceptions" open up or new ones are created in the name of flexibility. This is exactly the sort of manipulation of the administrative process by the political branches, the presidency especially, alluded to above. It also reflects the accumulated features of the "policy state" (Orren and Skowronek 2017). Particularly in the form of waivers and delays in enforcement, these developments are increasingly creating administrative action that is "procedurally unfettered and unchecked" (Sohoni 2016, 944). There is a mounting body of "unreviewable agency decisions made by unconfirmed acting agency heads or unconfirmed presidential aides" (944). Hence, the Senate check on the appointment power and the external checks triggered by formal administrative action are increasingly marginalized.

The capacity of the administrative constitution to force agencies to publicly provide good reasons—the legal, technical, and value substance behind their decisions—has also diminished. Political appointees at the heads of agencies are often particularly keen to obscure the political character of their decisions behind a legal facade—often leading to tortured legal reasoning. Administrative action is inescapably political, however. Politically appointed agency heads who make decisions on the basis of overtly political considerations should have the courage of their convictions. Instead, they too often attempt to hide the political roots of rulemaking, enforcement, and other actions behind the legal-process character of administrative constitutionalism. These attempts take the form of superficially legal rationales, some embarrassingly inept, that degrade both law and politics and pose increasing threats to administrative legitimacy and thus to administrative law generally.

A final form of erosion in administrative constitutionalism is regulation in the form of negotiated deals, epitomized by the design and implementation of the Toxic Asset Relief Program (TARP), and to a more limited extent the broad trade policymaking authority granted to the president. Such deals look like a fait accompli, with "no notice to the public or opportunity to comment," and "little in the way of contemporaneous explanation or justification" offered (Sohoni 2016, 957). In the case of TARP, the lack of transparency allowed corporate lobbying to significantly skew the distribution of bailout support (Blau, Brough, and Thomas 2013). Similar effects emerged in the "$669 billion Paycheck Protection Program," at the time "the U.S. government's largest coronavirus relief operation" (Niquette 2020). In the case of trade, the effects are more far reaching. Typically "courts will not review the reasoning behind a threshold determination made by the President, such as the existence of a national emergency, or the fact-finding involved in arriving at that determination, they will closely review whether the action taken in response bears a reasonable relationship to that determination." This is a conclusion, however, that courts almost always reach (Lewis 2016, 13). All of this suggests at least a "partial unraveling of administrative constitutional norms" (Sohoni 2016, 963).

Of particular concern is that these developments are feeding the aggrandizement of executive power, but they do not seem to be stimulating reaction and engagement from the other constitutional branches. The developments may in part reflect congressional dysfunction, as well as a genuine concern that the complexities of twenty-first-century governance demand a less-restrained executive. Nevertheless, the "political branches have not been openly debating or embracing some new set of principles for how the regulatory state should be governed. Nor does it appear that the courts and civil society are actively involved with the political branches in a cooperative enterprise of quasi-constitutional norm-articulation in administrative law" (Sohoni 2016, 968). At bottom, "the whole project of administrative law has become allied with an unappealing picture of overweening, tyrannical federal regulation—a picture that now has a powerful, unhealthy hold on the American psychology" (972). On these two counts, the tripartite separation of powers is failing to fulfill its design purposes.

There are many contributing factors to these developments indicating that an unwritten administrative constitution is weakening as a sufficient foundation for and constraint on an institutionally distinct fourth branch. From the point of view of the evolution of the commercial republic, however, one especially critical factor is the failure of the administrative separation of powers and other features of the administrative constitution to inhibit the privatization movement, broadly defined (Michaels 2017, 106). Privatization has been a key driver of the undercutting of administrative constitutional norms (Rosenbloom and Piotrowski 2005). This is not entirely surprising. Some of the transsubstantive features of the administrative constitution—procedural safeguards, the opportunity to weigh in on, and even sue to prevent, administrative action—have enhanced business influence because the resources that business can bring to bear enable it to exploit those features to a far greater extent than other interests (Bagley 2019, 391–394). Existing business privilege has thus been magnified in important respects by such features within the regulatory state. The privatization drive was possible because of a confluence of economic and political conditions, including a widespread concern about the economic cost and impact on government and the economy of the second administrative state—a concern partly driven by business advocacy (Michaels 2017, 85–98). Key to the privatization drive escaping the constraints imposed by the administrative constitution, however, was its success in turning the transsubstantive elements of administrative constitutionalism against the administrative constitution itself. Outsourcing and contracting in their various forms looked like neutral, business-like improvements that saved money and reduced the drag of complex administrative rules and procedures (Michaels 2017, chap. 5, esp. 126–130). Privatized government would function outside all those rules while still being watched by elected representatives and skilled civil servants.

Privatization writ large has been central to the lowering of the guardrails formed by administrative constitutionalism's transsubstantive components, however. The unwritten fourth branch has been weakened constitutionally precisely so that business can exploit what remains of the administrative state. The administrative constitution has not strayed into exile, it has been driven out by a business- and market-dominated movement. Whether a nonfactional majority of the electorate subsequently endorsed that movement's law and policy designs is dubious (Eskridge and Ferejohn 2010, 161). Although it may not amount to a "constitutional coup" (Michaels 2017), business control of the administrative state through the privatization endeavor certainly appears to serve interests far narrower than, if not entirely in opposition to, the general interest.

One answer to the weaknesses of the administrative constitution is a more radical reinterpretation of constitutional doctrine that establishes the administrative state as constitutionally obligatory. This argument rests on the premise that congressional delegation of power, to the executive branch generally and often to administrative agencies specifically, to interpret and carry out statutory law is constitutionally settled. It is more than just permissible, it is required, to fulfill government's constitutional duty to act (Metzger 2017, 87–95). From a constitutional and administrative-law perspective, such a sweeping reversal of long-standing doctrine and debates about delegation might obviate the need for the creation of a constitutionally formal fourth administrative branch. The approach, however, is entirely focused on sharply changing the interpretive direction of constitutional law. It lacks a "meta-theory for evaluating when changes in the constitutional regime of such potential scope and consequence are warranted" (Sohoni 2017, 25). It also relies almost exclusively on the persuasiveness of the argument, offering no perspective on what changes in the separate institutions sharing powers might be necessary to change their incentives so that they embrace the change in interpretive direction and accept that delegation is obligatory. Hence the reigning construct of an "unwritten" administrative constitution and the ways in which it might be reinforced is the primary target of those who seek to rectify, or at least ameliorate, the distressing conditions of administrative constitutionalism and the administrative state.

There are a number of modest reform proposals for addressing the corroding effects of privatization on the administrative state, such as reforming the federal civil service, improving the "multi-sector workforce," and a strong push to "re-professionalize government" (Verkuil 2017; see also Michaels 2017, 205–218). The most probing recent effort to rescue administrative constitutionalism constructs a "custodial model" akin to "the old balance-of-power geostrategic arrangements." In this model the constitutional branches "work together . . . to create and maintain rough parity among administrative actors and work to prevent the rise of administrative hegemonies that threaten the stability or order" in the administrative state. These potential hegemonies may be one of the constitutional branches—or may lurk within the administrative state. The key is that the coequal constitutional branches will ensure "truly rivalrous engagement" in the administrative state "even at the expense of advancing their own parochial interests" (Michaels 2017, 175).

The first and best place for this constitutional custodialism to develop is the judiciary, which does not face quite the same powerful incentives to control and manipulate the administrative state for institutionally parochial interests. This nevertheless still requires courts to develop a "workable jurisprudence" that can "deter and punish efforts to circumvent or weaken the administrative separation of powers" (Michaels 2017, 179). This workable jurisprudence will consist, among other things, of "new, process-perfecting tools" of judicial analysis along with either policing "administrative outcomes" or insisting more generally on "an administrative decision making framework that is more rivalrous, heterogenous, and inclusive" (200). It is unclear what would prompt the courts to adopt this more custodial orientation to the administrative state and develop the workable jurisprudence that actuates judicial custodialism. It depends on the "intuition, disposition, and practice" that make courts "already inclined to act in ways that promote a well-functioning administrative separation of powers" (202). That the courts allowed the dismantling of the existing administrative separation of powers via privatization raises serious questions about the vigor of this judicial inclination.

The question of what would prompt the president and Congress to embrace custodialism is even harder to answer. Part of the answer is that it is in the interests of both the president and Congress to do something about an administrative state that is in such serious disrepair. The key action they would need to take consists of "a set of legislative reforms to reverse the privatization agenda" (Michaels 2017, 202), restore and enhance the quality of the civil service, and "strengthen civil society" through the ways that the administrative state operates (218–230). Yet the strategy for realizing "legislative custodialism," given the incentives and ingrained practices of the political branches to control the administrative state for their parochial purposes, amounts to "nudging and obligating" the political branches to shift to a custodial orientation, with pressure from the courts (203).

The case for constitutional custodialism is compelling, and the envisioned outcome in the form of a constitutionally well-anchored administrative state without the need for fundamental structural change is enticing. Implicit within this model is that by reinvigorating and even expanding the administrative separation of powers, which turns on the rivalry of interests, business privilege within and through the administrative state will be kept in reasonable bounds. The nature of the market-state relationship, and reliance on major holders of productive capital as the social basis of the regime, might even be enhanced over previous versions of the working constitution. Getting the constitutional branches to take a custodial position with respect to the decidedly subordinate civil service and administrative state more generally, however, requires "nothing short of an administrative moon shot." If it is such a long shot to realize the constitutional custodialism that will achieve a new and more well-entrenched form of the administrative separation of power, why not aim even higher and farther and consider raising the status of administration to constitutional coequal? That would not only let the rivalries, deliberation, and cooperation unfold on that higher plane but also bring with it other regime design improvements beyond the separation of powers. In other words, there is nothing so outrageous about considering the question of how to raise administration to the status of a fourth branch, or at least to think about the possibility as an exercise in the design of a whole regime, that would place it radically outside the wide field of ongoing debate about the nature of the American regime, the administrative state, and the theory and practice of a commercial republic.

The fourth-branch idea is not any more impractical than schemes that require the major constitutive institutions of the regime to change their relations with one another and the administrative state without giving much thought to how to adjust the incentives that the institutions face, especially those that might prompt them to alter their regard for and approach to interacting with one another. An approach centered on a major structural change at least offers an argument for how it might produce a change in institutional incentives and thus a change in the dynamics of institutional interactions. It offers even more, however, by showing that any consideration of the problem of administration and an administrative state in the American constitutional system must take account of the design of the whole regime and its political and moral aspirations.

CONCLUSION

It may make sense to narrowly focus any effort aimed at constitutionalizing an administrative state on the existing structure of governmental institutions. The most obvious feature of that structure is a set of institutions with separate but overlapping powers. There is good evidence that the basics of an administrative structure are already delineated in the Constitution (Emerson 2021). Yet the Constitution does not provide for a separate administrative branch. Even if, moreover, successive versions of the working constitution built on the existing basics of constitutional structure for administration explicitly developed in ways intended to fit administration into the larger governmental structure and incorporate its essential character into the arrangements for checking and balancing interests, administration's fit within the tripartite scheme remains unsettled. It is a source of ongoing frustration and frequent contestation for many theorists and practitioners alike.

This unsettled condition became far more dramatic with the emergence of the second administrative state, which, in addition to its fusion of quasi-powers in various combinations, made it obvious that the administrative state is a constitutive institution of the regime in its own right. Administration in the form of an administrative state shapes aims and purposes, participates in deliberation on the nature of the public interest, and affects social and political relations in many forms, especially that between market and state. This continues to generate considerable friction with political treatment of administration as exclusively instrumental—and constitutionally and politically subordinate. It is no surprise, therefore, that many schemes have developed to legitimate administration and an administrative state's current place within the regime, or to tinker with its structure and role, both of which are aimed at addressing the fit and tensions with the tripartite scheme. The problems with such schemes, represented by the examples this chapter has examined, are threefold.

First, perhaps for necessary theoretical simplification, the schemes reduce the separation of powers to a matter of balancing institutional rivalry, or worse, balancing rival societal interests. The purpose of the separation of powers is not to reproduce factional strife institutionally or to enable factional rivalry to work itself out. Separation of powers is meant to enable governing by providing each institution with enough independence that it could defend against encroachments by the others, particularly if the others had fallen under the sway of faction, but not so much independence that any one institution could govern on its own. If the extended republic and the design of representation had done their work, factional government would be a residual threat that the separation of powers would then restrain and control. More so, however, if functioning properly, the separation of powers should give the occupants of the primary institutions enough relief from the threat of faction to allow them to articulate their particular perspectives on the meaning of the public interest, drawn from their distinct institutional roles and purposes. To get any governing done, they must cooperate to arrive at a concrete meaning of the public interest acceptable to all. If it were to work as well as could be expected, the separation of powers would help increase the likelihood that civic majorities would form by providing concrete lessons for citizens on what qualities might make representatives susceptible to having their interests broadened toward some meaningful conception of the public interest. Normative theories that aim to constitutionalize an administrative state by fitting it into the separation of powers and defending it as helping facilitate the functioning of interinstitutional rivalry, or redesigning it to inculcate an appreciation for and commitment to carrying out the results of such rivalry, or recreating within its structures and processes such rivalry, fall short of capturing the broader regime design purposes of the separation of powers.

Is it necessary to consider those broader regime design aims to better fit administration within the separation of powers given its explicit subordinate status? Perhaps not. Why forego the opportunity, however, to consider normative theorizing about the place of an administrative state in the American commercial republic in a form that *can* take account of those broader design aims?

Second, to a greater or lesser extent, schemes to constitutionalize public administration, either by defending it as constitutional in its current form, or by proposing design adjustments that better reconcile it to the constitutional system, rarely acknowledge, let alone confront the reality that it is a commercial republic the schemes are dealing with. That requires recognizing that the market plays a critical role in regime design, that relations between market and state are thus of central concern, and questions about the nature and extent of the political prerogatives of the holders of productive assets must be confronted. To ignore the role of administration in such central regime design matters has the potential to produce theorizing that may shore up one weakness only to perpetuate design deficiencies that have far greater potential to severely weaken the regime.

The third and last point is an extension of the first two. A focus on constitutionalizing public administration and an administrative state by justifying it as consistent with, or adjusting it to better fit with, the separation of powers misses the opportunity to explore how a civil service and an administrative state can contribute to the design of the whole regime. As the normative case for a fourth branch articulated in chapter 4 shows, there are ways to think constitutionally about the place of an administrative state in the American commercial republic that go beyond how to justify its relation to or fit within the separation of powers. How does administration relate to regime design questions not only about the structure and practice of market-state relations and business political prerogatives rightly understood, but also questions about how to structure and facilitate deliberative lawmaking and how to develop further the republican character of the citizenry?

The normative case for a fourth branch that takes account of the design of the whole regime thus can enrich already well-developed theory and practice about the political constitution of the American commercial republic. Enhancing that contribution further does call for an exploration of at least some specifics about which principles of design would guide the creation of a fourth branch and what structural elements might follow from such design principles. The next chapter takes up those tasks.

6. The Design of a Fourth Branch

To probe the possibilities for the design of a fourth administrative branch and its consequences for governing practice, the proposal for a simple yet dramatic constitutional change that Woodrow Wilson offered early in the development of his thinking about administration in American politics and government provides a useful point of departure. In "Committee or Cabinet Government" (Wilson 1884), he proposed a simple amendment to the last clause of Article I, Section 6, of the Constitution. The clause reads, "and no person holding any office under the United States shall be a member of either House during his continuance in office." Wilson proposed to add a mere four words, to wit: "and no person holding any *other than a Cabinet* office under the United States shall be a member of either House during his continuance in office" (25). Setting aside the problem that the Constitution nowhere refers to "cabinet" offices, Wilson's aim was to remove "the chief constitutional obstacle to the erection of Cabinet government in this country." He defined cabinet government as "government by means of an executive ministry chosen by the chief magistrate of the nation from the ranks of the legislative majority—a ministry sitting in the legislature and acting as its executive committee" (25). In one fell swoop, Wilson sought to breach the separation-of-powers wall between the legislative and executive branches, replace what he regarded as the corrupt, responsibility-hiding, and enervating system of national government by congressional committee chairs each controlling their own policy and fiscal fiefdom, and make government administration more efficient, more open to scrutiny, and thus more effective. Wilson admitted that other structural adjustments would probably be necessary to ensure sustained cabinet government, such as lengthening the terms of office of the president and members of the House of Representatives. This would in part reduce the likelihood of divided party control of the presidency and the House of Representatives. But the change central to his scheme for cabinet government remained the more overtly structural linkage between the very top positions in the executive branch and Congress.

Wilson was inspired in his pursuit of cabinet government by his youthful exasperation with raw majoritarian government, his general admiration for English government, and his subsequent acquaintance with Walter Baghot's *The English Constitution* (1867). He would later declare the United Kingdom the only regime that had reached what he regarded as the ultimate stage of development, a constitutional state (Cook 2007, 91). Wilson did not promote cabinet government simply because he adored English constitutionalism, however. The underlying problem that spurred Wilson to propose the constitutional change enabling cabinet government was the absence of responsible political parties in the United States, a problem that would become something of an obsession for American political science for at least the next seventy years. Wilson contended that representative government was government by majorities, and government by majority required parties to organize governing majorities. The separation of powers and the division of legislative work into standing committees in Congress, which concentrated power in the hands of committee chairs, enabled a majority party to escape responsibility. A party could promote a platform of policy actions and thereby gain a majority of seats in Congress and possibly the presidency as well. Yet citizens would not know whom to hold responsible for the success or failure of the party to deliver on its platform because there were only weak structural links between party leadership and leadership in national government. The solution, Wilson contended, was to make the "leaders of the dominant party in Congress the executive officers of the legislative will; by making them also members of the President's Cabinet, and thus at once the executive chiefs of the departments . . . and the leaders of their party on the floor of Congress" (Wilson 1884, 25). These legislative leaders would be the chairs of the standing committees. Whether they succeeded or failed to deliver the legislation embodying the party's platform and implement it successfully would determine whether the party would retain its control of one or both houses of Congress and the presidency in subsequent elections. The cabinet would be forced to craft legislation with an eye toward administrative design and capacity, and cabinet members would have to defend legislation, including its administrative design and impact in public during congressional debates. Neither lawmaking nor administration could be carried out in secret. Both would be open to citizen scrutiny.

Lest Wilson's ideas and arguments be dismissed as sepia-toned anachronisms, defenders of a "unitary executive" have contended that without the complete subordination of all administration and policy execution to the president, "bureaucratic agencies" would be subject to control "by the representatives of small, interest-group-captured committee chairs accountable only to the voters of one state or congressional district" (Calabresi and Terrell 2009, 1700). The irony should not be missed: polar-opposite solutions to the same essential problem. Wilson's scheme flies in the face of what proponents of a unitary executive point to as the constitutional keystone for their position, namely the rejection of an executive council as an appendage to the presidency in favor of a "single Executive" (Farrand 1911, 97) in the early weeks of the constitutional convention (Calabresi and Terrell 2009, 1696; but see Kitrosser 2009, 621–626). How a scheme for the creation of a fourth administrative branch can address this pivotal design choice in the creation of the commercial republic follows shortly. For now, however, it is helpful to close out the story of Wilson's cabinet government idea.

Wilson repackaged and expanded his critique of committee government and the barriers to effective governance created by the separation of powers in his first book *Congressional Government* (1981). Absent was the proposed remedy of constitutional change, however. Reviews of the book were generally favorable, with virtually no objections to the idea that something akin to cabinet government and its alleged advantages were needed to overcome the corrupt, desultory, and irresponsible character of government at the national level. In both a private letter to Wilson and in a published review, however, the retired Boston banker turned civil-service reformer, Gamaliel Bradford, insisted that the constitutional change Wilson had previously proposed would be impossible. Bradford declared that the change would never get a hearing in Congress, let alone the necessary two-thirds majority in both houses and the support of three-fourths of the states. Instead, Bradford suggested grassroots agitation to get the House of Representatives to grant the heads of departments non-voting committee and floor privileges, the idea being that with speech rights, department heads could shed light on committee machinations and publicize what they thought were administratively unwise legislative initiatives. That a future Congress could simply vote to cancel such department-head privileges never seemed to occur to Bradford. That was largely the end of Wilson's advocacy for cabinet government in most respects, however. Although never abandoning the aspiration for something akin to cabinet government, Wilson accepted the futility of formal constitutional restructuring to strengthen and improve administration in American national government. He turned instead to a reconception of the presidency as the path to making a vastly expanded administrative state more able and more legitimate.

Wilson's brief flirtation with simple yet profound constitutional change, along with both the immediate and long-term reactions to it, reflect the extreme resistance in American national politics to structurally fundamental constitutional change of any sort, let alone a change aimed at accommodating the reality and necessity of some form of administrative state. Of the twenty-seven amendments incorporated into the Constitution, only seven can be liberally interpreted to have made structural changes (Amendments 12, 13, 14, 17, 20, 22, 23). The remaining twenty amendments concern individual rights, decision processes, or particular policy choices. This reflects, of course, an Article V amendment process that places notoriously high hurdles in the way of constitutional change. A brief pause for reflection is in order, however.

On the one hand, the separation-of-powers doctrine behind the final clause in Article I, Section 6, that Wilson sought to amend was so deeply rooted and widely accepted at the time of the constitutional convention as to be considered the "backbone of our constitutional democracy" (Jacobs 2019, 378). This is a strange characterization for what Madison regarded as an auxiliary precaution. The essential point, however is that on the other hand, the shape and substance of this constitutional backbone is not strict separation (to the lament of some, e.g., Calabresi, Berghausen, and Albertson 2012) but partial blending and overlap, such as authorizing members of the branches to participate in the selection of members of other branches in a variety of ways, and facilitating members of the various branches to scrutinize one another's actions. There is thus more limberness in the backbone than may be generally supposed, allowing for stretching it beyond its current configuration without doing fatal damage to the essential character of a design for separating institutions but binding them nevertheless with shared powers and functions.

Setting aside the theory, tradition, or whatever is dictating that there are only three great governmental powers and thus there can be only three branches distinctly embodying each of those powers, it is possible to identify a set of basic textual changes to the existing Constitution that would enable the assembly of a fourth branch from elements that already exist within the first three articles. These existing textual elements include recognition of administration in the form of "executive departments" with "principal officers" and "inferior officers," and acknowledgment that appointment of the latter can be vested by law in the former. All these elements can be drawn together to form at least the initial textual basis of a new article spelling out the structure, powers, and limitations of the fourth branch with little change necessary to the existing constitutional procedures for creating administrative units and appointing principal officers. The best analogue is the judiciary. It is a separate branch, but the president and the Senate must cooperate on the appointment and confirmation of federal judges, and Congress has the power to determine the scope and structure of the courts. The only exceptions to Congress's power to structure the federal judiciary are the constitutionally specified judicial tenure of office, the original and appellate jurisdictions of the Supreme Court, and the existence of the only constitutionally named judicial officer, the chief justice of the United States. Additional text for a new branch may be derived from the structure and content of the administrative constitution and statutory designs reflecting separation-of-powers characteristics (Jacobs 2019), as well as other statutes that have structured the second administrative state, such as the system of selection by merit.

As intriguing as these possibilities are, however, no proposal of specific text for a fourth branch follows for two reasons. First, any specific proposed text is likely to become a lightning rod for reactions and criticisms that would inevitably devolve into disputes about text, right down to word choice and even punctuation. This book is not about the writing of a constitution. It is about a theory of regime design for a commercial republic that might (better) guide a written constitution's structure. There is no disputing that writing or rewriting a constitution to actuate what this book proposes is an enormous challenge. Perhaps, given the progression of "secular time" and the "more thickly institutionalized and interdependent" (Skowronek 2020, 202) operation of the working constitution, such an endeavor would be orders of magnitude harder than the task taken up in 1787, or in the period 1865–1870 when the Reconstruction amendments emerged.

Second, treating the Constitution as legal text and thus subject to the hunt for original meaning or interpretation in light of changed contexts reflects the legalization of the Constitution (Griffin 1996). This process has led to the granting of special privileges to a limited few with supposedly very special expertise enabling uncommon insight. The current Constitution is not primarily a legal document, however, despite its own declaration as the "supreme law of the land." It is the concrete but limited expression of a regime design, one intended to structure the politics of a particular regime. The theorist can, however, help lay the groundwork for the (collective) constitution writer seeking to revise or completely rewrite the text, and that is in part what this chapter offers.

It is best to approach the question of what a fourth branch should look like by following the example of James Madison and the other framers when they took on the challenge of responding to the governance problems posed by the Articles of Confederation. Neither Madison nor any other convention delegate arrived in Philadelphia with complete proposed text for a constitution. They had many analogues to draw on, including multiple state constitutions, as well as the existing text of the Articles, but they needed a foundation of ideas and principles to guide the debate, crafting, and refinement of the text. After his intensive period of study in preparation for the convention in Philadelphia, Madison brought with him a set of design principles deduced from theory and evidence. This came in the form of the Virginia Plan, formally introduced by his fellow delegate, Virginia Governor Edmund Randolph, and constructed as a series of resolutions that articulated the key principles for an integrated design upon which the Articles would be "corrected & enlarged as to accomplish the objects proposed by their institution; namely, 'common defence, security of liberty and general welfare'" (Rutland 1987, 25).

Translating the theoretical case for a fourth branch into structural framing—that like the Virginia Plan example might reconstitute politics to revitalize the peculiar aspirations for liberal justice that a commercial republic pursues—requires that two central design questions be satisfactorily addressed. First, how will authority, supervision, responsibility and accountability, and intragovernmental coordination be preserved after constitutionally detaching administration from subordination to and supervision by Congress, the courts, and especially the president? Second, what, if any, parts of the normative case for a fourth branch are not addressed by answers to the first question, and what design principles follow from them? Answering the first question must begin by confronting the historical and theoretical arguments for the framers' choice of a single executive and the subsequent interpretation and distillation of this decision into a claim of the necessity for strict presidential supervision and control of all interpretation and execution of policy and law—the so-called unitary executive. Answering the second question must consider what remains in the normative case for a fourth branch as part of a design for a whole regime that is not adequately addressed by the answer to the first question. Explication of principles and provisions for the design of a fourth branch can then follow.

ACCOUNTABILITY AND THE FOURTH BRANCH

It is best to begin with a handful of features of the separation of powers in the Constitution, often taken for granted, that highlight core power separations and overlaps. The first and most significant is that Congress has the primary authority to determine the organizational structure for the exercise of the executive power, and to preserve the distinction, administrative power as well. Setting aside constitutional amendments, which only Congress or the states are empowered to initiate, congressional design of the executive, and an administrative state, must be done by statute. Hence presidents have a role in this structuring too, through the presentment requirement and the veto power of Article I, Section 7.

American political development presents plenty of instances of presidential-congressional conflict over the reconfiguration or expansion of executive and administrative structures. Presidential-congressional agreement about the structure for exercising the executive power has more often than not prevailed, however, as has agreement about the construction and expansion of successive versions of an administrative state. With some exceptions provided for by statute, primarily with respect to units within the Executive Office of the President (EOP), presidents cannot create new administrative units on the basis of the executive power alone. Even for administrative units for which they have some design leeway outside the White House Office and EOP, presidentially proposed reorganizations must be approved, or not rejected, by Congress, depending on the authority in effect at the time (Hogue 2012). Similarly, neither presidents nor the Supreme Court can create any new type of federal court without prior congressional action. Creation of any new courts must come about by statute and thus requires presidential consent, most likely guided by input from the judiciary. With respect to the organizational structure of both the executive and the judicial power, therefore, Congress has primary authority to formally initiate as well as to flesh out the organizational details and determine the resources that will support the resulting structures. Subsequent articulation of executive or judicial structures is then more fully in the hands of the respective branches.

With respect to the general structuring of the government, therefore, the executive and the judiciary are subordinate to the legislative branch, despite being generally recognized as coequal branches, because how the executive and judiciary are structured and thus what they can do and how they do it is in considerable part predicated upon what Congress authorizes. How the former institutions operate is, moreover, subject to legislative supervision, even if the legislature is relatively derelict in performing such supervision. There is nothing in the constitutional text that prohibits Congress from demanding that the president account for his internal structuring and operation of the While House office, for example, although the president may have the political leverage to resist such demands. Similarly, there is no constitutional prohibition against a demand by Congress that the chief justice account for his oversight and administration of the federal judiciary. In both cases, however, norms have developed around the power-sharing structure that limit the acceptable reach and form such demands can take. Institutional incentives may also limit the reach and vigor of legislative supervision over the other branches.

The value of highlighting these basic realities about the separation of powers is twofold. First, it reveals that even under the current three-branch design, some superior-subordinate relations exist among the three branches. There is no obvious reason that the creation of a fourth administrative branch would alter these existing relations among the three original branches, nor would the fourth branch somehow acquire a distinctive position of superiority over the other branches in some formal sense. Certainly, a fourth administrative branch would possess some relative advantages in experience, knowledge, and expertise that would give it leverage in its dealings with the other branches with respect to such matters as the interpretation of statutes or the analysis of the evidence regarding the outcomes from the application of the law. The other branches would hardly lose any of their tools and capacities for countering the institutional advantages of a constitutionalized administrative state, however. Deference to Supreme Court opinions by all three other branches would very likely still be the case, for example, although an agency of the fourth branch might be emboldened to challenge a judicial statutory interpretation—and might even seek alliance with Congress to overturn a Supreme Court decision. Congress has done so on its own in the past, such in the Civil Rights Act of 1991, enacted in response to the majority opinion in *Wards Cove Packing Co. v. Antonio*, 490 U.S. 642 (1989), regarding disparate impact in employment discrimination. Whether that congressional action achieved its aims is debatable (Hart 2011), but the point is that the branches will defer to or confront one another in many and varied ways over both policy and constitutional principles.

The second value of highlighting the basic realities of interinstitutional relations and interactions under the aegis of the separation of powers is to show that thinking about these relations and interactions through the application of the language of authorization, supervision, and monitoring is analytically better for addressing the core concerns about accountability and responsibility that the existence of an administrative state raises than the traditionally and emotionally freighted language of powers and discretion (Rubin 2005a, chap. 3). This facilitates the analysis of the accountability implications of a fourth branch by getting past the needless, counterproductive handwringing and even fury over the seemingly frightening prospect of an administrative state with constitutional powers. Just as it is virtually meaningless to examine interbranch relations and actions in the tripartite scheme in terms of, for example, the Supreme Court having "power over" Congress and the presidency through its status as final arbiter in the interpretation of statutes and rights, there is little analytical purchase gained from trying to determine the powers a fourth branch might possess. It is better to probe the possible relationships between a constitutional fourth administrative branch and the other branches with questions about what a reconstructed constitution might authorize the fourth branch to do and what supervision and monitoring a fourth branch would be subject to by the other branches. An article creating a fourth branch in a new or reconstructed constitution for the commercial republic might, for example, authorize it to create a high-level coordinating body, a possibility explored further below.

The more general point is that the language of authorization and supervision enables clearer thinking about the shape and substance of a fourth administrative branch and its implications. There is considerable reason, for instance, to think that this fourth branch would be subject to authorization, supervision, and monitoring efforts by the other branches, much as the administrative state is now. One or more principles to guide the design of the fourth branch could ensure that this would be the case. To get to consideration of design principles in this regard requires first getting past prominent arguments about the necessary structure and substance of accountability, particularly the core claim about "democratic" accountability that necessitates a strict subordination of administration especially to the two elective branches.

The Problem of Democratic Accountability

For many critics and concerned citizens, the primary problem that the creation of a fourth administrative branch poses is that the administrative state already appears to suffer from inadequate connections and responsiveness to, and control by, the popular sovereign in the form of electoral majorities. As noted in chapter 3, this worry is only reinforced by the seeming vindication of the Whiggish fear of some of the founders that administration readily serves to facilitate factional rule. How will unelected bureaucrats be controlled, and held to account for their actions, if they are not subordinated to "political" authority? They must be subject to control by such authority so that they do not interpret the law and put it into execution in ways that serve their own interests rather the public's interests. Theorists and practitioners have attempted to analyze and address the perceived problem of political control of administration from many angles over the course of the commercial republic's development. Whatever the particulars, however, the essential diagnosis and remedy is that because elections are the means by which the public expresses its interests and holds elected representatives, including elected executives, to account, the public can only be assured of the bureaucracy's fidelity to the public's interests by subordinating administration to elected political authority.

It is an axiom of both democratic theory and practice that elections are the primary mechanism by which the public holds elected officials accountable and expresses its judgment about their performance. Because administrators are not elected, they must be subject to political control by those elected officials who are subject to direct electoral control and accountability by the public, at least that part of the public that regularly votes. As an aside, responses to questions about why an unelected judiciary is not subject to direct subordination and control of elected officials stress the importance of protecting minority rights from majority whim, that elected officials do exert some influence and control through the judicial appointment process and the structuring of the courts, and that the judiciary is restrained by internal professional norms, rules, and traditions, including a distinctive dedication to the rule of law. Still, it is the judiciary itself that has claimed the ultimate authority to say what the law is, and since elected officials have generally acquiesced, the logic of democratic accountability through elections requires the conclusion that the public must have acquiesced too.

James Madison articulated the necessity of subordinating administration to ensure democratic accountability for the execution of the law at the very beginning of the effort to build out the new commercial republican regime from the constitutional text, including its administrative structure. In the 1789 debate on the president's removal power, which arose as Congress was in the process of creating the first executive departments, Madison declared that subordinate executive officials had to be subject to removal by the president to ensure that they behaved. With the president possessing the sole power of removal, "those who are employed in the execution of the law will be in their proper situation, and the chain of dependence be preserved; the lowest officers, the middle grade, and the highest, will depend, as they ought, on the President, and the President on the community. The chain of dependence therefore terminates in the supreme body, namely, in the people" (*Annals of the Congress* 1834, 499). More generally, Madison referred to units within the executive as "subordinate departments," reinforcing his vision of a hierarchy for the exercise of the executive power. However, he also "envisioned both the principal departments established by the Constitution, and certain subordinate departments within the executive, as distributing power amongst officers so as to prevent abuse" (Emerson 2021, 21). This was most manifest in the structure of the Treasury Department, with its several statutorily designated officials having separate, specific grants of authority in revenue collection, expenditures, and auditing. It is also evident in the statutory authorization of "inferior officers" to keep an executive department's records (see 22–26).

Although Madison seemed concerned with distributing some of the constitutionally granted executive power to subordinate administrators in order to diminish the potential for abuse of that power by a single executive (Emerson 2021), it is his argument for the necessity of political subordination and control of administration that found repeated expression in theory and practice as the republic evolved and was reenergized as the second administrative state came into its own in the mid-twentieth century. This notion of hierarchical structuring, command and control, and even obedience (Finer 1941), of administration to political superiors is deeply embedded in American political philosophy despite the acceptance in both politics and law of some categories or gradations of administrative autonomy—or at least of indirect command and control. Projection of the hierarchical relationship of politics to administration captures what later economic and political theorists came to call the principal-agent problem. Even in that theoretical innovation, reflecting cross-pollination from the economic theory of the firm (Moe 1984), the public still holds the ends of Madison's chain of dependence as the ultimate principal. As inquiry into notions of political or democratic accountability has grown to epic proportions across constitutional and administrative law, political science, economics, and public administration, the contention that a distinctive form of political, or democratic, accountability secured primarily through elections provides the best security for the faithful performance of elected officials, and by extension administrative officials in a very bureaucratic administrative state, has become increasingly suspect, and may be in reality a merely comforting "myth" (Rubin 2005b).

Elections as the primary mechanism by which public officials can be held to account is problematic for two key reasons. First, elections as the pathway for the expression of a popular sovereign's will are suspect in any setting because they only capture a slice of whatever popular sentiment or opinion may exist. Elections are the aggregation of individual choices reflecting the expression of each individual voter's bundle of idiosyncrasies, including emotional affects and cognitive-processing limitations. These individual voter characteristics get funneled into what is most often a series of binary choices for each elective office on a ballot. That these individual ballot selections somehow express a general popular preference for one candidate over another has some validity—or at least liberal democracies have to accept that this is what elections produce. But what does this aggregated popular preference for one candidate over another mean?

This question points to the second reason to be skeptical that elections are the best, or at least primary, accountability mechanism. Elections serve two primary functions, they "solve the problem of succession" in elective offices, and they "produce a government" at every level that is generally "responsive to the people's basic desires" (Rubin 2005b, 2077, 2078). This is the representation function, the function that the design elements in the theory of political constitution of the commercial republic aimed at generating civic majorities are meant to fulfill. Civic majorities are those composed of individuals able to discern the qualities that make one candidate a better representative than another—in terms of abilities to understand, articulate, and respond to public desires—and transcend their self-interests through deliberation about the public interest in a way that is responsive to, but not necessarily an exact replication of, public desires. Although Madison envisioned elections as a means by which representatives could be judged at the bar of public opinion, he also envisioned such public opinion as cultivated in part by those same representatives. This suggests at the very least that even for Madison elections as an accountability mechanism would entail a complex, interactive, and somewhat inscrutable process.

Beyond fulfilling the succession and representation functions, which are enormous tasks in and of themselves, the electoral theory of accountability insists that elections also express the judgment of the general public, or at least the electorate, about the performance of public officials, including how they direct and control the administrative state. The theory and evidence accumulated for "retrospective voting" indicates that voters sometimes, in some circumstances, make judgments about the performance of elected officials, or at least of the institution they occupy. A particular election may thus amount to a collective judgment on government performance even if voters have serious knowledge and information-processing limitations (Healy and Malhotra 2013). There is also the possibility, however, that the combination of candidates' efforts to gain voter approval, combined with voter reaction to those efforts, can produce in perverse incentives that result in elected officials failing to serve voters' interests or the general welfare (Ashworth 2012).

At best, then, elections serve as a rough and relatively minor mechanism for ensuring accountable government. The linkage between the electoral process and accountability is too "highly attenuated" (Rubin 2005b, 2080) for elected officials generally, and even weaker as a mechanism for holding elected officials to account for their direction and control of the administrative state. To contend in particular that a quadrennial national election for a "chief magistrate" filtered through an eighteenth-century electoral contrivance that creates fifty-one separate elections, some more strategically important than others, can in any way be an expression of national public judgment, retrospective or prospective, about a president's management of an administrative state, is too farfetched to grant any credence. Whatever the good arguments are for keeping an administrative state strictly subordinate to presidential direction and command—the other principal one being the necessity for coordination, explored below—accountability achieved through an elective chief executive is not one of them.

That elected officials do make an effort to hold administrative agents to account is certainly widely evident. This is primarily a reflection, however, of an understanding of their jobs rather than a reflection of a significant electoral incentive to demonstrate to voters a sincere effort to improve government performance. What incentive there is for such a demonstration assumes the form of taking credit, or casting blame, for successes or failures. The true accountability structures and relationships within government are those internal to the administrative state because of its predominant hierarchical and bureaucratic structure. This is where a real "chain of accountability" resides (Rubin 2005b, 2122). Hence, it is possible to define and describe the nature of accountability achieved through intra- and interinstitutional operations in the presence of an administrative state that strongly suggests accountability will not be diminished, and may be enhanced, through the creation of a fourth administrative branch.

Authorization, Supervision, and Administrative Accountability

The concepts of authorization and supervision better capture the character of accountability relationships in a modern liberal democracy dominated by administrative action than the long-standing concepts of power and discretion. This is particularly so with respect to the representations of bureaucratic administration being held in check through subordination to the power of superior institutions. Those representations frame the process as superior institutions granting administrative agents a share of their power so that the agents may make decisions and take actions, that is, use their discretion, contingent on a satisfactory accounting of their exercise of discretion. Together, the concepts of authorization and supervision capture better than images of institutions doling out fragments of power or commanding agent behavior "the actions that each individual or institution within government is allowed to perform, and the way each one controls, or fails to control, any other individual or institution" in the highly articulated nature of a administratively centered modern state. "Authorization establishes a delineated identity and role for each governmental unit, and indicates that these features are established to achieve an explicit and identifiable purpose. Supervision provides the means by which the unit's ability to achieve that purpose can be monitored and measured" (Rubin 2005a, 92). This is a strongly instrumental expression of governance, consistent with the predominant nature of modern government, and administration especially. As considered further below, it also helps illuminate the instrumental-constitutive tension in administration that public administrators must contend with and elected officials must recognize if their authorization and supervision of administration is to be effective in terms of fulfilling designated aims.

Approaching questions of administrative accountability and responsibility from the perspective of authorization and supervision highlights that "authorization of the units that compose a modern state is generally derived from a multiplicity of sources" (Rubin 2005a, 93). Rather than from some Delphic expression of popular will or judgment of performance in the latest election, accountability is constituted out of prior institutional judgments, decisions, and commitments, including prior electoral choices regarding succession and representation. The ground source is a given government's original authorizations in a constitution that empower different institutions to generate different kinds of authorizations in furtherance of the original regime commitments. Recognizing that authorization of administrative action flows from multiple sources in turn highlights that accountability is a multisource, multidimensional phenomenon. In a modern liberal democracy, in sum, authorization and supervision occur, and thus accountability is realized, in a dense network of interactions within and across major governing institutions (chap. 2). Accountability is thus inescapably political (Heidelberg 2017). The interactive, political accountability process takes place in the general setting of popular acceptance of, or at least acquiescence to, "the state's ongoing practice" (Rubin 2005a, 94).

Using the concepts of authorization and supervision as a window into accountability, rather than the concepts of power and discretion, is also consistent with the theory of political constitution of a commercial republic, with its focus on the arrangement of institutions and other regime components to improve the chances that the public interest will be realized. Authorization and supervision as the conceptual anchors of accountability "enable us to evaluate the government we actually possess in terms of our genuine commitments to security, prosperity, and liberty" and to determine better whether that government is serving "the interests of its citizens rather than generating emergent interests of its own" (Rubin 2005a, 95). From the perspective of commercial republican theory, the latter phenomenon might well be an indicator that the government is under the sway of a minority faction—and thus that the interests of other citizens, and the general interest, may be in peril.

Approaching accountability through the concepts of authorization and supervision enables active monitoring of the state's ongoing practice because it stimulates useful analytical questions from individuals or groups of attentive citizens with the time, energy, and inclination to scrutinize government. Questions about which institutions have what powers, how they contest allocations of power, and how those conflicts facilitate administrative autonomy and discretion may be meaningful for political science study and theorizing, but they are not of much help for determining how particular institutional designs and interinstitutional relationships result in functioning governance. Questions concerning whether a particular administrative regulation or decision was authorized, how it was authorized, who authorized it, whether it was consistent with the authorization, and how and how well the administrative action is being monitored reveal to interested observers real information about lines of accountability and who can be called to account for missteps. This is in fact the way governance operates day to day throughout the regime, in the interactions among the constitutional branches and in their relationships with the administrative state. The creation of a fourth administrative branch would have little effect on the existence of such interactions, although it might alter the dynamics, which is part of the point. It is, moreover, consistent in general ways with the effect that Woodrow Wilson envisioned for his cabinet-government proposal, namely to enhance the opportunities for attentive citizens to scrutinize administration and to express their support or displeasure for administrative plans and performance (Cook 2007, 34–36). Wilson later concluded that this possibility was unrealistic given the everyday demands of modern life on people going about their business. With new tools and techniques for obtaining, processing, analyzing, and disseminating information, and new organizations actively engaged in using those tools and techniques, the original Wilsonian vision of active, organized citizen scrutiny of government through open, public debate, especially on big questions in which the public interest is implicated, may now be more practical than Wilson expected.

The analytical questions that flow from approaching the problem of accountability in terms of authorization and supervision rather than power and discretion open up not just the instrumental questions of who did what, where, when, how, and why, but also questions about the formative effect of policy design and administrative action. Failure to take account of formative, or constitutive, effects in policy design and administrative action results in the phenomenon commonly known as unintended consequences (Cook 2014, 221–230). Because the future state of the world is if not completely opaque at least very murky, unintended consequences cannot be eliminated entirely. Yet identifying potential formative effects from policy and administrative design, and adjusting designs accordingly, that is, articulating the specifics of authorization and supervision and what the consequences might be in a specific area of policy action, has the potential to reduce unintended consequences. This may reduce friction and disruption in state-society relations, reduce the burden on administrators to cope with the inevitable tension between their instrumental missions and the constitutive effect of fulfilling those missions, and improve the quality of outcomes in meeting policy aims. Creating a fourth administrative branch increases the chances that all this can occur by increasing the incentives for the other constitutive institutions to specify more carefully the terms of authorization and supervision for the various units in the administrative state. The constitutional autonomy of a fourth administrative branch in turn diminishes the incentives of the other branches to use the administrative state to hide from their own accountability, or to expect that administration will act effectively merely through commands for obedience, and despite the criticisms and condemnations that elective masters love to heap on nonelective public servants.

In addition to helping focus attention on the specific source and nature of the authorization that an administrative agency has for undertaking a decision process or putting a directive into action, accountability requires supervision in the form of guidance and requirements for monitoring and reporting. This allows the supervising institution to adjust its guidance in an ongoing fashion, including changes to formal authorization, whether it takes the form of an authorizing statute, substantive details in appropriations, or language in a committee report. For all this to work, administrative agents need some autonomy to act. Certainly such autonomy might enable them to resist some aspects of the authorization and supervision directed their way. This is likely to prompt contestation, dialogue, and negotiation in the relationship of supervising institutions and administrative agents. For the former to resort to command and demands for strict obedience, however, is to undermine accountability. Exercising such command and control through, for example, the threat of removal of top administrators at will or substituting for the judgments of experts a political superior's political judgments, does not create an accountability relationship. It creates a relationship of manipulation and submission. "Far from granting the subject autonomy or making it accountable for its own actions," control and demands for obedience "undermine its will to resist, making it an accomplice" merely in the effort at manipulation and control (Rubin 2005b, 2109). Furthermore, it squanders the intellectual and social capital generated in the creation of expert administrative entities and dilutes the special values and capacities that only administration can contribute to the regime.

True accountability, therefore, requires a level of autonomy, of independent thinking and self-directed action, sufficient to motivate administrative agents to develop and articulate reasons for the actions they take. Such behavior is already required by the rules of the administrative constitution and reinforced by professional norms and the rationality of bureaucracy. The point, however, is to think constitutionally about how better to facilitate such behavior and have it respected and encouraged by other institutional actors. This requires consideration of institutional designs and how to fit them together to achieve the kind of politics and lawmaking that the theory of political constitution of the commercial republic strives for, namely, a process of deliberation—the giving of reasons—as the road to finding, or fashioning, the concrete meaning of the public interest.

As noted previously, those engaged in deliberation need not be selfless. For the regime's design to work it is better that they have "morally ambiguous" motives (Elkin 2004, 64–65). As long as the pursuit of self-interest and ambition is done in public, where rationales for those interests and the expressions of others intermix, there is a chance that the public interest will come into view. None of this guarantees that the public interest will be discovered or well served. The rhetorical arts have been refined and fortified over centuries. Audiences can be manipulated to think as the speaker wishes, through many and subtle devices. There is, however, no other antidote to these possibilities than the open, public exchange of reasons and evidence supporting those reasons. Calling to account, and giving account, is already a part of politics in the commercial republic, however imperfectly practiced. Creating a fourth administrative branch will not diminish these tendencies, and it might very well enhance them by giving administrators greater legitimacy to offer in prominent public ways their distinctive perspectives on the public interest and to contest, when strategically appropriate, the public-interest perspectives of the other branches.

The complexity of accountability—varying forms of authorization and supervision, institutions that can be either principals or agents depending on the authorization and supervision at issue, and the range of options for standards employed to hold agents to account—point to the likelihood that mutual learning will be the best strategic relationship between the supervising entity and the one supervised and monitored. In public governance the vast majority of policy-administrative situations are those in which "the superior knows the result it is trying to achieve but does not know the means of achieving it, when circumstances are likely to change in ways that the superior cannot predict, or when the superior does not even know the precise result" desired (Rubin 2005b, 2131). A command-control-obedience relationship between principal and agent makes little sense in these situations because commands will have little substance that can form the basis by which agents can demonstrate obedience. Little learning useful for improving policy design or administration will emerge from such abstruseness. Even in conditions where there is some administrative autonomy, the effect of political superiors approaching the exercise of administrative autonomy from a starting point of mistrust "reduces information sharing between careerists and appointees and hurts agency performance" (Resh 2015, 2–3). A significant measure of designed administrative autonomy also increases the incentive that administrators will invest the time and energy necessary to acquire the information and expertise supportive of good policy making and implementation (Gailmard and Patty 2013, chap. 2–4). Interinstitutional relationships of mutual learning are thus likely to improve the capacity and quality of administration, and governance more generally, and make the regime more resilient.

Within administrative operations there are tactical situations in which command and faithful response are essential. When these are necessary, and well done, relationships of mutual respect and trust are established or reinforced between principals and agents. At the highest regime and institutional design level, however, command relationships are antithetical to liberal-democratic governance. Mutual learning, reflection, and deliberation are the essential qualities. The existence of a fourth administrative branch would not make the emergence of such highly valuable strategic mutual-learning relationships more difficult. It would instead make them easier, or at least more likely, because it would authorize administration to relate to the other branches on an equal legal and political plane and thus enable it to resist unwise efforts at control and manipulation that undermine accountability, corrode performance, and diminish the characteristics of bureaucratic administration that make it a distinctly valuable constitutive institution of the regime. All institutions with a major role in governance have their strengths and weaknesses—administration no more so than elected executives or legislatures or the judiciary. Setting the administrative state on an equal constitutional plane with the other branches will enhance their complementarities and increase the chances that mutual learning will take place.

This mutual learning might well include increased sensitivity to the formative effects of policy design and administration—and thus greater vigilance regarding unintended consequences—because, similar to the effect of trust on incentives for information acquisition and sharing, attentiveness to formative effects is likely a function of trust or distrust in the relationship between political principals, including their appointees, and career administrators. This raises questions about the nature and extent of the presence of political appointees in an administrative state lodged in a separate branch. The elective branches are likely to fight furiously to maintain an extensive layer of political appointees in administration in order to maintain control and influence over administration and diminish its strength as a coequal branch. To ensure sufficient political autonomy, however, the number of political appointments at the top of the administrative branch would have to be reduced from current design and practice. How far a reduction in political appointees must go is an open question. There are, however, indications that some kind of balance of "politicized and autonomous" personnel selection systems are associated with more administrative competence and stronger administrative performance (Krause, Lewis, and Douglas 2006, 770). Such balancing "provides politicians with a formal mechanism to engage in 'institutional hedging,' whereby both political responsiveness and bureaucratic autonomy are not incompatible for maximizing bureaucratic competence" (785).

In sum, there are multiple reasons to conclude that a well-designed fourth, administrative branch would result in no deficit of accountability or administrative competence and performance in comparison with current arrangements. An accountable administrative state does not require strict subordination to three branches, and it especially does not require subordination and subjugation to an elected executive with the capacity and legal or constitutional authorization to manipulate personnel, substitute personal judgment for that of the expert bureaucracy, or tamper with structures and resources without discernible consequence. The administrative state is enmeshed in accountability relationships now, and it would be no less so with its own constitutional status and level of authorization. Those accountability relationships might even prove better and stronger, giving the regime greater internal integrity, with the creation of a fourth branch.

There is, however, another argument favoring subordination of administration to an elected executive specifically—the need for coordination of a vast administrative apparatus—that must be addressed. Delineating how the responses to the accountability and coordination concerns in the current analysis point to one or more design principles and associated structural provisions for a fourth, administrative branch, one that has approximately the same political and legal autonomy and dependence as the existing branches, can then proceed.

COORDINATION IN THE ADMINISTRATIVE STATE

In addition to claims that strictly subordinating administration to the president will result in the most politically accountable administrative state obtainable, proponents of a unitary executive (for example, Calabresi and Yoo 2008) contend that strict subordination of administration to presidential command and control is essential for optimum policy and administrative prioritization and coordination reflecting public preferences in the vast and unwieldy administrative state. "Coordination is essential to efficiency and energy in the executive. Without coordination, . . . policies may run at cross purposes, leading to waste, increases in taxes, and a decrease in services" (Calabresi and Terrell 2009, 1717). Without some form of "centralized hub-and-spoke network," information costs and bargaining costs become excessive. "Information is more easily collected and distributed when it travels through the President than when it must pass directly from each" administrative unit involved in a policy area to every other involved unit. "These information costs alone discourage coordination at the outset" (1717–1718). This contention that administration must be kept strictly subordinate to and thus under direct command and control of the president to avoid an administrative state that is inefficient, internally conflicted, and aimless, as well as insufficiently responsive and accountable to aggregate public desires and preferences as embodied in the nationally elected president, are surprisingly weak for at least two reasons.

First, no president can manage the collection and distribution of more than an infinitesimal fraction of the information generated in the vast expanses of the modern American state. There is no "uniquely presidential capacity vis-à-vis the other branches" (Farina 2010, 395) for the collection and distribution of information critical for administrative coordination and policy direction. Every president "faces the same cognitive challenges as the rest of us in managing information flows, prioritizing multiple demands for attention, and comprehending and analyzing novel situations" (397). Presidents have always needed help, as the Brownlow Committee intoned, and under both the first and second administrative states such presidential help grew to the point that there is now a vast presidential bureaucracy with several layers or spokes of its own, including most critically the White House Office. There are certainly identifiable incentives for Congress to accept the necessity for the creation of such a support structure, in order to increase the chances that presidents will make use of information in policy decisions (Gailmard and Patty 2013, chap. 5–6). Since the emergence of the managerial, or institutional, presidency, however, presidents have not gained extraordinary new cognitive and information-processing capacities of their own. Hence their ability to manage even their own in-house bureaucracy is limited. Span of control matters, although it is not entirely clear how (Meier and Bohte 2003). What is clear, however, is that most of the units within the presidential bureaucracy operate on their own and coordinate with one another without needing direct presidential authorization or direction. This often empowers particular presidential staff—chiefs of staff, domestic-policy advisors, and the like—to raise concerns of their own about both coordination and accountability. It also highlights that the reality, and claims about the necessity, of the unitary executive are suspect at this stage in the republic's development.

With proponents of the unitary executive portraying the constitutional convention's rejection of a proposal for an executive council in favor of a single-headed executive as a "famous and celebrated" decision (Calabresi and Terrell 2009, 1696), it is particularly ironic that there has been in effect something like an executive council in the form of the president's key advisors and support staff since the mid-twentieth century. Certainly the president is the only and ultimate constitutionally authorized wielder of executive power. Nevertheless, "staff members have zero legal authority in their own right, yet 100 percent of presidential authority passes through their hands" (Patterson 2000, 2, cited in Farina 2010, 403). What goes on within those structures for presidential support are among the least transparent in government. Decision processes within these structures are often hidden behind the veil of "secrecy and despatch" claimed as essential for effective executive action. The problem is not just hidden policy making but manipulation of "the very 'facts' upon which policies purport to be based" (Kitrosser 2009, 1774). Furthermore, given their biases and other cognitive and physical limitations, presidents don't create such close-in circles of support merely for convenience. They must depend on these supporting players to make most decisions (Farina 2010, 403 and works cited there), many of which leave them with only a final sign-off.

The claim for presidentially centered coordination as essential for an efficient, properly directed administrative state is weak for a second key reason. Centralized presidential direction and coordination may create the very problems it supposedly solves. If administrators, whether within the direct presidential orbit or in the many agencies of the administrative state, must ultimately go through the president for authorization to interpret statutes and put them into action, intense competition and conflict will arise for the president's attention. Direct presidential surrogates have the inside track on this, of course, but more generally the spreading of a kind of court politics throughout the administrative state is not only disruptive, it is wasteful and inefficient as time and energy are funneled into the attention-getting effort. It can also distort the efforts that administrative agencies direct toward fulfilling their missions and statutory mandates or responding promptly and effectively to immediate issues or crises. In addition, on what basis will the president decide to allocate her limited attention resources? We may hope, with the proponents of the unitary executive, that such presidential choices are guided by the enunciated national priorities supposedly ratified in the last election. Yet such electoral mandates are at best elusive—and almost always claimed after the fact (Conley 2001; Azari 2013). In other words, having won election, presidents can claim a mandate for whatever priorities they choose. Despite whatever mandate claims they make, however, when presidents choose to weigh in on a policy question under consideration within the administrative state, there are few obstacles to their doing so in ways that favor particular interests, especially business. As noted in chapter 4, most presidential electoral coalitions are idiosyncratic assemblages of interests that don't necessarily reflect broad, general interests. Neither can presidents push against the political prerogatives of business if they want to have sufficient campaign resources to be competitive for the magic number of 270 electoral votes.

Identifying national policy priorities and proposing an agenda for action is certainly a valuable and constitutionally designated role for the president. Beyond that, the idea of extensive formal presidential coordination and direction of the administrative state not only weakens the incentives of bureaucrats to be accountable for what they do best—committing the time and energy toward acquiring the knowledge and expertise needed for good policy making and implementation—it also runs counter to well-established knowledge about the limitations of formal administrative coordination and the advantages of informal, ad hoc coordination. Formal, centralized coordination is only most effective under very limited conditions, "where the task environment is known and unchanging" and "it can be treated as a closed system" (Chisholm 1992, 10). There are very few instances of such conditions in the public realm. Even in military operations, where centralized hierarchy and coordination are so deeply ingrained, improvisation and horizontal coordination and communication are often the keys to success, whether in logistics or battle at the front lines. More generally, formal, centralized coordination can backfire in several ways.

First, it generates "routines [that] tend to take on a life of their own, commonly undergoing a conversion from purely instrumental devices" to becoming intrinsically valuable, resulting in goal displacement (Chisholm 1992, 11). Second, the "gap between the formal authority to make decisions and the capacity to make them," means either that the formal authority must beef up its capacity to gain and process expert knowledge, creating all the follow-on accountability and coordination problems in the presidency already noted, or coordination responsibility falls to staff "with the requisite professional skills" and knowledge to coordinate informally, negating the reason for formal coordination (11). Nevertheless, presidents have considerable incentive to continue to centralize control over the administrative state. The effect is to hollow out the bureaucracy of those committed to helping shape policy but less extreme in their policy views (Cameron and De Figueiredo 2020). In other words, over time there will be fewer of those policy-oriented bureaucrats most likely to be effective, because of their moderate policy positions, in coordinating efforts across agencies where there may be clashes over shared policy domains.

Finally, centralized formal coordination is "time consuming and the results are generally inconclusive" (Chisholm 1992, 11, citing Seidman 1980, 206). Consider the effectiveness of national emergency management and disaster response. Few would contend that coordination in response to a disaster is improved by having all the information flow up to and then out from a central node in the person of the president himself. A presidential disaster declaration is needed to release federal resources to respond to the disaster. From then on, however, coordination of the deployment of those resources flows to those with the requisite experience, professional training, and expertise. Even the centralization of the initial authorization can have deleterious effects—such as delaying critical action as the relevant agencies sit and wait for a president to make up his or her mind about whether to issue a declaration. Such decisions may also be influenced by overt political considerations (Reeves 2011; Husted and Nickerson 2014).

In sum, the fourth, administrative branch may pose control and coordination complications for presidents in terms of their particular aims and interests, service of their electoral coalitions, and a general system preference that presidents make policy decisions on the basis of good information. However, placing the administrative state in its own constitutional branch poses no serious obstacles to effecting coordination within the administrative state. It might actually improve coordination, by protecting the special values and capacities of administration and the incentives for bureaucrats to sustain those values and capacities and protect them from the manipulation of political overseers, as well as increasing the likelihood that coordination will be emergent because it is in the hands of those with the requisite professional skills and knowledge. This is a question in part about whether any sort of high-level coordinating mechanism is needed in a constitutionally independent administrative state. A brief consideration of that possibility will round out this treatment of the claims that accountability and coordination require strict constitutional and political subordination of administration in the commercial republic.

Central Coordination for the Administrative State

Policy fragmentation and overlap, statutory ambiguity, and contrasting professional values and organizational cultures can engender horizontal and vertical conflicts between agencies in an administrative state. The frequency of such interagency conflict is unclear, but its importance is mostly discounted or dismissed as battles over turf or other forms of friction that reveal the pathologies of bureaucracy. It may not be wise to scoff at or condemn such encounters as petty bureaucratic politics, however, because many such encounters may actually be indicators not of bureaucratic dysfunction but of efforts at informal coordination. Such coordination efforts will inevitably be less than seamless. As frustrating as it may be for both those engaged in the coordination effort and those waiting for the results, it takes time, energy, focus, experience, and skill to iron out differences and parcel out roles where multiple public values are involved and statutory authorizations overlap. Sometimes these coordination efforts among mostly mid-level managers and policy and legal specialists do not resolve all conflicts and the search for resolution must be elevated to higher levels of authorization. Must there be a final, perhaps single, arbiter for the most stubborn areas of irresolution? The ubiquitous use of moderators and arbitrators, and of course the courts, to help resolve social, economic, and political conflicts of widely varying sorts suggests that the answer is yes, although the need for such an arbiter might be less frequent or extensive in an arena of skilled professionals engaged in important public work and thus motivated by both internal values and external demands to resolve differences. Two alternative forms of high-level coordination and conflict resolution seem the most likely options in association with the creation of a fourth, administrative branch.

The first alternative is that the president retain a specific and limited role for coordination and conflict resolution. Only the most critical and contentious policy and administrative questions would be brought to the president for consideration and possible resolution. What qualifies for such presidential consideration could, as one possibility, be determined by the heads of the agencies involved. Given the vast reach and complex policy profile of the administrative state, there might still be considerable demand for the president's attention. This suggests that there would then still be a gatekeeper role for key presidential advisors. On the other hand, knowing that the president's time, energy, attention, and decision-making capacity are limited might create considerable incentive for the agencies involved to resolve the final areas of contestation, perhaps with additional outside help, such as consultation with senators and representatives or staff on relevant committees. None of this guarantees crisp final resolution of policy and administrative conflicts. Even under the dominance of unitary executive thinking, presidents often deflect or finesse hard decisions or simply fail to make up their minds.

The second probable alternative is some form of multimember body at the top of the fourth branch that would be responsible for any coordination, arbitration, and final resolution of difficult-to-resolve policy and administrative questions. Two possible forms would be a more constitutionally formalized cabinet, which raises the question of the nature and extent of a presidential role in appointments, considered further below, or a distinct central administrative board or commission.

The president's cabinet, so called, has at best an ephemeral existence and generally unimpressive utility in national governance. As a collective body it has no constitutional or statutory authority or status, nor does it possess any independent source of political support whatsoever. It is a protean creature whose shifting shape reflects the widely varying aims and preferences of presidents for advice. Since the mid-twentieth century, presidents have used the cabinet in varying, and not necessarily mutually exclusive, ways. They have used the cabinet "as a 'sounding-board' . . . to try out alternative strategies before deciding upon a particular course of action." The have also "used the cabinet meeting as an occasion on which to play the role of honest broker between departmental heads who disagreed with each other," as "a forum for the exchange of information" and cross-agency collaboration, and as a conduit for conveying decisions outward and downward into the administrative state. Cabinet meetings also serve as a form of presidential spectacle for publicly demonstrating that a president is serious about seeking consultation and advice and to "impress on the electorate that the president [is] in control" and "running a competent, open administration." Furthermore, presidents use "members of their cabinet as evangelists, spreading the word around the country of their decisions, policies and plans." Most presidents endeavor to show at least early in their terms that they are relying on their cabinets for important matters. As time wears on, however, they increasingly resort to reliance on and consultation with their closest and most trusted advisors (Bennett 1996, 4).

Even those most dismissive of any collective role for a cabinet closely tied to presidential predilections have found some potential for "modest advances in coordination and integration of legislation and administration . . . through the cabinet as a collective entity . . . under current institutional arrangements and the talents and aims of individual presidents" (Cook 2007, 236; see Fenno 1959). Yet presidents now have such capabilities through alternative structures within the institutional presidency, reflecting their very strong tendency to rely on their closest and most ideologically compatible advisors (Gailmard and Patty 2013, chap. 5–6). Such incentives and tendencies will not diminish with any attempt to make the cabinet a coordinating body for the administrative state, whether in its current condition of strict subordination or lodged in a separate constitutional branch. In the case of the latter arrangement, a cabinet made up of department heads appointed and confirmed as they are now might exercise a high-level coordinating function. As a bridge to the executive or legislative branches, however, the cabinet's actual function and effectiveness remains difficult to conjure even if it were granted formal constitutional existence and authority for such a role.

A different way to think about this question of some form of central, formal coordination in a constitutionally independent administrative state is to create a high-level body not so dependent on the president or the other constitutional branches. This body might consist of a specific number of individuals not drawn from the political-appointee ranks but from the top ranks of the civil service—the highest-ranking merit-protected executives representing a diverse cross-section of agencies. Authority and responsibility for making these appointments could be distributed across the other branches, and term lengths and possibility of reeligibility specified. The body's specific authorizations and supervisory mandates might be left quite general, as is the jurisdictional scope of the Article III courts in the Constitution, with details left to subsequent enabling statutes. This is exactly how the First Congress articulated the structure of the executive and the judiciary from the very general text of Articles II and III.

One existing entity might serve as a template for this high-level administrative coordinating body: the Administrative Conference of the United States (ACUS). In its current form, the ACUS is an independent executive agency, with a membership "drawn from other federal agencies and from private-sector persons with expertise and experience in law and government" (ACUS 2017, 2). It has a full-time chairman by presidential appointment and senate confirmation with a five-year term, and a governing council of roughly ten members, no more than five drawn from "senior officials at other government agencies" (3). By statute these must be the heads of executive departments and agencies and independent boards and commissions or their designees, or the president's designees. They serve three-year terms by presidential appointment with no senate confirmation. There are also "public members" from the private sector with specializations in law, management, technology, and policy. The ACUS mission is "to study administrative procedures in federal programs and recommend improvements" (2). It thus has a policy, law, and management orientation but is heavily dominated by lawyers. Its effectiveness in bridging the separate specialties of administrative law and public administration and management is debatable (Metzger 2015), but it does have a committee on administration and management. It also previously had a committee on collaborative governance, suggesting the possibility that some concern for coordination is part of the ACUS culture. However, that committee was disbanded in 2016 because of overlapping jurisdiction with other standing committees.

It is possible to imagine a general provision in the text for a fourth, administrative branch empowering Congress to create a high-level coordinating body for the national administrative system and specifying a few requirements such as those spelled out in the Administrative Conference Act (5 U.S.C., Part I, Chapter 5, Subchapter V). The question remains, however, whether centralized coordination is a necessary principle for the organization of a fourth branch—the details to be left to actual constitution writers—or better yet, the practices and experiences that coalesce into a working constitution. Following the latter path would assuredly spark the kind of "pragmatic state building" indicative of the early republic (Mashaw 2012, chap. 2), with its improvisation through a variety of administrative forms and processes much like that in the early republic.

Would a fourth administrative branch still need some form of centralized coordination and direction? Consider the example of the federal judiciary. Do the federal courts get "direction" from within, from the chief justice and the Supreme Court? Yes, with respect to the interpretation of the law, up to a point. The Supreme Court renders decisions on only a small fraction of all the cases taken on by the federal courts. Much of the coordination and direction in applying and interpreting the law takes place outside the direct purview of SCOTUS, following the deep and generally stable tradition and norm of *stare decisis*. The courts also receive direction, or at least authorization and supervision, from statutes delineating court jurisdiction and from the government's presence as a party to suits. Again, however, the court system achieves coordination by relying on core principles, theories of interpretation developed within the legal profession, and the common law. To whom or what are judges accountable for the interpretation of the law and the decisions they render? The answer is other judges, the various forms of the law, tradition, legal norms, public values, and at least to some extent public opinion. No one claims that the courts must be subordinated to "political" authority to achieve coordination or to be accountable, however. In fact, just the opposite has been the prevailing wisdom about the function and value of the courts since before the American founding.

Although it is far larger, far greater in the scope of its mandates and responsibilities, more diverse and more fragmented, administration in a separate branch is just as likely to develop coordinating and accountability structures and processes, norms, values, and traditions as the courts have done. Much of this exists now in the administrative state, not all of which is a function of coordination and direction from the institutional presidency. Law, policy, and norms of administrative operations are already well developed—and have been since early in the republic's development. A fourth branch can stand on and operate by these principles with little disruption from current structure and practice because they reflect the highly interactive nature of the administrative state's relationships with the three branches and the interactions among the three branches regarding the administrative state. Administrative agency statutory and constitutional interpretation will be anchored in greater formal authority, so perhaps a high-level arbiter within the administrative state to address conflicting agency interpretations may be wise. Alternatively, the courts can play that role, much as they do now. Certainly, the legislative and executive branches will seek to weigh in on agency decisions and actions. Except for the sheer additional volume of decisions and actions they may face, however, the reactions and responses of the other branches to the decisions and actions of an administrative branch are likely to be little different from the ways in which they respond to one another's decisions and actions in the existing tripartite scheme. Constitution writers might consider some additional safeguards in the form of limited legislative and executive vetoes of administrative interpretations, rulemaking, and adjudications, or they may not if judicial review remains a central norm and practice respected by the other branches.

The lack of strict hierarchy and subordination of administration to the political branches, replaced by authority and supervision exercised in a shared way across all the constitutive institutions, will not be satisfactory to many. It flies in the face of more than two hundred years of ideology, theory, practice, and tradition, as well as the rejection of a multiheaded executive in favor of unity in the executive at the founding. Yet in the normal politics of successive working constitutions, such consultation and shared decision making, with administration as a distinctive player and an at least quasi-independent voice, are more frequent than commonly recognized, especially since the mid-nineteenth century. The loss of what many regard as the critical necessity for authority to rest with a single executive who can order action with little resistance and no defiance from those so ordered will be especially unsettling. This partly reflects the unfortunate legal and normative expansion of the president's commander-in-chief role beyond the national security and regime self-preservation roles where the office's "energy and despatch" are best directed. In the gray area between clear existential threats and normal public-interest politics, presidents have sometimes met with resistance from Congress when it was called on to act swiftly in response to serious exigencies. There are also examples of presidents themselves *not* making decisions even when they have been pressed by advisers and agencies, or even one or both of their coequal branches, to do so. Furthermore, presidential orders for action do not spring out of nowhere. They are likely to be the result of prior consultation and debate with varying casts of characters of assorted formal positions and informal roles. Even in the national security domain, the image of a president astutely recognizing an existential threat and saving the republic through the force of unity of command is pure dramatic myth.

In the broader sphere of normal politics, the creation of a fourth, administrative branch will not perceptively change the dynamics by which a regime designed with multiple devices to protect rights and regulate factions responds to the problems and serious threats it confronts. A constitutionally autonomous fourth branch might even save the regime from the unprecedented instance that is now possible, in which an especially factious or even corrupt president attempts to use the powers of command to exploit a crisis and enrich himself and his faction, all while a politically subjugated administrative state is forced to facilitate the deeds because it is incapable by law, norm, and tradition of putting up much of a fight.

DESIGN POSSIBILITIES FOR A FOURTH BRANCH

It is the contention of this book that reconstructing the commercial republic by transforming a structurally and politically subordinated administrative state into a constitutionally autonomous fourth administrative branch affords multiple and varied advantages to the regime with respect to its original design aims and aspirations. It is a necessary part of, and advances, a theory of political constitution of a commercial republic that is derived from and seeks to improve on that original design. The evidence from past and current practices—working constitutions—further informs and enriches those advantages, and highlights their limits. There will of course be trade-offs, as no one design alteration can resolve all troubles the regime currently faces. The advantages to the quality and depth of the information and expertise developed in the administrative state to guide policy making and implementation, for example, may come at the price of even less trust between the executive branch and the public administration—and less use by the institutional presidency of information and advice coming from an administrative state further distanced from presidential control.

Readers, commentators, and critics will draw their own conclusions about whether the advantages of a fourth branch outweigh the disadvantages. The preceding pages have shown, however, that those advantages are substantial, at least theoretically, and more far-reaching than most theorists and practitioners have been able or willing to appreciate. The final task of this chapter is to translate some of those advantages into one plausible design for a fourth branch.

As already noted, James Madison's Virginia Plan (see the appendix), which Edmund Randolph introduced to the constitutional convention on May 29, 1787, consisted of a set of resolutions, the first being to fix the Articles of Confederation to better fulfill its purposes. Within those resolutions were embedded several design principles expressed through specific authorities and structures. Madison's preparatory materials and correspondence before the convention indicate that he always thought about the principles and concrete specifics in tandem (Rutland 1987). He regarded the essential design principles as: 1) representation of people, not states; 2) separate institutions with distinct authorities and functions; 3) national supremacy; and 4) a guarantee of republican government to all states. Under the second principle were additional subprinciples and structural elements: 1) bicameralism; 2) no dual office holding horizontally within a level of government or vertically between levels of government; 3) a national executive with "general authority" to execute national laws and a council of revision with veto authority; and 4) a national judiciary with service during good behavior, and a structure of superior and inferior tribunals and trial and appellate jurisdictions. The national supremacy principle was further articulated through a veto over state laws and an oath required of all federal and state officials.

As is well known, the 1787 convention quickly dispensed with the idea of trying to amend the Articles of Confederation. The result was a substantially new plan of government and regime design reflecting to a considerable extent the Virginia Plan, but also other plans and compromises. Not unlike the situation in the mid-1780s, Americans are now grappling with an existing plan of government and regime design that are in considerable distress. However the critical reconstruction proposed in these pages might come about, it ought to follow the spirit of Madison's stated motivation for the Virginia Plan, to better "accomplish the objects" of the original compact. If it is to be consistent with the aims and aspirations of the American commercial republic, in other words, the creation of a fourth branch must first and foremost take into account the regime's core design aims and aspirations: limited but vigorous government, acceptance and preservation of the political value of a commercial society, and a continuous striving toward liberal justice. This in turn means a central concern with the regulation of faction, and thus the acceptance of the preservation of the regime's commitment to a design of separate institutions sharing the authorities and supervisory functions enumerated in the written compact. Because Madison sought to design a whole regime, his plan had to express multiple design principles and corresponding structural elements. For the creation of a fourth branch, the task is simpler because only one design principle is essential: the creation of institutional autonomy for administration and calibration of that autonomy against a certain measure of interdependence with the other constitutive institutions of the regime. The advantages that flow from this restructuring, not just for the separation of powers but for the design of the whole regime, originate in this single design principle.

For the fourth, administrative branch, this calibration must be such that it creates the incentives for the other branches to relate to and treat administration in a manner that increases its unique contributions to the regime. This means, in particular, bringing its long time horizon to bear on questions of the public interest, enabling the acquisition and deployment of expertise, and experience with the law in action, including the tensions between the instrumental and the constitutive that arise. This calibration, in short, requires both sufficient structure and scope of autonomy to enable the fourth branch to operate as a constitutional coequal, but also a more-than-minimal say on the part of the other branches in the structure, character, and function of the fourth branch. One possible combination of provisions that might lay a firm foundation for articulating the primary design principle of autonomy and interdependence and creating a "real civil service" (Elkin 2006, 291) is as follows.

> The administrative power is vested in a national administration, which consists of all the principal, inferior, and other public officers, as well as all departments, offices, bureaus, boards, commissions, and other agencies within which they operate, as may be created by law.
>
> The national administration is mandated to take care that the laws be faithfully administered. Congress is mandated to ensure that the administration has the structures and resources necessary to fulfill its mandate. The scope of the executive is concomitantly adjusted to center on regime self-preservation, which requires a leading role in national security, defense, diplomacy, and serving as head of state.
>
> Within the administrative branch, presidential appointment and senatorial confirmation is restricted to the principal officers of any department, office, bureau,

board, commission, or other agency, as, for example, in the structure of the US Bureau of Labor Statistics, in which only the commissioner is subject to presidential appointment and Senate confirmation, for a four-year term. The presidential removal power is restricted to some form of for-cause removal, such as might be found in the enabling statute of one of the independent regulatory commissions. Removal must be accompanied by publicly stated reasons for removal and evidence of conformance with the for-cause criteria.

All other administrative offices and officers are part of a constitutionally mandated, merit-protected civil service, which is governed by an independent board that Congress is mandated to create.

Because a great deal of adjudication takes place within the administrative state, Congress is mandated to create a system of administrative courts that balance the specialized expertise associated with agency missions and the general norms of adjudication, such as due process, associated with Article III courts. Administrative law judges, or whatever those presiding in administrative courts may be called, are subject to removal only for specified cause, such causes to be limited and specified in enabling statutes.

The extent to which the legislature, the executive, and the judiciary have authorization over creating, organizing or reorganizing, and eliminating components of the administrative state beyond those specified in this plan, as well as general supervision of operations in the fourth branch, need not be specified as those aspects will be worked out within the sphere of administrative autonomy and interdependence defined by the first four provisions.

The creation of a fourth branch is especially aimed at addressing the problems of business-state relations, which is essential for pulling the nation back onto a path more conducive to meeting its aspirations to be a commercial republic and all that entails for questions of justice and the general good. If the analysis in chapter 4 and in the sections above regarding accountability and coordination are correct, or at least persuasive, then no particular provision for the creation of the fourth branch need address business-administrative state relations directly. The autonomy and interdependence created by the provisions above will raise administration from the depths of subordination to private interests generally and the facilitation of business privilege specifically that have pushed the regime toward a virulent form of factional rule and away from the path of a fully realized commercial republic.

Nevertheless, there will inescapably be areas of ambiguity regarding the scope of authorization and supervision of the four branches. This is particularly so with respect to national security, defense, and diplomacy. One possibility for addressing this ambiguity is to keep the institutional presidency relatively intact precisely because the executive would be responsible for supervising national security, defense, intelligence, and diplomatic functions. However, the major administrative agencies for carrying out these functions and reevaluating them at appropriate times might still be placed in the administrative branch and thus subject to less day-to-day presidential command and control. Even under current constitutional and statutory arrangements, these units operate on their own much of the time. Hence, the disjunction that would occur with the creation of a fourth branch might not be so wrenching even within the reconfigured sphere of primary presidential authority. To stabilize the arrangement further, the administrative units within the executive's national security purview might come under more direct presidential command control in the event that constitutionally or statutorily specified conditions are met. Such a set-up is similar to the Constitution's provision authorizing the president to assume command of "the Militia of the several States, when called into the actual Service of the United States" (US Constitution, Article II, Section 2).

One final set of provisions not included above that constitution writers might propose and debate concerns the creation of a central coordinating body for the administrative branch, and the establishment of a true higher civil service, the latter comprised of "an elite corps of career public officials who fill key positions in governmental administration" (Huddleston 1988–89, 407). Relevant considerations and options regarding the creation of a central administrative coordinator have already been explored. The creation of a higher civil service could be roughly analogous to permanent secretaries in the British civil service, or in France to the "*hauts fonctionnaires* . . . who interpret and execute the 'general will' that equates primarily to their pursuit of the public interest" (Haraway and Haraway 2004, 111). Creation of such a new and more prominent top-level corps of career civil servants might necessitate a constitutional provision authorizing the establishment of one or more national civil-service academies. If several were created, they might provide in common for the moral, ethical, political, and administrative development of generalist leadership and management but distinguish themselves by different technical specializations, similar to the armed-services academies.

How well these ideas sit with American political history, traditions, and sentiments is surely a matter of debate. Yet some enterprising delegates to a gathering to consider the creation of a fourth branch might advance proposals along these lines to help facilitate the development of an institutional-level perspective for those serving in the fourth branch similar to what has developed in the judiciary. Although these ideas put into practice might not achieve the kind of norm and practice cohesion of the courts, they might at least serve as a way to moderate the extreme fragmentation and narrow mission orientation that prevails in the administrative state under current constitutional and legal structures and political norms. Manifestations of such current structures and norms are likely to remain because some of the authority for and supervision of the organization and operation of the fourth branch will still be in the hands of the other branches.

CONCLUSION

Reconstruction of the foundational structures of the commercial republic to incorporate a separate administrative branch with the aim of fulfilling the core principle of a calibrated autonomy and interdependence is well within the capabilities and imagination of constitution makers who might take up the cause. Several national constitutions currently in force create or reference a civil service and provide various constitutionally specified structures and protections. The constitutions of France and India, for example, provide specific provisions for a merit-based public service and include procedural protections that political authorities are constitutionally bound to follow and respect. The French Constitution of 1958 as amended recognizes "fundamental guarantees granted to civil servants and members of the Armed Forces" (Title V, Article 34). The Indian Constitution of 1949 as amended provides for the creation of a public-service commission to oversee all aspects of the administrative services at the national, state, and local levels (Part XIV, Chapter II). The 1999 Constitution of the Federal Republic of Nigeria creates within the executive a "Public Service of the Federation," which encompasses all offices and officers up to and including the "Permanent Secretary in any Ministry or Head of any Extra-Ministerial Department of the Government of the Federation howsoever designated" (Chapter VI, Part D, Section 171 [d]). The 1987 constitution of the Philippines perhaps goes the farthest. Its Article IX specifies several "constitutional commissions," including a civil service commission. This commission oversees a civil service that "embraces all branches, subdivisions, instrumentalities, and agencies of the Government, including government-owned or controlled corporations with original charters" (Section 2[1]). It also requires appointment by "merit and fitness" and removal only "for cause provided by law" (Section 2, clauses 2 and 3).

Despite these real-world examples, the reconstruction of the commercial republic to incorporate a fourth administrative branch will rile many a political or constitutional theorist, elected official, and attentive citizen. This is especially so because American exceptionalism remains strong, as does the veneration of the hallowed Constitution, no matter how much it has been modified in practice. The essential principle and interconnected provisions outlined above would in the eyes of many go well beyond the arrangements for a civil service and administrative state that can be found in any other national constitution currently in force.

Nevertheless, perhaps all those who might adamantly oppose the creation of a fourth administrative branch would be willing to join in agreement on one essential point with the few who are at least intrigued enough to consider the possibility of a fourth branch. The American administrative state is in a wretched condition, and something more far-reaching must be done than anything that has been tried before.

Perhaps, then, all can agree to strive toward a "public serve model" for the calibration of politics and merit in the administrative state (Ingraham and Ban 1988). That model achieves such calibration by centering on four essential characteristics: 1) "consistent awareness of the public service as a democratic institution for political appointees and for career managers"; 2) "joint commitment to management competency" and recognition of "the unique qualities and demands of public management"; 3) "mutual respect for the skills, perspectives and values" that political and career executives and managers bring to governance; and most important 4) "consistent awareness of, and active concern for, the public interest broadly defined" (14). This public-service model might serve well as a lodestar for new efforts at reform of administration and its relationship with other governing institutions. A firm warning must accompany any such effort, however. Any reform that fails to take account of the whole regime, including the critical centrality of state-market relations and the nature of administration as a distinct form of politics and constitutive institution of that whole regime, is doomed to fail. What the creation of a fourth, administrative branch grounded in a theory of political constitution of the commercial republic especially offers is to elevate an institutional definition of the public interest. This requires a focus on preserving and enhancing the constitutive institutions that enable a particular kind of regime. This regime, a commercial republic, is one in which energetic, imaginative popular government creates—but then respects and protects—the boundaries defining a broad sphere of personal and communal liberty, including liberty expressed as the pursuit of material gain. Whatever might be said about the prospects for the creation of a fourth branch that might push the commercial republic forward toward realization of its highest aspirations, the possibility must not be dismissed on the grounds that the effort is politically impossible or that the work will be hard.

Conclusion:
Setting Administration in Its Rightful Place

Before the emergence of the SARS-CoV-2 pandemic, the greatest public-health emergency of the past fifty years in the United States was probably the opioid abuse epidemic. In this still ongoing tragedy, 128 people died of opioid overdoses every day on average in 2018, and the economic burden of prescription opioid misuse was $78.5 billion a year (NIDA 2020). The primary federal agency responsible for monitoring and regulating the distribution of the opioids at the center of this scourge is the US Drug Enforcement Administration (DEA) in the Department of Justice. Because of the immensity of the flow of pharmaceuticals in the American economy, DEA largely relied on self-regulation. "Drug manufacturers, distributors, and large pharmacies" had to "police themselves by monitoring suspicious orders and reporting them to the agency" (Higham et al. 2019). By 2005, however, opioid overdose deaths had risen to roughly 10,000 a year. DEA began stepping up its regulatory scrutiny and enforcement, employing a set of graduated enforcement actions to put pressure on distributors and pharmacies to act more aggressively to stem the flow of illegal opioid distribution. The agency's two more forceful tools were to "issue 'an immediate suspension order' instantly halting operations" and bringing "a civil or criminal enforcement case with heavy fines" (Higham et al. 2019). Enforcement cases against big, economically important drug companies were hard to build and win, however. Nevertheless, between 2006 and 2012 the DEA took action against a number of large drug distribution facilities, issuing "show cause" demand letters and suspending facility licenses.

At first, the industry, represented by the Healthcare Distribution Alliance (HDA), worked with the DEA to develop best-practices guidelines for its member companies. When the guidelines failed to make a dent in the flood of opioids illegally circulating in American communities and DEA continued its more aggressive actions, however, the HDA turned to combative political activism to curb the DEA's formal enforcement authority. In addition to finding media and organizational allies to help it battle "overzealous regulators," the HDA cultivated support in Congress to legislate weakening of DEA enforcement tools. Twice such efforts died before final formal votes, but on the third try, and with far more congressional support and Obama administration acquiescence, the innocuously titled Ensuring Patient Access and Effective Drug Enforcement Act became law (Pub. L. no. 114-145). Although the language of its principal provision was softened slightly from the preceding versions that failed to win congressional approval, the law nevertheless narrowed the definition of an "imminent danger to the public health or safety," imposing "a dramatic diminution of the Agency's authority to issue Immediate Suspension Orders (ISOs)" (Mulrooney and Legel 2017, 346).

The HDA used other tactics, including pushing for an investigation by the Office of Inspector General of the DEA's lead enforcement official tackling the opioid crisis and the ever-popular business tactic of campaign contributions, amounting to $1.4 million flowing to the law's sponsors and cosponsors. Industry representatives defended all their tactics, insisting that the law was "intended to provide greater clarity to one element of DEA's enforcement standards and encourage communication and coordination that was much-needed between the DEA and the industry" (Higham et al. 2019). Yet DEA issuance of immediate-suspension orders declined dramatically after the law went into effect. One major drug distributor also insisted that there was "nothing inappropriate about companies communicating with policymakers in a transparent, law-abiding way to foster a more effective working relationship with the government." The industry's tactics were far from transparent, however, with many of its more aggressive tactics only coming to light during the discovery process of a massive lawsuit against the industry filed by Ohio localities in federal court.

Nine companies agreed to a settlement of the Ohio lawsuit just before opening statements in the trial were to begin, reaching settlements "worth more than $325 million" with two counties in northeast Ohio (Heisig 2019). The 2016 law has been the subject of considerable subsequent criticism, with both legislative sponsors and drug companies insisting that the law seems to have had "unintended consequences" (Higham et al. 2019). If that is truly so, it suggests insufficient deliberation within and across the executive and legislative branches about the effects of the law and what the concrete meaning of the public interest should be in shaping public action in response to this horrifying episode. The DEA did assert its views in the lawmaking process, as did the Department of Justice, but the DEA "eventually yielded to industry pressure that had created a wave of support for it in Congress" (Higham et al. 2019).

Was the industry pressure within the scope of acceptable business political privilege in a commercial republic? Observers and commentators, as well as public officials, are so inured to the aggressive assertion of political influence by well-organized and well-resourced business interests that it may now be nearly impossible to make such distinctions clearly. Would a DEA that was part of a separate fourth branch have better withstood this drug-industry pressure and influence on public policy and administration? If so, would that have been more in the public interest and better in keeping with the political value of a commercial society in the American commercial republic? It is at least plausible to suppose that a DEA as part of a fourth branch might have succeeded in fending off the critical definitional change that the 2016 law codified because it was not so subservient to elected officials in both the executive and legislative branches as to allow the drug industry to work its will. The agency might then have sustained its enforcement efforts and perhaps have convinced the industry to follow the suggestion of its own lawyers that it would be "better off averting DEA actions by taking even stronger compliance measures" (Higham et al. 2019). Surely forestalling an appreciable number of the roughly 450,000 opioid overdose deaths since 1999 (Boslett, Denham, and Hill 2020) would have been more in keeping with the public interest than what actually transpired.

The case for a fourth, administrative branch cannot really resolve such policy dilemmas with any clarity, however. The aim of the effort is not to fix policy and administrative failures but instead to shed light on the nature of the American regime, to make clear the design features and fundamental aims and aspirations of the commercial republic, and to offer the kind of far-reaching change required to redirect the path of American constitutional politics to improve the chances that those core aims and aspirations might be realized.

In constructing their commercial republic, the American founders recognized that the challenges confronting their new regime would be predominantly administrative. They went some way toward structuring their national government design accordingly, yet they proceeded to hobble its administrative capabilities, partly from confusion about the relationship between popular sovereignty and administration, but far more so from fear of the dangers of a designing ministry. Those putting the Constitution into practice sometimes succeeded in pushing the age-old fear to the margins, working around the obstacles of weak and fragmented founding-law authority and subordination to elective legitimacy to meet their obligations to govern. Nevertheless, the fear was never wholly absent, and certainly some wariness about any kind of formal authority is reasonable.

Whether out of a good-faith but confused commitment to the public interest or narrowly self-interested and demagogic motivations, however, some political leaders and self-appointed speakers for the people in nearly every era have reanimated the fear of administration and bureaucracy. A generation ago, one of the sagest voices in the study of public administration pegged this reanimated fear as particularly virulent, "a raging pandemic" (Kaufman 1981). Although an unfortunate characterization in the context of the actual and horrifically deadly pandemic raging as this book was reaching completion, this fear of bureaucracy, or at least its self-serving articulation, harbors a tragedy of its own in the irony that "government workers who are so often depicted as drab, 'faceless,' timid, and obscure should be called self-directing, dominant, and sinister, especially since the indictment is so confused and supported by such antinomic evidence" (7). What is the proper response to this recurring antipathy and the real-world damage it can precipitate in the lives of the American people?

From the perspective of the theory of the political constitution of the American commercial republic, it is time to take seriously the "deeper constitutive" (Elkin 2006, 269) implications of this question. In a world of inconstancy and conflict, chasing ever more policy reforms and tinkering around the margins of institutions and processes no longer suffices to properly confront the problems of the American administrative state and of the republic as a whole. Those problems are rooted in the design weaknesses of the regime and their exacerbation as the regime has evolved in practice. Before Americans conclude that they are in the throes of the republic's demise from an excess of its virtues, however, they might want to seize the reins and seriously consider more far-reaching change. This need not require wholesale destruction and rebirth. Trying to improve on what already exists, but also accepting the necessity of more profound adjustments to realize improvement, is the order of the day. A broad and deep form of practical reason—thinking constitutionally—is requisite. That means thinking about a particular part not in isolation but with attention to how it best fits with other parts to make a whole regime.

The whole of the regime that Americans have chosen, a commercial republic, is constituted in multiple ways—deliberation on the public interest in the legislature, reason and judgment about the law and rights in the courts, energy and dispatch in the executive in response to external threats—and administration is one of those ways. It is where collective aims are tested against reality, and the state's capacity for and efforts to learn from such testing begins. Because thinking constitutionally about public administration is in short supply, however, Americans remain trapped by their fear and confusion about public bureaucracy, allowing it to become, if not wholly an instrument of cynical political manipulation and base corruption, than at least an instrument over which they sense little influence of their own. This is the true root of the misery they feel when struggling with burdensome forms, complex procedures, and insulting officiousness.

Most Americans say they want to live their lives as they see fit, and to do so with a minimum of interference from those who might be inclined to tell them what to do and how to do it. They want to enjoy work, family, and friends in reasonable comfort, safety, peace, and security. Yet they also want strong communities, broad opportunity to use their talents for creativity and financial gain to the extent their ambitions allow, and a society in which everyone, no matter what their starting circumstances, has a fair chance to succeed as they so choose. They desire a moderate regime, in other words, one suited to moderate aspirations and a moderate sense of justice. It is a form of self-government in which government is energetic in pursuit of well-defined purposes, and "can gain and keep the affections of a people free to consider the merits of the political way of life of which they are a part" (Elkin 2006, 302). It is a republican regime they have embraced, and, it can be hoped, one they still aspire to realize.

Within those aspirations two great sources of confusion have emerged. The first is confusion about how to distinguish the essential political value of a commercial society from the need to keep business happy and productive. The second is confusion about what it means in a modern commercial republic to have an administrative state sufficiently robust yet respectfully limited so that it helps rather than hinders the realization of liberal justice. The account in these pages of how Americans and their representatives have struggled with both those challenges over time, how they have arrived at the present confusions, and how they might resolve or at least reduce them, offers an essential message. It is that administration properly understood as a constitutive institution of a modern commercial republican regime and accordingly placed among the other constitutive institutions will mean a less bloated and grasping national state and one more capable of regulating those who would conspire to engineer government for the sole purpose of serving their own narrow but unlimited ends of self-enrichment at the expense of everyone else.

Creating a fourth, administrative branch will break the link between an administrative state and the service of business interests. Public administrators, freed from the worst features and effects of subordination to the existing branches that force them to be the principal conduit for delivering business inducements, can draw on their distinctive strengths and character to help increase the chances that their companion public officials will see how actions to respond to business demands either sustain or subvert the political value of a commercial society. Even more than that, an administrative state accepted as constitutive of the regime because it is grounded in fundamental law, would establish, preserve, and promote good governance and in turn more tightly bind the union.

This central message will be hard for almost all Americans, erstwhile heirs to liberal constitutionalism, to hear and take seriously. Can a republic in which bureaucratic administration, that great bugbear of both liberalism and common law communalism, enjoys autonomy rooted in a more systemic claim to a share of governance, be more just? Even if this book convinces Americans of that possibility, their reaction may be to contend that extracting administration from its current entanglement in a subordinate capacity serving the other branches and business, under the separation of powers, is well-nigh impossible. But is it really? The constant grinding dissatisfaction with management and governance under the current arrangement strongly implies that some more drastic measures are needed. The current working constitution, and the underlying formal constitution and broader regime design, are more than just frayed around the edges. They are increasingly dysfunctional with respect to sustaining a politics of self-limitation that is capable of giving concrete meaning to a republican public interest.

Administration's dual character—instrumental *and* constitutive—is the great dilemma in this regard. Over time, there is a tendency to suppress the latter, at least in public philosophy and political rhetoric, which only sharpens the tensions and strains within the regime. There is, moreover, a great contradiction entailed in this orientation to administration in a republic, the United States in particular. Other institutional components of governance, courts especially, are also both instrumental and constitutive in character. Yet few question the legitimacy of the constitutiveness of the courts. Nor are the courts treated as strictly a means to an end. They both embody and shape what justice under law means. Perhaps political leaders and thoughtful members of the public understand courts in more comprehensive terms because they have such a long history and tradition of making visible their instrumental and constitutive contributions to the regime through the common-law tradition. There is also the obvious fact that in the Constitution's structure the courts are granted their own status as an autonomous governing institution. Yet administration is as old as the common law and tied at its origins to systems marked by a single, reigning sovereign. The subordination of administration specifically to a single-headed executive is a remnant of that history. Now that it is in a system with a constituent sovereign, the reasons to keep administration subordinate in the old way rather than tied to popular sovereignty directly through the basic compact are no longer compelling. To give administration its own constitutional home is a way for the regime finally to tap into and enjoy safely the full power of administration. It will securely place administration in service to the public interest, in a moderate regime, for the good of ordinary people who wish to govern.

APPENDIX

VARIANT TEXT A OF THE VIRGINIA PLAN, PRESENTED BY EDMUND RANDOLPH TO THE FEDERAL CONVENTION, MAY 29, 1787.

Source: The Avalon Project, Lillian Goldman Law Library, Yale Law School. https://avalon.law.yale.edu/18th_century/vatexta.asp.

1. Resolved that the Articles of Confederation ought to be so corrected & enlarged as to accomplish the objects proposed by their institution; namely, "common defence, security of liberty and general welfare."

2. Res[d] therefore that the rights of suffrage in the National Legislature ought to be proportioned to the Quotas of contribution, or to the number of free inhabitants, as the one or the other rule may seem best in different cases.

3. Res[d] that the National Legislature ought to consist of two branches.

4. Res[d] that the members of the first branch of the National Legislature ought to be elected by the people of the several States every _______ for the term of ______ ; to be of the age of years at least, to receive liberal stipends by which they may be compensated for the devotion of their time to public service; to be ineligible to any office established by a particular State, or under the authority of the United States, except those peculiarly belonging to the functions of the first branch, during the term of service, and for the space of after its expiration; to be incapable of reelection for the space of after the expiration of their term of service, and to be subject to recall.

5. Resol[d] that the members of the second branch of the National Legislature ought to be elected by those of the first, out of a proper number of persons nominated by the individual Legislatures, to be of the age of _____ years at least; to hold their offices for a term sufficient to ensure their independency; to receive liberal stipends, by which they may be compensated for the devotion of their time to public service; and to be ineligible to any office established by a particular State, or under the authority of the United States, except those peculiarly belonging to the functions of the second branch, during the term of service, and for the space of _____ after the expiration thereof.

6. Resolved that each branch ought to possess the right of originating Acts; that the National Legislature ought to be impowered to enjoy the Legislative Rights vested in Congress bar the Confederation & moreover to legislate in all cases to which the separate States are incompetent, or in which the harmony of the United States may be interrupted by the exercise of individual Legislation; to negative all laws passed by the several States, contravening in the opinion of the National Legislature the articles of Union; and to call

forth the force of the Union agst any member of the Union failing to fulfill its duty under the articles thereof.

7. Res[d] that a National Executive be instituted; to be chosen by the National Legislature for the term of years, to receive punctually at stated times, a fixed compensation for the services rendered, in which no increase or diminution shall be made so as to affect the Magistracy, existing at the time of increase or diminution, and to be ineligible a second time; and that besides a general authority to execute the National laws, it ought to enjoy the Executive rights vested in Congress by the Confederation.

8. Res[d] that the Executive and a convenient number of the National Judiciary, ought to compose a Council of revision with authority to examine every act of the National Legislature before it shall operate, & every act of a particular Legislature before a Negative thereon shall be final; and that the dissent of the said Council shall amount to a rejection, unless the Act of the National Legislature be again passed, or that of a particular Legislature be again negatived by of the members of each branch.

9. Res[d] that a National Judiciary be established to consist of one or more supreme tribunals, and of inferior tribunals to be chosen by the National Legislature, to hold their offices during good behaviour; and to receive punctually at stated times fixed compensation for their services, in which no increase or diminution shall be made so as to affect the persons actually in office at the time of such increase or diminution. that the jurisdiction of the inferior tribunals shall be to hear & determine in the first instance, and of the supreme tribunal to hear and determine in the dernier resort, all piracies & felonies on the high seas, captures from an enemy; cases in which foreigners or citizens of other States applying to such jurisdictions may be interested, or which respect the collection of the National revenue; impeachments of any National officers, and questions which may involve the national peace and harmony.

10. Resolv[d] that provision ought to be made for the admission of States lawfully arising within the limits of the United States, whether from a voluntary junction of Government & Territory on otherwise, with the consent of a number of voices in the National legislature less than the whole.

11. Res[d] that a Republican Government & the territory of each State, except in the instance of a voluntary junction of Government & territory, ought to be guarantied by the United States to each State

12. Res[d] that provision ought to be made for the continuance of Congress and their authorities and privileges, until a given day after the reform of the articles of Union shall be adopted, and for the completion of all their engagements.

13. Res[d] that provision ought to be made for the amendment of the Articles of Union whensoever it shall seem necessary, and that the assent of the National Legislature ought not to be required thereto.

14. Res[d] that the Legislative Executive & Judiciary powers within the several States ought to be bound by oath to support the articles of Union.

15. Res[d] that the amendments which shall be offered to the Confederation, by the Convention ought at a proper time, or times, after the approbation of Congress to be submitted to an assembly or assemblies of Representatives, recommended by the several Legislatures to be expressly chosen by the people, to consider & decide thereon.

REFERENCES

Aberbach, Joel, and Bert A. Rockman. 1997. "Back to the Future? Senior Federal Executives in the United States." *Governance: An International Journal of Policy and Administration* 10 (4): 323–349.

Ackerman, Bruce A. 2010. *The Decline and Fall of the American Republic*. Cambridge, MA: Harvard University Press.

ACUS. 2017. "Guide for Members." Administrative Conference of the United States. January 3. https://www.acus.gov/sites/default/files/documents/Guide%20for%20Members%20FINAL%201-3-2017.pdf.

Adler, William D. 2012. "State Capacity and Bureaucratic Autonomy in the Early United States: The Case of the Army Corps of Topographical Engineers." *Studies in American Political Development* 26 (2): 107–124.

Allison, Graham T., and Philip D. Zelikow. 1999. *Essence of Decision: Explaining the Cuban Missile Crisis*. 2nd ed. New York: Longman.

Angresano, James. 2016. *A Corporate Welfare Economy*. New York: Routledge.

Annals of the Congress of the United States. 1834. 1st Congress, part 1. Washington, DC: Gales & Seaton.

Arestis, Philip. 2016. "Main and Contributory Causes of the Recent Financial Crisis and Economic Policy Implications." In *Emerging Economies during and after the Great Recession*, edited by Philip Arestis and Malcom Sawyer, 1–36. New York: Palgrave Macmillan.

Arnold, Peri E. 1998. *Making the Managerial Presidency: Comprehensive Reorganization Planning, 1905–1996*. 2nd ed. Lawrence: University Press of Kansas.

———. 2003. "Democracy and Corruption in the 19th Century United States: Parties, 'Spoils' and Political Participation." In *The History of Corruption in Central Government*, edited by Seppo Tihonen, 197–212. Amsterdam: IOS Press.

———. 2007. "The Brownlow Committee, Regulation, and the Presidency: Seventy Years Later." *Public Administration Review* 67 (6): 1030–1040.

———. 2011. "Federalist No. 70: Can the Public Service Survive in the Contest between Hamilton's Aspirations and Madison's Reality?" *Public Administration Review* 71, s1: s105–s111.

Aron, Cyndi S. 2001. "The Evolution of the Middle Class." In *A Companion to 19th-Century America*, edited by William L. Barney. Malden, MA: Blackwell Publishers.

Ashworth, Scott. 2012. "Electoral Accountability: Recent Theoretical and Empirical Work." *Annual Review of Political Science* 15: 183–201.

Atkinson, Glen, Eric R. Hake, and Stephen P. Paschall. 2019. "Evolution of the Corporation in the United States: Stabilized Scarcity and Vested Interests." *Journal of Economic Issues* 53 (1): 1–25.

Azari, Julia R. 2013. "Institutional Change and the Presidential Mandate." *Social Science History* 37 (4): 483–514.

Baghot, Walter. 1867. *The English Constitution.* London: Chapman & Hall.

Bagley, Nicholas. 2019. "The Procedure Fetish." *Michigan Law Review* 118 (3): 345–401.

Bailey, Jeremy D. 2008. "The New Unitary Executive and Democratic Theory: The Problem of Alexander Hamilton." *American Political Science Review* 102 (4): 453–465.

———. 2015. *James Madison and Constitutional Imperfection.* New York: Cambridge University Press.

Bailyn, Bernard. 1967. *The Ideological Origins of the American Revolution.* Cambridge, MA: Harvard University Press.

Baker, Dean. 2016. *Rigged: How Globalization and the Rules of the Modern Economy Were Structured to Make the Rich Richer.* Washington, DC: Center for Economic and Policy Research.

Balla, Steven J., and Christopher J. Deering. 2013. "Police Patrols and Fire Alarms: An Empirical Examination of the Legislative Preference for Oversight." *Congress and the Presidency* 40 (1): 27–40.

Balogh, Brian. 2009. *A Government out of Sight: The Mystery of National Authority in Nineteenth-Century America.* New York: Cambridge University Press.

Banning, Lance. 1978. *The Jeffersonian Persuasion: Evolution of a Party Ideology.* Ithaca, NY: Cornell University Press.

———. 1995. *Jefferson and Madison: Three Conversations from the Founding.* Lanham, MD: Madison House.

Baritz, Loren. 1989. *The Good Life: The Meaning of Success for the American Middle Class.* New York: Knopf.

Barkin, J. Samuel. 2016. "Sovereignty." In *The Wiley Blackwell Encyclopedia of Race, Ethnicity, and Nationalism*, edited by John Stone, Rutledge M. Dennis, Polly S. Rizona, and Xiaoshuo Hou, 1–2. New York: John Wiley & Sons.

Barth, Thomas J. 1993. "Constitutional Subordinate Autonomy: Serving Multiple Masters—A Normative Theory in Practice." *Administration & Society* 25 (2): 160–182.

———. 1995. "Autonomy Grounded in Subordination: A Framework for Responding to Competing Institutional Norms." *American Review of Public Administration* 25 (3): 231–246.

Bauer, Dorothea, and Hans Peter Schmitz. 2012. "Corporations and NGOs: When Accountability Leads to Co-optation." *Journal of Business Ethics* 106 (2): 9–21.

Baumgartner, Frank R., Jeffrey M. Berry, Marie Hojnacki, David C. Kimball, and Beth L. Leech. 2009. *Lobbying and Policy Change: Who Wins, Who Loses, and Why.* Chicago: University of Chicago Press.

Baxter, Maurice G. 1995. *Henry Clay and the American System.* Lexington: University Press of Kentucky.

Beach, Jon C., Elaine D. Carter, Martha J. Dede, Charles T. Goodsell, William M. Haraway, Monisha Kumar, Betty N. Morgan, Virginia K. Sweet. 1997. "State Administration and the Founding Fathers During the Critical Period." *Administration & Society* 28 (4): 511–530.

Bearfield, Dominic A. 2009. "What Is Patronage? A Critical Reexamination." *Public Administration Review* 69 (1): 64–76.

Beaulac, Stephane. 2003. "Emer de Vattel and the Externalization of Sovereignty." *Journal of the History of International Law* 5 (2): 237–292.

Béland, Daniel, and Edella Schlager. 2019. "Varieties of Policy Feedback Research: Looking Backward, Moving Forward." *Policy Studies Journal* 47 (2): 184–205.

Bennett, Anthony J. 1996. *The American President's Cabinet: From Kennedy to Bush.* New York: St. Martin's Press.

Bensel, Richard Franklin. 1990. *Yankee Leviathan: The Origins of Central State Authority in America, 1859–1877.* New York: Cambridge University Press.

Bergmann, William H. 2012. *The American National State and the Early West.* New York: Cambridge University Press.

Bernstein, Jonathan. 2019. "Is U.S. Republic or Democracy? Why Some Conservatives Pick a Side." *Bloomberg.com,* April 11. https://www.bloomberg.com/opinion/articles/2019-04-11/is-u-s-republic-or-democracy-why-some-conservatives-pick-a-side.

Bertelli, Anthony E., and Laurence E. Lynn. 2006a. *Madison's Managers: Public Administration and the Constitution.* Baltimore, MD: Johns Hopkins University Press.

———. 2006b. Public Management in the Shadow of the Constitution." *Administration & Society* 38 (1): 31–57.

Bevir, Mark. 2010. *Democratic Governance.* Princeton, NJ: Princeton University Press.

Bien, Morris. 1910. "The Public Lands of the United States." *North American Review* 192 (658): 387–402.

Bierele, Thomas C., and Rebecca J. Long. 1999. "Chilling Collaboration: The Federal Advisory Committee Act and Stakeholder Involvement in Environmental Decisionmaking." *Environmental Law Reporter* 29 (7): 10399–10418.

Binder, Sarah, and Mark Spindel. 2017. *The Myth of Independence: How Congress Governs the Federal Reserve.* Princeton: Princeton University Press.

Birdsall, Nancy. 2016. "Middle-Class Heroes: The Best Guarantee of Good Governance." *Foreign Affairs* 95 (2): 25–32.

Blair, Margaret M., and Elizabeth Pollman. 2017. "The Supreme Court's View of Corporate Rights: Two Centuries of Evolution and Controversy." In *Corporations and American Democracy,* edited by Naomi R. Lamoreaux and William J. Novak, 231–270. Cambridge, MA: Tobin Project.

Blau, Benjamin M., Tyler J. Brough, and Diana W. Thomas. 2013. "Corporate Lobbying, Political Connections, and the Bailout of Banks." *Journal of Banking & Finance* 37 (8): 3007–3017.

Bledstein, Burton J., and Robert D. Johnston. 2001. *The Middling Sorts: Explorations in the History of the American Middle Class.* New York: Routledge.

Bonica, Adam. 2016. "Avenues of Influence: On the Political Expenditures of Corporations and Their Directors and Executives." *Business and Politics* 18 (4): 367–394.

Boslett, Andrew J., Alina Denham, and Elaine L. Hill. 2020. "Using Contributing Causes of Death Improves Opioid Involvement in Unclassified Drug Overdoses in US Death Records." *Addiction* 115 (7): 1308–1317.

Bovaird, Tony. 2007. "Beyond Engagement and Participation: User and Community Coproduction of Public Services." *Public Administration Review* 67 (5): 846–860.

Bozeman, Barry, and Xuhong Su. 2015. "Public Service Motivation Concepts and Theory: A Critique." *Public Administration Review* 75 (5): 700–710.

Bradley, Curtis A., and Trevor W. Morrison. 2012. "Historical Gloss and the Separation of Powers." *Harvard Law Review* 126 (2): 411–485.

Bremer, Emily S. 2015. "The Unwritten Administrative Constitution." *Florida Law Review* 66 (3): 1215–1273.

Bressman, L. S., and Vanderbergh, M. P. 2006. "Inside the Administrative State: A Critical Look at the Practice of Presidential Control." *Michigan Law Review* 105 (1): 47–99.

Brown, Kate Elizabeth. 2017. *Alexander Hamilton and the Development of American Law.* Lawrence: University Press of Kansas.

Brown, Trevor L., Matthew Potoski, and David M. Van Slyke. 2018. "Complex Contracting: Management Challenges and Solutions." *Public Administration Review* 78 (5): 739–747.

Bull, Reeve T. 2013. "Making the Administrative State 'Safe for Democracy': A Theoretical and Practical Analysis of Citizen Participation in Agency Decisionmaking." *Administrative Law Review* 65 (3): 611–664.

Calabresi, Steven G., and Nicholas Terrell. 2009. "The Fatally Flawed Theory of the Unbundled Executive." *Minnesota Law Review* 96 (5): 1696–1740.

Calabresi, Steven G., and Christopher S. Yoo. 2008. *The Unitary Executive: Presidential Power from Washington to Bush.* New Haven, CT: Yale University Press.

Calabresi, Steven G., Mark E. Berghausen, and Skylar Albertson. 2012. "The Rise and Fall of the Separation of Powers." *Northwestern University Law Review* 106 (2): 527–549.

Caldwell, Lynton K. 1988. *The Administrative Theories of Hamilton and Jefferson: Their Contributions to Thought on Public Administration.* 2nd ed. New York: Holmes & Meier.

Cameron, Charles M., and John M. De Figueiredo. 2020. "Quitting in Protest: Presidential Policymaking and Civil Service Response." NBER Working Paper no. 26944. https://www.nber.org/papers/w26944.

Campaign Finance Institute. 2018. "Table 2–1: The Cost of Winning an Election, 1986–2018." http://www.cfinst.org/pdf/federal/HistoricalTables/pdf/CFI_Federal-CF_18_Table2-01.pdf.

Carolan, Eoin. 2009. *The New Separation of Powers: A Theory of the Modern State.* Oxford, UK: Oxford University Press.

Carpenter, Daniel P. 2001. *The Forging of Bureaucratic Autonomy: Reputations, Networks, and Policy Innovation in Executive Agencies, 1862–1928.* Princeton, NJ: Princeton University Press.

Carpenter, Daniel P., and David A. Moss, eds. 2014. *Preventing Regulatory Capture: Special Interest Influence and How to Limit It.* New York: Cambridge University Press.

Chisholm, Donald. 1992. *Coordination without Hierarchy: Informal Structures in Multiorganizational Systems.* Berkeley: University of California Press.

Cohen, Jeffrey E. 1988. *The Politics of the U.S. Cabinet: Representation in the Executive Branch, 1798–1984.* Pittsburgh: University of Pittsburgh Press.

Conley, Patricia Heidotting. 2001. *Presidential Mandates: How Elections Set the National Agenda.* Chicago: University of Chicago Press.

Conover, Milton. 1923. *The General Land Office: Its History, Activities and Organization.* Baltimore, MD: Johns Hopkins University Press.

Cook, Brian J. 1992. "The Representative Function of Bureaucracy: Public Administration in Constitutive Perspective." *Administration & Society* 23 (4): 403–429.

———. 2007. *Democracy and Administration: Woodrow Wilson's Ideas and the Challenges of Public Management.* Baltimore, MD: Johns Hopkins University Press.

———. 2010. "The Organ of Experience: A Defense of the Primacy of Public Administrators in the Design and Reform of Policy and Law." *Administration & Society* 42 (3): 263–286.

———. 2014. *Bureaucracy and Self-Government: Reconsidering the Role of Public Administration in American Politics.* 2nd ed. Baltimore, MD: Johns Hopkins University Press.

Cooper, Philip J. 1988. *Public Law and Public Administration.* Englewood Cliffs, NJ: Prentice Hall.

Cooper, Rebecca, Caroline Heldman, Alissa R. Ackerman, and Victoria A. Farrar-Meyers. 2016. "Hidden Corporate Profits in the U.S. Prison System: The Unorthodox Policymaking of the American Legislative Exchange Council." *Contemporary Justice Review* 19 (3): 380–400.

Cordero, Carrie F., Heidi Li Feldman, and Chimene I. Keitner. 2020. "The Law against Family Separation." *Columbia Human Rights Law Review* 51 (2): 432–508.

Costello, Jennifer L. 2019. "Testimony of Acting Inspector General Jennifer L. Costello before the Committee on Oversight and Reform, U.S. House of Representatives, July 12, 2019." www.oig.dhs.gov.

Cotlar, Seth. 2013. "Languages of Democracy in America from the Revolution to the Election of 1800." In *Re-imagining Democracy in the Age of Revolutions: America, France, Britain, Ireland, 1750–1850*, edited by Joanna Innes and Mark Philip, 13–27. New York: Oxford University Press.

Crane, Daniel A. 2017. "The Disassociation of Incorporation and Regulation in the Progressive Era and the New Deal." In *Corporations and American Democracy*, edited by Naomi R. Lamoreaux and William J. Novak, 102–130. Cambridge, MA: Tobin Project.

Crenson, Matthew A. 1975. *The Federal Machine: Beginnings of Bureaucracy in Jacksonian America*. Baltimore, MD: Johns Hopkins University Press.

Croley, Steven P. 2008. *Regulation and Public Interests: The Possibility of Good Regulatory Governance*. Princeton, NJ: Princeton University Press.

Crouch, Jeffrey. 2008. "The Law: Presidential Misuse of the Pardon Power." *Presidential Studies Quarterly* 38 (4): 722–734.

DeCanio, Samuel. 2015. *Democracy and the Origins of the American Regulatory State*. New Haven, CT: Yale University Press.

Delrahim, Makan. 2019. "Ensuring the Legacy of the Consumer Welfare Standard." Opening Remarks as Prepared for the Federalist Society National Lawyers Convention. Washington, DC: U.S. Department of Justice, November 14.

Devins, Neal. 2009. "Presidential Unilateralism and Political Polarization: Why Today's Congress Lacks the Will and the Way to Stop Presidential Initiatives." *Willamette Law Review* 45 (3): 395–416.

Diamond, Martin. 1959. "Democracy and *The Federalist:* A Reconsideration of the Framers' Intent. *American Political Science Review* 53 (1): 52–68.

Dietsch, Peter. 2010. "The Market, Competition, and Equality." *Politics, Philosophy & Economics* 9 (2): 213–244.

Dudley, Larkin, Kathryn E. Webb Farley, and Noel Gniady Banford. 2018. "Looking Back to Look Forward: Federal Officials' Perceptions of Public Engagement." *Administration & Society* 50 (5): 679–698.

Durant, Robert F. 2014. "Progressivism, Corporate Capitalism, and the Social Sciences: Confronting the Paradox of Federal Administrative Reform in America." *Administration & Society* 46 (6): 599–631.

———. 2015. "Whither Power in Public Administration? Attainment, Dissipation, and Loss." *Public Administration Review* 75 (2): 206–218.

Eden, Lynn. 2004. *Whole World on Fire: Organizations, Knowledge, and Nuclear Weapons Devastation*. Ithaca, NY: Cornell University Press.

Eikenberry, Angela M., and Jodie Drapal Kluver. "The Marketization of the Nonprofit Sector: Civil Society at Risk?" 2004. *Public Administration Review* 64 (2): 132–140.

Eisner, Marc Allen. 1991. *Antitrust and the Triumph of Economics: Institutions, Expertise, and Policy Change*. Chapel Hill: University of North Carolina Press.

Elkin, Stephen L. 1985. "Pluralism in Its Place: State and Regime in Liberal Democracy."

In *The Democratic State*, edited by Roger Benjamin and Stephen L. Elkin. Lawrence: University Press of Kansas.

———. 1987. *City and Regime in the American Republic*. Chicago: University of Chicago Press.

———. 1994. "Business-State Relations in the Commercial Republic." *Journal of Political Philosophy* 2 (2): 115–139.

———. 2004. "Thinking Constitutionally: The Problem of Deliberative Democracy." *Social Philosophy and Policy* 21 (1): 39–75.

———. 2006. *Reconstructing the Commercial Republic: Constitutional Design after Madison*. Chicago: University of Chicago Press.

Ellison, Brian A., and Adam J. Newmark. 2010. "Building the Reservoir to Nowhere: The Role of Agencies in Advocacy Coalitions." *Policy Studies Review* 38 (4): 653–678.

Emerson, Blake. 2021. "The Departmental Structure of Executive Power: Subordinate Checks from Madison to Mueller." *Yale Journal on Regulation* 38 (1): forthcoming.

Ericson, David F. 2017. "The United States Military, State Development, and Slavery in the Early Republic." *Studies in American Political Development* 31 (1): 130–148.

Eskridge, William N., Jr., and John Ferejohn. 2010. *A Republic of Statutes: The New American Constitution*. New Haven, CT: Yale University Press.

Farina, Cynthia R. 2010. "False Comfort and Impossible Promises: Uncertainty, Information Overload, and the Unitary Executive." *Journal of Constitutional Law* 12 (2): 357–424.

Farrand, Max, ed. 1911. *The Records of the Federal Convention of 1787*. Vol. 3. New Haven, CT: Yale University Press.

The Federalist Papers. 2001. Edited by Jim Manis. Pennsylvania State University, Electronic Classics Series. Hazleton: Pennsylvania State University. https://www.sisd.net/cms/lib/TX01001452/Centricity/Domain/729/Federalist_Papers.pdf.

Fenno, Richard F., Jr. 1959. *The President's Cabinet: An Analysis in the Period from Wilson to Eisenhower*. Cambridge, MA: Harvard University Press.

Ferguson, Thomas, and Joel Rogers. 1986. *Right Turn: The Decline of the Democrats and the Future of American Politics*. New York: Hill & Wang.

Finer, Herman. 1941. "Administrative Responsibility in Democratic Government." *Public Administration Review* 1 (4): 335–350.

Fiorina, Morris P. 1989. *Congress: Keystone of the Washington Establishment*. 2nd ed. New Haven, CT: Yale University Press.

Fishkin, Joseph, and William E. Forbath. 2014. "The Anti-Oligarchy Constitution." *Boston University Law Review* 94 (3):669–696.

Flynn, Meagan. 2020. "'Not Good Enough': How Rep. Katie Porter's Relentless Questioning Led the CDC Chief to Commit to Free Coronavirus Testing." *Washington Post*. https://www.washingtonpost.com/nation/2020/03/13/coronavirus-testing-katie-porter/.

Ford, Carmel. 2017. "Homeownership by Race and Ethnicity." *Eye on Housing*. National Association of Home Builders, December 15. https://eyeonhousing.org/2017/12/homeownership-by-race-and-ethnicity/.

Formisano. Ron. 2017. *American Oligarchy: The Permanent Political Class*. Urbana: University of Illinois Press.

Fraser, Nancy, and Linda Gordon. 1994. "A Genealogy of *Dependency:* Tracing a Keyword of the U.S. Welfare State." *Signs: Journal of Women in Culture and Society* 19 (2): 309–336.

Froomkin, A. Michael. 1987. "In Defense of Administrative Agency Autonomy." *Yale Law Journal* 96 (4): 787–814.

Gailmard, Sean, and John W. Patty. 2013. *Learning While Governing: Expertise and Accountability in the Executive Branch.* Chicago: University of Chicago Press.

Garcia, Eric. 2016. "A History of 'Draining the Swamp.'" *Roll Call*, October 18. https://www.rollcall.com/2016/10/18/a-history-of-draining-the-swamp/.

Garrett, R. Sam, James A. Thurber, A. Lee Fritschler, and David H. Rosenbloom. 2006. "Assessing the Impact of Bureaucracy Bashing by Electoral Campaigns." *Public Administration Review* 66 (2): 228–240.

Geisst, Charles R. 1997. *Wall Street: A History*. 4th ed. New York: Oxford University Press.

Genovese, Michael A. 1987. "The Presidency and Styles of Economic Management." *Congress and the Presidency* 14 (2): 51–67.

Gibson, Alan. 1993. "The Commercial Republic and the Pluralist Critique of Marxism: An Analysis of Martin Diamond's Interpretation of 'Federalist' 10." *Polity* 25 (4): 497–528.

———. 2012. "Madison's 'Great Desideratum': Impartial Administration and the Extended Republic." *American Political Thought* 1 (2): 181–207.

Gilbert, Jess, Spencer D. Wood, and Gwen Sharp. 2002. "Who Owns the Land? Agricultural Land Ownership by Race/Ethnicity." *Rural America* 17 (4): 55–62.

Ginsberg, Tom, and Aziz Z. Huq. 2018. *How to Save a Democracy.* Chicago: University of Chicago Press.

Goldberg, Joseph P., and William T. Moye. 1985. *The First Hundred Years of the Bureau of Labor Statistics.* Washington, DC: U.S. Department of Labor, Bulletin 2235.

Gordon, Sanford C., and Catherine Hafer. 2005. "Flexing Muscle: Corporate Political Expenditures as Signals to the Bureaucracy." *American Political Science Review* 99 (2): 245–261.

Green, Richard T. 2014. "Institutional History and New Public Governance." In *New Public Governance: A Regime-Centered Perspective*, edited by Douglas F. Morgan and Brian J. Cook. Armonk, NY: M. E. Sharpe.

———. 2019. *Alexander Hamilton's Public Administration.* Tuscaloosa: University of Alabama Press.

Griffin, Charles J. 1992. "New Light on Eisenhower's Farewell Address." *Presidential Studies Quarterly* 22 (3): 469–479.

Griffin, Stephen M. 1996. *American Constitutionalism: From Theory to Politics.* Princeton, NJ: Princeton University Press.

Grossman, Andrew D. 2002. "The Early Cold War and American Political Development: Reflections on Recent Research." *International Journal of Politics, Culture, and Society* 15 (3): 471–483.

Grullon, Gustavo, Yelena Larkin, and Roni Michaely. 2015. "The Disappearance of Public Firms and the Changing Nature of U.S. Industries." March. https://pdfs.semanticscholar.org/3af3/51b2d8a83546cc361e15a6f9ac87b7fa32ca.pdf.

Haeder, Simon F., and Yackee, Susan Webb. 2015. "Influence and the Administrative Process: Lobbying the U.S. President's Office of Management and Budget." *American Political Science Review* 10 (3): 507–522.

Haines, Michael R. 2006. "Components of Population Growth, by Decade: 1790–2000." Table Aa15–21. In *Historical Statistics of the United States, Earliest Times to the Present: Millennial Edition*, edited by Susan B. Carter, Scott Sigmund Gartner, Michael R. Haines, Alan L. Olmstead, Richard Sutch, and Gavin Wright. New York: Cambridge University Press. http://dx.doi.org/10.1017/ISBN-9780511132971.Aa1-109.

Halliday, Daniel, and Janine O'Flynn. 2018. "Economic Rent, Rent-Seeking Behavior, and the Case of Privatized Incarceration." In *The Palgrave Handbook of Philosophy and Public Policy*, edited by David Boonin, 455–467. New York: Palgrave Macmillan.

Hamburger, Philip. 2014. *Is Administrative Law Unlawful?* Chicago: University of Chicago Press.

Hammack, David C. 2002. "Nonprofit Organizations in American History: Research Opportunities and Sources." *American Behavioral Scientist* 45 (11): 1638–1674.

Haraway, William M., and Dana L. Haraway. 2004. "American Civil Service Reform: Using France as a Model to Develop Administrative Statesmen in the Senior Executive Service." *International Social Science Review* 79 (3 and 4): 108–123.

Hart, Melissa. 2011. "From *Wards Cove* to *Ricci:* Struggling Against the 'Built-in Headwinds' of a Skeptical Court." *Wake Forest Law Review* 46 (2): 261–279.

Hayek, Frederick A. von. 1945. *The Road to Serfdom.* Chicago: University of Chicago Press.

Healy, Andrew, and Neil Malhotra. 2013. "Retrospective Voting Reconsidered." *Annual Review of Political Science* 16: 285–306

Heidelberg, Roy L. 2017. "Political Accountability and Spaces of Contestation." *Administration & Society* 49 (10): 1379–1402.

———. 2019. "The Becoming of the Policy Maker." *Administration & Society*, Online First. https://doi.org/10.1177%2F0095399719890301.

Heisig, Eric. 2019. "Cuyahoga, Summit Counties Received Millions of Dollars through Opioid Litigation." Cleveland.com, October 23. https://www.cleveland.com/court-justice/2019/10/cuyahoga-summit-counties-received-millions-of-dollars-through-opioid-litigation-see-the-breakdown.html.

Hennessey, Jessica L., and John Joseph Wallis. 2017. "Corporations and Organizations in the United States after 1840." In *Corporations and American Democracy*, edited by Naomi R. Lamoreaux and William J. Novak, 77–100. Cambridge, MA: Tobin Project.

Hertel-Fernandez, Alexander. 2016. "Explaining Durable Business Coalitions in U.S. Politics: Conservatives and Corporate Interests across America's Statehouses." *Studies in American Political Development* 30 (1): 1–18.

Higham, Scott, Sari Horowitz, Steven Rich, and Meryl Kornfield. 2019. "Inside the Drug Industry's Plan to Defeat the DEA." Washingtonpost.com, September 13. https://www.washingtonpost.com/graphics/2019/investigations/drug-industry-plan-to-defeat-dea/?nid=top_pb_signin.

Hilt, Eric. 2017. "Early American Corporations and the State." In *Corporations and American Democracy*, edited by Naomi R. Lamoreaux and William J. Novak, 41–76. Cambridge, MA: Tobin Project.

Hoffer, Williamjames Hull. 2007. *To Enlarge the Machinery of Government: Congressional Debates on the Growth of the American State, 1858–1891.* Baltimore, MD: Johns Hopkins University Press.

Hogue, Henry B. 2012. "Presidential Reorganization Authority: History, Recent Initiatives, and Options for Congress." *Congressional Research Service*, December 11. https://fas.org/sgp/crs/misc/R44909.pdf.

Hohle, Randolph. 2015. *Race and the Origins of American Neoliberalism.* New York: Routledge.

Hollis-Brusky, Amanda. 2015. *Ideas with Consequences: The Federalist Society and the Conservative Counterrevolution.* New York: Oxford University Press.

Howell, William G. 2003. *Power without Persuasion: The Politics of Direct Presidential Action.* Princeton, NJ: Princeton University Press.

Huddleston, Mark W. 1988–89. "Is the SES a Higher Civil Service?" *Policy Studies Journal* 17 (2): 406–419.
Hummel, Ralph P. 2008. *The Bureaucratic Experience: The Post-Modern Challenge*. 5th ed. Armonk, NY: M. E. Sharpe.
Huq, Aziz Z. 2014. "The Negotiated Structural Constitution." *Columbia Law Review* 114 (7): 1595–1686.
Husted, Thomas, and David Nickerson. 2014. "Political Economy of Presidential Disaster Declarations and Federal Disaster Assistance." *Public Finance Review* 42 (1): 35–57.
Inequality.org. N.d. "Wealth Inequality in the United States." https://inequality.org/facts/wealth-inequality/.
Ingraham, Patricia W., and Carolyn Ban. 1988. "Politics and Merit: Can They Meet in a Public Service Model?" *Review of Public Personnel Administration* 8 (2): 7–19.
Ingrams, Alex. 2020. "Organizational Citizenship Behavior in the Public and Private Sectors: A Multilevel Test of Public Service Motivation and Traditional Antecedents." *Review of Public Personnel Administration* 40 (2): 222–244.
Jacobs, Sharon B. 2019. "The Statutory Separation of Powers." *Yale Law Journal* 129 (2): 378–444.
Jefferson, Thomas. 1795. "From Thomas Jefferson to Jean Nicolas Démeunier, 29 April 1975." Founders Online, National Archives. http://founders.archives.gov/documents/Jefferson/01-28-02-0259. [Original source: *The Papers of Thomas Jefferson*, vol. 28, 1 January 1794–29 February 1796, edited by John Catanzariti. Princeton, NJ: Princeton University Press, 2000, 340–342.]
———. 1801. "First Inaugural Address, 4 March 1801." Founders Online, National Archives, https://founders.archives.gov/documents/Jefferson/01-33-02-0116-0004. [Original source: The Papers of Thomas Jefferson, vol. 33, 17 February–30 April 1801, edited by Barbara B. Oberg. Princeton, NJ: Princeton University Press, 2006, 148–152.]
John, Richard R. 1995. *Spreading the News: The American Postal System from Franklin to Morse*. Cambridge, MA: Harvard University Press.
———. 1997. "Governmental Institutions as Agents of Change: Rethinking American Political Development in the Early Republic, 1787–1835." *Studies in American Political Development* 11 (2): 347–380.
———. 2003. "Affairs of Office: The Executive Departments, the Election of 1828, and the Making of the Democratic Party." In *The Democratic Experiment: New Directions in American Political History*, edited by Meg Jacobs, William J. Novak, and Julian E. Zelizer, 50–84. Princeton, NJ: Princeton University Press.
Johnson, Paul. 1991. *The Birth of the Modern: World Society 1815–1830*. New York: HarperCollins.
Johnston, Judy, and Alexander Kouzmin. 1998. "Who Are the Rent Seekers?: From the Ideological Attack on Public Officials to the 'Pork Barrel' Par Excellence—Privatization and Out-Sourcing as Oligarchic Corruption." *Administrative Theory & Praxis* 20 (4): 491–507.
Karl, Barry D. 1988. "The Constitution and Central Planning: The Third New Deal Revisited." *Supreme Court Review 1988*: 163–201. https://www.journals.uchicago.edu/doi/abs/10.1086/scr.1988.3109624.
Karty, K. D. 2002. "Closure and Capture in Federal Advisory Committees." *Business and Politics* 4 (2): 213–238.
Kathi, Pradeep Chandra, and Terry L. Cooper. 2005. "Democratizing the Administrative

State: Connecting Neighborhood Councils and City Agencies." *Public Administration Review* 65 (5): 559–567.

Kaufman, Herbert. 1981. "Fear of Bureaucracy: A Raging Pandemic." *Public Administration Review* 41 (1): 1–9.

Kelleher, Christine A., and Susan Webb Yackee. 2006. "Who's Whispering in Your Ear? The Influence of Third Parties over State Agency Decisions." *Political Research Quarterly* 59 (4): 629–643.

Kerwin, Keith, Scott Furlong, and William West. 2010. "Interest Groups, Rulemaking, and American Bureaucracy." In *The Oxford Handbook of American Bureaucracy*, edited by Robert F. Durant, 590–611. New York: Oxford University Press.

Kitrosser, Heidi. 2009. "Accountability and Administrative Structure." *Willamette Law Review* 45: 607–658.

Kovacs, Kathryn E. 2018. "Rules about Rulemaking and the Rise of the Unitary Executive." *Administrative Law Review* 70, 3: 515–567.

Krause, George A., David E. Lewis, and James W. Douglas. 2006. "Political Appointments, Civil Service Systems, and Bureaucratic Competence: Organizational Balancing and Executive Branch Revenue Forecasts in the American States." *American Journal of Political Science* 50 (3): 770–787.

Kruse, Kevin M. 2005. *White Flight: Atlanta and the Making of Modern Conservatism*. Princeton, NJ: Princeton University Press.

Kwak, James. 2013. "Cultural Capture and the Financial Crisis." In *Preventing Regulatory Capture: Special Interest Influence and How to Limit It*, edited by Daniel Carpenter and David A. Moss, 98–125. New York: Cambridge University Press.

Lasswell, Harold D. 1936. *Politics: Who Gets What, When, and How.* New York: Whittlesey House.

Lavertu, Stéphane, Daniel E. Walters, and David L. Weimer. 2011. "Scientific Expertise and the Balance of Political Interests: MEDCAC and Medicare Coverage Decisions." *Journal of Public Administration Research and Theory* 21 (2): 211–237.

Lawson, Gary. 2010. "Burying the Constitution Under a TARP." *Harvard Journal of Law and Public Policy* 33 (1): 55–72.

Lewis, Catherine Devereaux. 2016. "Presidential Authority over Trade: Imposing Tariffs and Duties." Washington, DC: Congressional Research Service, December 9. https://fas.org/sgp/crs/misc/R44707.pdf.

Lindbloom, Charles E. 1977. *Politics and Markets.* New York: Basic Books.

Lindert, Peter H., and Jeffrey G. Williamson. 2012. "American Incomes 1774–1860." *National Bureau of Economic Research*, Working Paper 18396. http://www.nber.org/papers/w18396.

Lindsey, Brink, and Steven M. Teles. 2017. *The Captured Economy: How the Powerful Enrich Themselves, Slow Down Growth and Increase Inequality.* New York: Oxford University Press.

Link, Arthur S., ed. 1968. *The Papers of Woodrow Wilson*, vol. 5. Princeton, NJ: Princeton University Press.

———. 1969. *The Papers of Woodrow Wilson*, vol. 7. Princeton, NJ: Princeton University Press.

———. 1975. *The Papers of Woodrow Wilson*, vol. 20. Princeton, NJ: Princeton University Press.

Long, Heather. 2020. "Railroads are Slashing Workers, Cheered on by Wall Street to Stay Profitable amid Trump's Trade War." *Washington Post*, January 3. https://www.washingtonpost.com/business/economy/railroads-are-slashing-workers-cheered-on-by-wall-street-to-stay-profitable-amid-trumps-trade-war/2020/01/02/dc757ed4-1603-11ea-a659-7d69641c6ff7_story.html.

Long, Norton E. 1949. "Power and Administration." *Public Administration Review* 9 (4): 257–264.

———. 1952. "Bureaucracy and Constitutionalism." *American Political Science Review* 46 (3): 808–818.

Lowery, David. 1993. "A Bureaucratic-Centered Image of Governance: The Founders' Thought in Modern Perspective." *Journal of Public Administration Research and Theory* 3 (2): 182–208.

Lowi, Theodore E. 1979. *The End of Liberalism*. 2nd ed. New York: W. W. Norton.

———. 1985. *The Personal President: Power Invested, Promise Unfulfilled*. Ithaca, NY: Cornell University Press.

Lusk, Jayson L. 2016. "The Evolving Role of the USDA in the Food and Agricultural Economy." Mercatus Research, Mercatus Center at George Mason University, Arlington, VA, June. https://www.mercatus.org/system/files/Lusk-USDA-v1.pdf.

Magill, M. Elizabeth. 2001. "Beyond Powers and Branches in Separation of Powers Law." *University of Pennsylvania Law Review* 150 (2): 603–660.

Maritain, Jacques. 1951. *Man and the State*. Washington, DC: Catholic University of America Press.

Mashaw, Jerry L. 2006. "Recovering American Administrative Law: Federalist Foundations, 1787–1801." *Yale Law Journal* 115 (6): 1256–1344.

———. 2007. "Reluctant Nationalists: Federal Administration and Administrative Law in the Republican Era,1801–1829." *Yale Law Journal* 116 (8): 1636–1740.

———. 2010. "Federal Administration and Administrative Law in the Gilded Age." *Yale Law Journal* 119 (7): 1362–1472.

———. 2012. *Creating the Administrative Constitution: The Lost One Hundred Years of American Administrative Law*. New Haven, CT: Yale University Press.

Mayer, Jane. 2016. *Dark Money: The Hidden History of the Billionaires Behind the Rise of the Radical Right*. New York: Doubleday.

Mazur, Christopher. 2017. "Rural Residents More Likely to Own Homes Than Urban Residents." United States Census Bureau, September 27. https://www.census.gov/library/stories/2017/09/rural-home-ownership.html.

McCormick, Richard L. 1981. "The Discovery That Business Corrupts Politics: A Reappraisal of the Origins of Progressivism." *American Historical Review* 86 (2): 247–274.

McCoy, Drew R. 1980. *The Elusive Republic: Political Economy in Jeffersonian America*. Chapel Hill: University of North Carolina Press.

———. 1989. *The Last of the Fathers: James Madison and the Republican Legacy*. New York: Cambridge University Press.

McCubbins, Matthew D., and Thomas Schwartz. 1984. "Congressional Oversight Overlooked: Police Patrols versus Fire Alarms." *American Journal of Political Science* 28 (1): 165–179.

McDonald, Forrest. 1958. *We the People: The Economic Origins of the Constitution*. Chicago: University of Chicago Press.

McGuire, Michael, and Robert Agranoff. 2010. "Networking in the Shadow of Bureaucracy." In *The Oxford Handbook of American Bureaucracy*, edited by Robert F. Durant, 372–395. New York: Oxford University Press.

Meier, Kenneth J., and John Bohte. 2003. "Span of Control and Public Organizations: Implementing Luther Gulick's Research Design." *Public Administration Review* 63 (1): 61–70.

Meier, Kenneth J., and Laurence J. O'Toole, Jr. 2006. *Bureaucracy in a Democratic State: A Governance Perspective.* Baltimore, MD: Johns Hopkins University Press.

Mettler, Suzanne, and Mallory SoRelle. 2014. "Policy Feedback Theory." In *Theories of the Policy Process.* 3rd ed., edited by Paul A. Sabatier and Christopher M. Weible, 151–182. Boulder, CO: Westview Press.

Metzger, Gillian E. 2013. "Administrative Constitutionalism." *Texas Law Review* 91 (7): 1897–1935.

———. 2015. "The Constitutional Duty to Supervise." *Yale Law Journal* 124 (6): 1836–2201.

———. 2017. "Foreword: 1930s Redux: The Administrative State under Siege." *Harvard Law Review* 131 (1):1–95.

Michaels, Jon D. 2015. "An Enduring, Evolving Separation of Powers." *Columbia Law Review* 115 (3): 515–597.

———. 2017. *Constitutional Coup: Privatization's Threat to the American Republic.* Cambridge, MA: Harvard University Press.

Miller, Susan M. 2013. "Administering Representation: The Role of Elected Administrators in Translating Citizens' Preference into Public Policy." *Journal of Public Administration Research and Theory* 23 (4): 865–897.

Minsky, Hyman. 1992. "Schumpeter and Finance." In *Markets and Institutions: Essays in Honor of Paulo Sylas Labini*, edited by Salvatore Bisasco, Allesandro Roncaglia, and Michele Salvati, 103–115. New York: St. Martin's Press.

Moe, Terry M. 1984. "The New Economics of Organization." *American Journal of Political Science* 28 (4): 739–777.

———. 2012. "Delegation, Control, and the Study of Public Bureaucracy." *Forum* 10, 2 ISSN (Online) 1540–8884, https://doi.org/10.1515/1540-8884.1508.

Moe, Terry M., and William D. Howell. 1999. "The Presidential Power of Unilateral Action." *Journal of Law, Economics and Organization* 15 (1): 132–179.

Morgan, Douglas F., and Brian J. Cook, eds. 2014. *New Public Governance: A Regime-Centered Perspective.* Armonk, NY: M. E. Sharpe.

Moynihan, Donald P. 2008. "The Normative Model in Decline? Public Service Motivation in the Age of Governance." In *Motivation in Public Service: The Call of Public Service*, edited by James L. Perry and Annie Hondeghem, 247–267. New York: Oxford University Press.

Mulrooney, John J., II, and Katherine E. Legel. 2017. "Current Navigation Points in Drug Diversion Law: Hidden Rocks in Shallow, Murky, Drug-Infested Waters." *Marquette Law Review* 101 (2): 333–451.

Nadelsky, Jennifer. 1990. *Private Property and the Limits of American Constitutionalism: The Madison Framework and Its Legacy.* Chicago: University of Chicago Press.

Nash, George H. 2006. *The Conservative Intellectual Movement in America since 1945.* Thirtieth-Anniversary Edition. Wilmington, DE: ISI Books.

Nelson, David, and Susan Webb Yackee. 2012. "Lobbying Coalitions and Government Policy Change: An Analysis of Federal Agency Rulemaking." *Journal of Politics* 74 (2): 339–353.

Nelson, William E. 2006. *The Roots of American Bureaucracy, 1830–1900.* Originally published 1982, Harvard University Press. Reprinted with a new preface, Washington, DC: Beard Books.

Neshkova, Milena I. 2014. "Does Agency Autonomy Foster Public Participation? *Public Administration Review* 74 (1): 64–74.

Newswander, Chad B. 2015. "The Balance Wheel Reconsidered: Addressing Constitutional Principle Disputes in Practice." *Administrative Theory and Practice* 37 (1): 18–33.

Nickel, Patricia Mooney, and Angela M. Eikenberry. 2009. "A Critique of the Discourse of Marketized Philanthropy." *American Behavioral Scientist* 52 (7): 974–989.

NIDA. 2020. "Opioid Overdose Crisis." National Institute on Drug Abuse, National Institutes of Health, May 27. https://www.drugabuse.gov/drug-topics/opioids/opioid-over dose-crisis.

Niquette, Mark. 2020. "U.S. Virus Bailout: Trump Ties, Investors, Chinese Companies." Washingtonpost.com, July 7. https://www.washingtonpost.com/business/on-small-business /us-virus-bailout-trump-ties-investors-chinese-companies/2020/07/07/65aeca62-c030-1 1ea-8908-68a2b9eae9e0_story.html.

Nirappil, Fenit. 2019. "A Private School Saved a Public D.C. Field. Should It Get Preference for Playing Time?" *Washington Post*, October 22.

Novak, William J. 1996. *The People's Welfare: Law and Regulation in Nineteenth-Century America.* Chapel Hill: University of North Carolina Press.

———. 2008. "The Myth of the 'Weak' American State." *American Historical Review* 113(3): 752–772.

———. 2010. "Law and the Social Control of Capitalism." *Emory Law Journal* 60 (2): 377–405.

———. 2017. "The Public Utility Idea and the Origins of Modern Business Regulation." In *Corporations and American Democracy*, edited by Naomi R. Lamoreaux and William J. Novak, 135–166. Cambridge, MA: Tobin Project.

Nzelibe, Jide Okechuku. 2006. "The Fable of the Nationalist President and the Parochial Congress." *UCLA Law Review* 53 (5): 1217–1273.

O'Connor, Mike. 2014. *A Commercial Republic: America's Enduring Debate over Democratic Capitalism.* Lawrence: University of Kansas Press.

Olivo, Antonio. 2019. "Fairfax Solar Plan Could Spur Change to Va. Law Meant to Shield Dominion Energy from Competitors." *Washington Post*, December 25. https://www .washingtonpost.com/local/virginia-politics/fairfax-solar-plan-could-spur-change -to-va-law-meant-to-shield-dominion-energy-from-competitors/2019/12/25/bfde04ca -21f8-11ea-a153-dce4b94e4249_story.html.

Olson, Paulette, and Dell Champlin. 1998. "Ending Corporate Welfare As We Know It: An Institutional Analysis of the Dual Structure of Welfare." *Journal of Economic Issues* 32 (3): 759–771.

Orren, Karen, and Stephen Skowronek. 2017. *The Policy State: An American Predicament.* Cambridge, MA: Harvard University Press.

Osborne, Stephen P., ed. 2010. *The New Public Governance? Emerging Perspectives on the Theory and Practice of Public Governance.* New York: Routledge.

O'Toole, Laurence J., Jr. 1987. "Doctrines and Developments: Separation of Powers, the Politics-Administration Dichotomy, and the Rise of the Administrative State." *Public Administration Review* 47 (1): 17–25.

O'Toole, Laurence J., Jr., and Kenneth J. Meier. 2004. "Desperately Seeking Selznick: Cooptation and the Dark Side of Public Management in Networks." *Public Administration Review* 64 (6): 681–693.

Page, Benjamin I., Jason Seawright, and Matthew J. Lacombe. 2018. *Billionaires and Stealth Politics.* Chicago: University of Chicago Press.

Park, Sung Min, and Jessica Word. 2012. "Driven to Service: Intrinsic and Extrinsic Motivation for Public and Nonprofit Managers." *Public Personnel Management* 41 (4): 705–734.

Patterson, Bradley H., Jr. 2000. *The White House Staff: Inside the West Wing and Beyond.* Washington, DC: Brookings Institution Press.

Pestoff, Victor. 2012. "Co-production and New Public Governance in Europe." In *Towards Peer Production in Public Services: Cases from Finland*, edited by Andrea Botero, Andrew Paterson, and Johanna Saad-Sulonen, 13–32. Helsinki, Finland: Aalto University Publication Series.

Petit, Philip. 2012. *On the People's Terms: A Republican Theory and Model of Democracy.* New York: Cambridge University Press.

Pew Research Center. 2015. "Most Say Government Policies Since Recession Have Done Little to Help Middle Class, Poor." March 4. https://www.people-press.org/2015/03/04/most-say-government-policies-since-recession-have-done-little-to-help-middle-class-poor/.

———. 2017. "Public Trust in Government Remains Near Historic Lows as Partisan Attitudes Shift." May 3. https://www.people-press.org/2017/05/03/public-trust-in-government-remains-near-historic-lows-as-partisan-attitudes-shift/.

Pistor, Katharina. 2019. *The Code of Capital: How the Law Creates Wealth and Inequality.* Princeton, NJ: Princeton University Press.

Pocock, J. G. A. 1975. *The Machiavellian Moment: Florentine Political Thought and the Atlantic Republican Tradition.* Princeton, NJ: Princeton University Press.

Polsky, Andrew. 2000. "When Business Speaks: Political Entrepreneurship, Discourse, and Mobilization in American Partisan Regimes." *Journal of Theoretical Politics* 12 (4): 455–476.

Posner, Eric A., and Adrian Vermeule. 2010. *The Executive Unbound: After the Madisonian Republic.* New York: Oxford University Press.

Postell, Joseph. 2017. *Bureaucracy in America: The Administrative State's Challenge to Constitutional Government.* Columbia: University of Missouri Press.

Potoski, Michael, and Neal D. Woods. 2001. "Designing State Clean Air Agencies: Administrative Procedures and Bureaucratic Autonomy." *Journal of Public Administration Research and Theory* 11 (2): 203–221.

President's Committee. 1937. Report of the Committee: With Studies of Administrative Management in the Federal Government/Submitted to the President and to the Congress in Accordance with Public Law No. 739, 74th Congress, 2d session. Washington, DC: U.S. Government Printing Office. Retrieved from http://hdl.handle.net/2027/mdp.39015019768939.

Pressman, Steven. 2007. "The Decline of the Middle Class: An International Perspective." *Journal of Economic Issues* 16 (1): 181–200.

Rahman, K. Sabeel. 2017. *Democracy Against Domination.* New York: Oxford University Press.

Rao, Gautham. 2014. "William E. Nelson's *The Roots of American Bureaucracy* and the Resuscitation of the Early American State." *Chicago-Kent Law Review* 89 (3): 997–1018.

———. 2016. *National Duties: Custom Houses and the Making of the American State.* Chicago: University of Chicago Press.

Reenock, Christopher M., and Brian J. Gerber. 2007. "Political Insulation, Information Exchange, and Interest Group Access to the Bureaucracy." *Journal of Public Administration Research and Theory* 18 (4): 415–440.

Reeves, Andrew. 2011. "Political Disaster: Unilateral Powers, Electoral Incentives, and Presidential Disaster Declarations." *Journal of Politics* 73 (4): 1142–1151.

Reimer, Neal. 1958. "Two Conceptions of the Genius of American Politics." *Journal of Politics* 20 (4): 695–717.

Resh, William G. 2015. *Rethinking the Administrative Presidency: Trust, Intellectual Capital, and Appointee-Career Relations in the George W. Bush Administration.* Baltimore, MD: Johns Hopkins University Press.

Ritz, Adrian, Gene A. Brewer, and Oliver Neumann. 2016. "Public Service Motivation: A Systematic Literature Review and Outlook." *Public Administration Review* 76 (3): 414–426.

Roberts, Alasdair. 2010. *The Logic of Discipline: Global Capitalism and the Architecture of Government.* New York: Oxford University Press.

———. 2020. "Should We Defend the Administrative State?" *Public Administration Review* 80 (3): 391–401.

Robertson, David Brian, and David R. Judd. 1989. *The Development of Public Policy: The Structure of Policy Restraint.* Glenview, IL: Scott, Foresman.

Rockwell, Stephen J. 2010. *Indian Affairs and the Administrative State in the Nineteenth Century.* New York: Cambridge University Press.

Rohr, John A. 1986. *To Run a Constitution: The Legitimacy of the Administrative State.* Lawrence: University Press of Kansas.

———. 1998. *Public Service, Ethics, and Constitutional Practice.* Lawrence: University Press of Kansas.

Rohrbough, Malcolm J. 1968. *The Land Office Business: The Settlement and Administration of American Public Lands, 1789–1837.* New York: Oxford University Press.

Rosenbloom, David H. 1983. "Public Administrative Theory and the Separation of Powers." *Public Administration Review* 43 (3): 219–227.

———. 2000. *Building a Legislative-Centered Public Administration: Congress and the Administrative State, 1946–1999.* Tuscaloosa: University of Alabama Press.

———. 2010. "Reevaluating Executive-Centered Public Administration Theory." In *The Oxford Handbook of American Bureaucracy*, edited by Robert F. Durant, 101–127. New York: Oxford University Press.

Rosenbloom, David H., and Suzanne J. Piotrowski. 2005. "Outsourcing the Constitution and Administrative Law Norms." *American Review of Public Administration* 35 (2): 103–121.

Rosenbloom David H., Stephanie P. Newbold, and Meghan Doughty. 2018. "Madison's Ratchet: Ambition Counteracting Ambition and the Aggregation of Political, Managerial, and Legal Controls Over Federal Administration." *American Review of Public Administration* 48 (6): 495–505.

Rubin, Edward L. 2005a. *Beyond Camelot: Rethinking Politics and Law for the Modern State.* Princeton, NJ: Princeton University Press.

———. 2005b. "The Myth of Accountability and the Anti-administrative Impulse." *Michigan Law Review* 103 (8): 2073–2136.

Rutland, Robert A. 1987. "The Virginia Plan of 1787: James Madison's Outline of a Model

Constitution." *This Constitution: A Bicentennial Chronicle*, 197–201. Washington, DC: National Endowment for the Humanities.

Saez, Emmanuel, and Gabriel Zucman. 2019. *The Triumph of Injustice: How the Rich Dodge Taxes and How to Make Them Pay.* New York: W. W. Norton.

Salamon, Lester M. 1997. *Holding the Center: America's Nonprofit Sector at a Crossroads.* New York: Nathan Cummings Foundation. January 16. http://www.ncf.org/.

Samuel, Lawrence R. 2014. *The Middle Class: A Cultural History.* New York: Routledge.

Scheffler, Gabriel. 2020. "Failure to Capture: Why Business Does Not Control the Rulemaking Process." *Maryland Law Review* 79 (3): 700–770.

Schmidt, Diane E. 2002. "Politicization and Responsiveness in the Regional Offices of the NLRB." *American Review of Public Administration.* 32 (2): 188–215.

Schneider, Saundra K., and William G. Jacoby. 2003. "A Culture of Dependence? The Relationship between Public Assistance and Public Opinion." *British Journal of Political Science* 33 (2): 213–231.

Seidman, Harold. 1980. *Politics, Position, and Power: The Dynamics of Federal Organization.* 3rd ed. New York: Oxford University Press.

Sellers, Charles. 1991. *The Market Revolution: Jacksonian America, 1815–1846.* New York: Oxford University Press.

Shane, Peter M. 2009. *Madison's Nightmare: How Executive Power Threatens American Democracy.* Chicago: University of Chicago Press.

Shankman, Andrew. 2003. "'A New Thing on Earth': Alexander Hamilton, Pro-Manufacturing Republicans, and the Democratization of American Political Economy." *Journal of the Early Republic* 23 (3): 323–352.

Shapiro, Sydney A. 2012. "The Complexity of Regulatory Capture: Diagnosis, Causality, and Remediation." *Roger Williams University Law Review* 17 (1): 221–257.

Sheehan, Colleen A. 2004. "Madison v. Hamilton: The Battle over Republicanism and the Role of Public Opinion." *American Political Science Review* 98 (3): 405–424.

Short, Lloyd Milton. 1923. *The Development of National Administrative Organization in the United States.* Baltimore, MD: Johns Hopkins University Press.

Shugerman, Jed Handelsman. 2020. "The Indecisions of 1789: Strategic Ambiguity and the Imaginary Unitary Executive (Part I)." Fordham Law Legal Studies Research Paper No. 3596566, available at SSRN: https://ssrn.com/abstract=3596566.

Sklar, Martin J. 1988. *The Corporate Reconstruction of American Capitalism, 1890–1916: The Market, the Law, and Politics.* New York: Cambridge University Press.

Skowronek, Stephen. 2020. *Presidential Leadership in Political Time: Reprise and Reappraisal.* 3rd ed., revised and expanded. Lawrence: University Press of Kansas.

Smith, Kevin B., and Michael J. Licari. 2006. *Public Administration: Power and Politics in the Fourth Branch of Government.* New York: Oxford University Press.

Sohoni, Mila. 2016. "The Administrative Constitution in Exile." *William and Mary Law Review* 57 (3): 923–974.

———. 2017. "A Bureaucracy—If You Can Keep It." *Harvard Law Review* 131 (1): 13–31.

Sorensen, Eva, and Jacob Torfling, eds. 2007. *Theories of Democratic Network Governance.* New York: Palgrave Macmillan.

Soss, Joe, Richard C. Fording, and Sanford F. Schram. 2011. *Disciplining the Poor: Neoliberal Paternalism and the Persistent Power of Race.* Chicago: University of Chicago Press.

Spicer, Michael W. 2010. *In Defense of Politics in Public Administration: A Value Pluralist Perspective.* Tuscaloosa: University of Alabama Press.

Standing, Guy. 2016. *The Corruption of Capitalism: Why Rentiers Thrive and Work Does Not Pay.* London: Biteback Publishing.

Stapleford, Thomas A. 2010. "Shaping Knowledge about American Labor: External Advising at the U.S. Bureau of Labor Statistics in the Twentieth Century." *Science in Context* 23 (2): 187–220.

Steen, Trui P. S., and Mark R. Rutgers. 2011. "The Double-Edged Sword: Public Service Motivation, the Oath of Office and the Backlash of an Instrumental Approach." *Public Management Review* 13 (3): 343–361.

Steen, Trui, Taco Brandsen, and Bram Verschuere. 2018. "The Dark Side of Co-Creation and Co-Production: Seven Evils." In *Co-Production and Co-Creation: Engaging Citizens in Public Services*, edited by Trui Steen, Taco Brandsen, and Bram Verschuere, 284–293. New York: Routledge.

Stephanson, Anders. 1995. *Manifest Destiny: American Expansionism and the Empire of Right.* New York: Hill & Wang.

Storing, Herbert J. 1995. "Political Parties and the Bureaucracy." In *Toward a More Perfect Union: Writings of Herbert J. Storing*, edited by Joseph M. Bessette, 307–326. Washington, DC: American Enterprise Institute.

Storrs, Landon R. Y. 2013. *The Second Red Scare and the Unmaking of the New Deal Left.* Princeton, NJ: Princeton University Press.

Strahan, Derek. 2016. "Worcester County Courthouse, Worcester, Mass." *Lost New England*, September 14. https://lostnewengland.com/2016/09/worcester-county-courthouse-worcester-mass/.

Straus, Jacob R., Wendy R. Ginsberg, Amanda K. Mullan, and Jaclyn D. Petruzzelli. 2015. "Restricting Membership: Assessing Agency Compliance and the Effects of Banning Federal Lobbyists from Executive Branch Advisory Committee Service." *Presidential Studies Quarterly* 45 (2): 310–334.

Stromquist, Shelton. 2006. *Reinventing "The People": The Progressive Movement, the Class Problem, and the Origins of Modern Liberalism.* Urbana: University of Illinois Press.

Styhre, Alexander. 2017. *Precarious Professional Work: Entrepreneurialism, Risk and Economic Compensation in the Knowledge Economy.* Cham, Switzerland: Palgrave Macmillan.

Sunstein, Cass R. 2015. "The Most Knowledgeable Branch." *University of Pennsylvania Law Review* 164 (7): 1607–1686.

Szymanski, Ann-Marie. 2008. "Transformations in Regulatory Policy and the Decline of the Amateur." Presented at the 2008 Policy History Conference, St. Louis, MO, May 29–June 1, 2008.

Terry, Larry D. 2003. *Leadership of Public Bureaucracies: The Administrator as Conservator.* 2nd ed. Armonk, NY: M. E. Sharpe.

Tocqueville, Alexis de. 2000. *Democracy in America*, edited by Harvey C. Mansfield and Delba Winthrop. Chicago: University of Chicago Press.

Tulis, Jeffrey K. 1987. *The Rhetorical Presidency.* Princeton, NJ: Princeton University Press.

Twenge, Jean M., W. Keith Campbell, and Nathan T. Carter. 2014. "Declines in Trust in Others and Confidence in Institutions among American Adults and Late Adolescents, 1972–2012." *Psychological Science* 25 (10): 1914–1923.

Unger, Abraham. 2019. *The Death and Life of the American Middle Class: A Policy Agenda for American Jobs Creation.* Cham, Switzerland: Palgrave Macmillan.

US Congress. 1793. "List of Civil Officers of the United States, Except Judges, with Their

Emoluments, for the Year Ending October 1, 1792." *American State Papers*, Senate, 2nd Congress, 2nd Session. https://memory.loc.gov/cgi-bin/ampage?collId=llsp&fileName=037/llsp037.db&recNum=64.

U-S-History.org. N.d. "U.S. Population, Land Area and Density, 1790–2000. https://u-s-history.com/pages/h986.html.

US Official Register. 1818. *A Register of Officers and Agents, Civil, Military, and Naval, in the Service of the United States.* Washington, DC: Department of State.

———. 1845. *A Register of Officers and Agents, Civil, Military, and Naval, in the Service of the United States.* Washington, DC: Department of State.

———. 1874. *A Register of Officers and Agents, Civil, Military, and Naval, in the Service of the United States.* Washington, DC: Department of State.

US OPM. 2017. "Federal Civilian Employment by Major Geographic Area, State, and Selected Agency Executive Branch and Selected Other Agencies, Non-Postal, Non-Seasonal, Full-time, Permanent Employees and All Annuitants." U.S. Office of Personnel Management, September. https://www.opm.gov/policy-data-oversight/data-analysis-documentation/federal-employment-reports/reports-publications/federal-civilian-employment/.

Van Riper, Paul P. 1958. *History of the United States Civil Service.* Evanston, IL: Row, Peterson.

Vattel, Emer de. 1835. *The Law of Nations; or Principles of the Law of Nature Applied to the Conduct and Affairs of Nations and Sovereigns.* 4th ed. Philadelphia, PA: Nicklin & Johnson.

Veblen, Thorstein. 1904. *The Theory of the Business Enterprise.* New York: Charles Scribner.

Verkuil, Paul R. 2017. *Valuing Bureaucracy: The Case for Professional Government.* New York: Cambridge University Press.

Vibert, Frank. 2007. *The Rise of the Unelected: Democracy and the New Separation of Powers.* Cambridge: Cambridge University Press.

Vyse, Graham. 2019. "How a Fight over a City Athletic Field Turned into a Woke-off of Washington's Well-off." *Washington Post Magazine,* December 9. https://www.washingtonpost.com/lifestyle/magazine/how-a-fight-over-a-city-athletic-field-turned-into-a-woke-off-of-washingtons-well-off/2019/12/06/fc2d14dc-07c9-11ea-818c-fcc65139e8c2_story.html.

Waldo, Dwight. 1984. "Further Discussion." *Public Administration Review* 44 (2): 191–192.

———. 2007. *The Administrative State: A Study of the Political Theory of American Public Administration.* New Brunswick, NJ: Transaction Publishers. Originally published 1948.

Wallis, John Joseph. 2006. "Federal Government Employees, by Government Branch and Location Relative to the Capital: 1816–1992." Table Ea894–903. In *Historical Statistics of the United States, Earliest Times to the Present: Millennial Edition*, edited by Susan B. Carter, Scott Sigmund Gartner, Michael R. Haines, Alan L. Olmstead, Richard Sutch, and Gavin Wright. New York: Cambridge University Press. http://dx.doi.org/10.1017/ISBN-9780511132971.Ea827-985.

———. 2008. "Founding Errors: Making Democracy Safe for America." December. http://econweb.umd.edu/~wallis/MyPapers/Wallis%20Founding%20Errors%20Colorado%2012.12.08.pdf.

Wang, Tova Andrea. 2014. *The Politics of Voter Suppression: Defending and Expanding Americans' Right to Vote.* Ithaca, NY: Cornell University Press.

Weber, Gustavus A. 1923. *The Bureau of Pensions: Its History, Activities and Organization.* Baltimore, MD: Johns Hopkins University Press.

Weber, Max. 1968. *Economy and Society*, edited by Gunter Roth and Clause Wittich. Los Angeles: University of California Press.

Weiner, Rachel. 2014. "New Va. Law Shields Dominion Power from Financial Reviews. *Washington Post*. February 24. http://www.washingtonpost.com/local/virginia-politics/new-va-law-shields-dominion-power-from-financial-reviews/2015/02/24/9cd64026-bc51-11e4-b274-e5209a3bc9a9_story.html.

Weiss, Thomas. 1992. "U.S. Labor Force Estimates and Economic Growth, 1800–1860." In *American Economic Growth and Standards of Living before the Civil War*, edited by Robert E. R. Gallman and John Joseph Wallis, 19–78. Chicago: University of Chicago Press.

West, William F., and Connor Raso. 2013. "Who Shapes the Rulemaking Agenda? Implications for Bureaucratic Responsiveness and Bureaucratic Control." *Journal of Public Administration Research and Theory* 23 (4): 495–519.

White, Leonard D. 1948. *The Federalists: A Study in Administrative History*. New York: Macmillan.

———. 1951. *The Jeffersonians: A Study in Administrative History*. New York: Macmillan.

———. 1954. *The Jacksonians: A Study in Administrative History*. New York: Macmillan.

———. 1958. *The Republican Era, 1869–1901: A Study in Administrative History*. New York: Macmillan.

Whittington, Keith E. 2007. *Political Foundations of Judicial Supremacy: The Presidency, The Supreme Court, and Constitutional Leadership in U.S. History*. Princeton, NJ: Princeton University Press.

Wilkins, Mira. 2001. "A History of Multinational Enterprise." In *The Oxford Handbook of International Business*, edited by Alan M. Rugman and Thomas L. Brewer, 3–35. New York: Oxford University Press.

Williams, Brian N., Seong-Cheol Kang, and Japera Johnson. 2016. "(Co)-Contamination as the Dark Side of Co-Production: Public Values Failures in Co-Production Processes." *Public Management Review* 18 (5): 692–717.

Willoughby, William F. 1919. *An Introduction to the Study of the Government of Modern States*. New York: Century Co.

Wilson, James Q. 1990. "Juridical Democracy versus American Democracy." *PS: Political Science and Politics* 23 (4): 570–72.

Wilson, Mark R. 2003. "The Business of Civil War: Military Enterprise, the State, and Political Economy in the United States, 1850–1880." *Enterprise and Society* 4 (4): 599–605.

———. 2006. "The Politics of Procurement: Military Origins of Bureaucratic Autonomy." *Journal of Policy History* 18 (1): 44–73.

Wilson, Woodrow. 1884. "Committee or Cabinet Government?" *Overland Monthly* 3 (1): 17–33.

———. 1887. "The Study of Administration." *Political Science Quarterly* 2 (3): 197–222.

———. 1981. *Congressional Government: A Study in American Politics*. Baltimore, MD: Johns Hopkins University Press.

Winkler, Adam. 2017. "*Citizens United*, Personhood, and the Corporation in Politics." In *Corporations and American Democracy*, edited by Naomi R. Lamoreaux and William J. Novak, 340–367. Cambridge, MA: Tobin Project.

Wise, Charles R. 1993. "Public Administration Is Constitutional and Legitimate." *Public Administration Review* 53 (3): 257–261.

Wood, Gordon S. 1969. *The Creation of the American Republic: 1776–1787*. New York: W. W. Norton.

Workman, Samuel. 2015. *The Dynamics of Bureaucracy in the U.S. Government: How Congress and Federal Agencies Process Information and Solve Problems*. New York: Cambridge University Press.

Wright, Robert E. 2002. *The Wealth of Nations Rediscovered: Integration and Expansion in American Financial Markets, 1780–1850*. New York: Cambridge University Press.

Wu, Tim. 2018. *The Curse of Bigness: Antitrust in the New Gilded Age*. New York: Columbia Global Reports.

Yackee, Susan W. 2006a. "Assessing Inter-institutional Attention to and Influence on Government Regulations." *British Journal of Political Science* 36 (4): 723–744.

———. 2006b. "Sweet-Talking the Fourth Branch: The Influence of Interest Group Comments on Federal Agency Rulemaking." *Journal of Public Administration Research and Theory* 16 (1): 103–124.

———. 2012. "The Politics of Ex Parte Lobbying: Pre-proposal Agenda Building and Blocking during Agency Rulemaking." *Journal of Public Administration Research and Theory* 22 (3): 373–393.

———. 2014. "Reconsidering Agency Capture during Regulatory Policymaking." In *Preventing Regulatory Capture: Special Interest Influence and How to Limit It*, edited by Daniel P. Carpenter and David A. Moss. New York: Cambridge University Press.

Yackee, Jason Webb, and Susan Webb Yackee. 2006. "A Bias Toward Business? Assessing Interest Group Influence on the U.S. Bureaucracy. *Journal of Politics* 68 (1): 128–139.

Zavodnyik, Peter. 2007. *The Age of Strict Construction: A History of the Growth of Federal Power, 1789–1861*. Washington, DC: Catholic University Press of America.

INDEX